Living in
Two Worlds

THE SEQUEL TO
Crossing Life's Many Bridges

LEM BURNHAM

CANADIAN CATALOGUING IN PUBLICATION DATA

Burnham, Lem, 1926–
    Living in two worlds

ISBN 09699035-1-0

    1. Burnham, Lem, 1926– 2. Missionaries—China—Hong Kong—
Biography. 3. United Church of Canada—Biography.
I. Title. II. Title: Crossing life's many bridges.

BX9883.B94A3 2000   266'.792'092   C00-911510-2

Layout and design by Vancouver Desktop Publishing Centre Ltd.
Printed in Canada by Kromar Printing

Dedicated
to
all members of the
the Coquitlam Stroke Recovery Association,
Dogwood Pavilion
and
Phyllis Florence Delaney
who contributed so much to the growth and success of the
Stroke Recovery Association of British Columbia

Contents

Appreciation and Thanks

MY SINCERE APPRECIATION and thanks to all who have enabled this publication to become a reality; without their invaluable assistance, I could never have completed my story.

Foremost, I wish to thank my sister Betty for her unlimited patience by assisting me in routine matters like helping to keep me organized, punching holes in the manuscript for placing in large binders, carrying and moving reference books, plus countless other routine tasks necessary because of my limited physical ability due to the stroke I experienced nine years ago.

A special thanks to Jonathan Lau for granting his permission to use one of his most interesting and attractive photographs on the cover of this publication. Jonathan is an exceedingly skillful, artistic, devoted calligrapher and photographer who has travelled extensively throughout most regions of China plus Southeast Asia. Jonathan kindly selected an attractive and beautiful photo for me to use on the cover.

The bridge depicted in the photo is known as the Flying Rainbow Bridge, which crosses the swiftly flowing Min River. It's a wooden suspension bridge located in a remote area of the northern Sichuan (Szechuan) province in China.

My thanks to West Country Photo Limited in Saskatoon, Saskatchewan for granting permission to use their beautiful aerial photo of the Burnham farm situated north of the village of Summerberry, Saskatchewan. The photo was taken on August 20, 1995.

I wish to thank various local museums in Saskatchewan including Grenfell, Wolseley, Abernethy, Fort Qu'Appelle and the Yorkton Heritage Museum. Each of the museums cooperated in all respects to make their facilities available; the museum staff enabled me to recreate and reconstruct the life of the early pioneers in Saskatchewan in a vivid and realistic manner. Congratulations to the prairie museums for capturing the essence and pioneering spirit of the early settlers as they moved to Western Canada.

My thanks to the Lutheran World Federation Department of World Service in Hong Kong for photographs of the destructive nature of Typhoon Wanda which struck Hong Kong on September 1st, 1962, killing 123 and making 46,550 homeless besides injuring others who were detained in local hospitals.

I wish to express my thanks to Norma (Fleming) Wagner for providing the early photograph of our grandfather Thomas Fleming's first house built in the 1880s when the family migrated from Ontario, settling in the Northwest Territories, later to become known as Saskatchewan in 1905.

My appreciation to professor Chen Chan Yuen for his informative and profoundly interesting publication in Chinese and English, *History of Chinese Medical Science*, illustrated with photos, published in Hong Kong in 1968. It provides valuable information tracing the early development of Chinese medicine throughout the ages.

To the Information Services Department of the Hong Kong government for material used from various yearbooks throughout the years—my thanks and appreciation.

A special thanks to *Scientific American* for their exceedingly informative article regarding Hong Kong's return to China and to Western Tunnel Company from the article "Building a New Gateway to China," by John J. Kosowatz (December 1997, pp. 102, 104, approx. 335 words). It's a splendid summary of the development of transportation in Hong Kong.

Thanks to the Women's Department of the Hong Kong Council of the Church of Christ in China, who wrote and produced "A Silent Witness" in Petburi, Thailand in November 1962. It vividly describes the courageous, fascinating and inspiring story of Che Kam Kong, the first Protestant martyr in southern China.

Thanks to the family of Dr. Siu Choh Leung for the vivid and fascinating account of the life, work and times of Dr. Robert Morrison, first Protestant missionary to China. I was privileged to attend Dr. Leung's lecture presented in Chi-to church, Macau, held September 2, 1952. Following the lecture all who attended proceeded to the Old Protestant Cemetery in Macau, paying their respect to Dr. Robert Morrison and his family. May their souls rest in eternal peace.

Thanks also to the Tourist Association of Macau, for the detailed historical information regarding the early background of Macau.

Likewise to Dr. Basil Mathews, a former professor of mine at Union College (now known as Vancouver School of Theology) in Vancouver, B.C., for his book *Forward through the Ages*. His chapter, on the outreach of the Nestorian church (pp. 64-65) provided invaluable information regarding the growth of the Nestorian faith in China during the T'ang dynasty (618-907 A.D.).

Likewise thanks to Friendship Press, the New York publisher of the book (1951).

To Norma Mar for permission to use several splendid photographs taken by her in China and Vancouver.

To my fine friend, Aziz Khaki, president of the Pacific Interfaith Citizenship Association of B.C., for so kindly preparing his generous introduction to this publication.

Last, but by no means least, I must express my sincere thanks to Isabel Nanton for her exceedingly kind introduction on the cover of this publication. Isabel is a veteran author who has had tremendous experience and success publishing books that are widely read.

Once more my thanks and deep appreciation to all who have so generously helped with this publication, and to any whom I may have inadvertently omitted from my appreciation and thanks, my humble and sincere apologies.

Introductory Remarks

I FIRST MET REV. LEM BURNHAM in 1975 at a meeting of the Interfaith Council at 622 Seymour Street in Vancouver. As chair of the council, Lem made me feel very welcome and this marked the beginning of our friendship.

Lem in a lucid and entertaining way deals with his experience beginning with the pioneering days of his family. He details the readiness of the farmers to fight prairie fires at all times during the hot, dry summer season and the state of farming in the 1930s. His family came to Canada two and half centuries ago and finally settled in what is now known as Saskatchewan. Very recently Lem was delighted to have had the opportunity to go back to the farm and had the joy of sleeping in the same room where he was born.

Lem arrived in his present home—British Columbia—in 1945 and rightly he calls it a "new beginning." His observation of valued Chinese customs and traditions make indeed very interesting reading for us, especially for those who have not had the opportunity to visit that part of the world but now come in everyday contact with Canadians of Chinese background.

Lem and his sister Betty continue to benefit from the use of Chinese medicine and in chapter five he is appreciative of it. He acknowledges that the Chinese medicine at the very early days registered important achievements in the identification, classification and treatment of various diseases. The discovery well in advance of Western medicine. Lem had a productive eighteen years of his stay in Hong Kong. He shares with his readers the transportation system in Hong Kong. According to him, "housing in Hong Kong is nothing less than a modern miracle deserving our attention."

In Chapter 8 of his book, Lem tells us about his visit to Britain, the land of his ancestors. He then talks of his visits to Turkey and Iran. Turkey is a predominantly Sunni Muslim country and Iran is a Shiite Muslim strong hold. Describing his visit to Topkapi Palace in Istanbul Turkey, Lem was dazed by "the wealth amassed by the sultans (rulers) of bygone days." in Teheran, Iran he was able to visit the "Gulistan " palace. Within the palace he was thrilled to see " many Persian rugs covering the floors, attractive and colourful chandeliers were evident. "

Lem talks of his experience with a stroke and his brave and courageous struggle to overcome damage done by the disease. It is indeed a very clear manifestation of the triumph of human spirit with the power of prayers.

The courage of his ancestors to come to Canada was not lost on Lem. With the questing spirit of the explorer, he cultivated the courage and determination to visit and meet people of different backgrounds and ethnicities.

In his opening remarks in chapter one Lem starts with these remarks: "Our memories are an invaluable asset each of us has the responsibility to pass on to future generations. It is through such memorie, we are able to pass along the wisdom/folly of first hand experience by sharing our thoughts, experiences and memories with others." Lem has a very secure feeling of his own Christian faith and at the same time he has a deep appreciation of the beliefs and practices of other faiths. I have very much enjoyed the manuscript of Part Two of *Crossing Life's Many Bridges*, and I am sure it will be well received by the reading public even more than his successful publication of Part One. I hope readers will enjoy this book as much as I have.

—*Aziz Khaki*
President, Pacific Interfaith Citizenship Council
September 22, 2000.

A century of farming: 1995 aerial photo of the Burnham farm.

CHAPTER I

Pioneering Days

OUR MEMORIES ARE an invaluable asset each of us has the responsibility to pass on to future generations. It is through such memories we are able to pass along the wisdom/folly of first hand experience by sharing our thoughts, experiences and memories with others. It is a responsibility we should not neglect nor consider lightly, since once our memories have passed beyond our reach, they are lost within the annals of time and eternity, never to be recalled or recaptured again.

I fully recognize there are those who have already recorded many such precious memories. Nevertheless, as a former resident and son of Saskatchewan of which I'm proud, it's my desire to complete a small corner by recording some valued experiences and memories. This publication is a sequel to the previous publication entitled *Crossing Life's Many Bridges.* It's my sincere hope both publications may be of some general interest to others in the years to come.

My mother, Jemima May Fleming, and others of the Fleming family were born in what was originally known as the Northwest Territories (Saskatchewan), south of the village of Summerberry (district of Assiniboia). Please note in the 1880s that specific part of the Northwest Territories later became known as the province of Saskatchewan in 1905.

In 1882 Thomas Fleming and Sophia Jane (McKenzie), my maternal grandparents, commenced their journey from Ontario to Western Canada by train. In the spring of 1882, they moved all their possessions in confidence, hope, and trust from the place of their roots: Ontario, Canada. They were accompanied by their three sons George, Benjamin, and John. The family travelled by rail from Ontario via St. Paul Minneapolis, Minnesota, U.S.A., THEN TRANSFERRED TO ANOTHER TRAIN HEADING NORTHWEST TO WINNIPEG, MANITOBA, CANADA. FROM WINNIPEG THEY TRANSFERRED TO A WESTBOUND EXPRESS FOR BRANDON, MANITOBA (CANADA). IN 1882 Brandon was the end of the steel (Canadian Pacific Railway) in Western Canada. The railway crossing Canada was still under construction; it was not completed across the continent from the Atlantic to the Pacific until November 7, 1885. The last spike was driven at a small place known as Craigellachie, B.C., west of Revelstoke, by Lord Strathcona.

Upon their arrival in Brandon, Manitoba, they purchased "Red River carts," especially designed for and used by many of the early pioneers in those days. The carts were similar to two wheeled chariots drawn by teams of oxen. The Red River carts were light in weight, made entirely from wood, held together by wooden pegs and rawhide, transported such pioneer families and their possessions to their newly established dwellings in the Northwest Territories. The Red River carts slowly moved their precious cargos across the lone prairie. However, due to the lack of grease, squeaked, squealed and groaned as they proceeded westward from Brandon, Manitoba. Their passengers were journeying in faith, hope and confidence not knowing what the future may hold for them and their families. The Red River carts literally could be heard for miles as they slowly proceeded westwards, crossing the flat prairie with all of the family possessions for a distance of nearly 150 miles.

Upon arriving at their destination in the Northwest Territories, they felt the land their eyes gazed and feasted upon had distinct possibilities for the immediate future. The Flemings concluded their journey four miles south of the tiny village of Summerberry, arriving at their destination on the 30th of May 1882.

The family initially staked claim to the land they chose to settle upon, registered their names on the government's homestead list and paid the standard fee of $10.00 at the land registry office in Moosomin, Saskatchewan. The agreement indicated they were expected to plough and break at least five acres of land during the first year, besides break and cultivate 10 acres per year for the next three years. It was mandatory too they construct a house (see photo) that was livable, and dwell in their house for a minimum of six months per year. Their first house was made of wood, but later in the year 1900 it was replaced it by a dwelling made of bricks. They erected a plaque in the house recording the momentous event for the family.

Besides building their home other essential farm buildings were erected for the animals and implements. They dug a well to supply drinking water, a matter for survival; they cleared off the bluffs from around their home. The trees consisted mostly of poplars, birch and willows. They drained many of the nearby sloughs, picked up endless rocks of all sizes, shapes and description found on the land. They used some stones to help construct the farm buildings like the barn, milk house, storage bins etc. They gathered the stones on a stone boat, similar to a sleigh but pulled by a team of horses. The stone boat was exceedingly heavy when loaded with stones.

The early settlers worked long arduous hours, as did their neighbours and friends. There were no short cuts or easy methods in those days. They were exceedingly diligent hard working people, sharing their tools and implements with their neighbours. The settlers were always willing to extend a helping hand to others in times of need, trouble, or disaster. For example, if a house, barn or other farm building was destroyed due to a severe electrical storm or perhaps internal combustion by overheating of the hay that had been stored, the entire community rallied around the family to help them reconstruct their building. Life in general consisted of a more communal sharing process than it does nowadays.

One of the first buildings required by the community was an elementary school for the children, built by the farmers from the surrounding district. The school assured the younger generation they would receive a basic education for the future. A one-room schoolhouse was erected and named after the district of Summerhill. The children ordinarily walked to school, except during extremely cold sub-zero weather, frequently accompanied by heavy winds in the winter. The rural country school was considered the main focal point for the community. The local school helped weld the community together in the common goal of providing an education. The school was also used for dances and other such recreational or community activities.

The Flemings originated from a former Methodist church

background and tradition in Ontario. The first recorded Methodist church service held in the area was Sunday August 26, 1883 in Uncle Sam Fleming's home. Several years later a Methodist church was constructed within the village of Summerberry (1906), later it became an integral part of the United Church of Canada in 1925 by the union of the Methodists, Presbyterian and Congregational churches in Western Canada on June 10, 1925. The church was one of the principal focal points within the community.

My mother, Jemima May Fleming, was born on May 4, 1888 in the Northwest Territories. She frequently recalled many of her childhood memories on the farm. She indicated they were not fearful or nervous concerning the native Indian people living in the community; however, they were extremely cautious of a prairie fire breaking out, then spreading across the land, which periodically occurred. Mother likewise claimed that during the heat of the summer, every evening before retiring to bed, they carefully scanned the horizon for any possible evidence of smoke or fire, which could affect the well-being of the community. She also claimed prairie fires were one of the greatest nightmares for the early settlers.

In order to protect their home and farm buildings from prairie fires sweeping over the land, they ploughed several furrows of black soil around the home and farm buildings, serving as a protective fireguard. However, if the wind was exceedingly strong, the fire occasionally jumped over the fireguard, continuing on its path of destruction. The farmers had to be ready to fight prairie fires at all times during the hot dry summer season. They usually did so by using burlap bags soaked in barrels of cold water.

Families had to create their own recreational activities. Often they would go ice-skating with their friends on a slough or nearby lake. Horseback riding was also a popular sport and pastime. The women rode on sidesaddles placed on the back of the horses to accommodate their long skirts. During the summer everyone travelled by horse and carriage (also known as a buggy or democrat). They eagerly read the local newspapers, since radios had not yet been invented. Many young people participated in the local church choir, held church picnics, Christmas concerts, curling and other such community activities.

My father, Harry, was born on a farm near Cobourg, Ontario in

1872. He was a descendant of a United Empire Loyalist family. In 1797 they migrated from New Hampshire in the United States to Nova Scotia, eventually settling down in Cobourg, Ontario.

During his youth, Father heard many stories about the development of Western Canada; therefore, he was determined to follow through on some of the stories commonly rumoured in his day. In 1903 Father was freely offered the opportunity to go west by a friend of the family named Sam Clarke. Harry was requested to accompany a carload of horses being shipped by train to Wolseley, Saskatchewan. He happily accepted Sam Clarke's offer and conditions. Upon arrival at his destination in Wolseley, Father decided to remain there, where he worked for some time as a carpenter.

Following his arrival on the Prairies, Harry Burnham, along with a friend named Bill Jeff, worked in the local community as carpenters. They built an extension to the Osler home and helped erect a new barn for them. Not long afterwards Harry himself commenced farming. Harry married my mother Jemima May Fleming on January 4, 1912.

Father purchased the former Waugh farm from Albert Todd. Years later it was operated by his eldest son, George. In 1997 the farm was passed over to George's son Trevor Burnham.

Harry Burnham purchased a Sawyer Massey steam engine to assist with the farm work during the harvest season. He used the threshing machine to help other farmers with their harvesting, earning money in that way. Unfortunately Harry had a very serious accident during the harvest of 1925. He was accidentally crushed against the boiler of his steam engine, severely burning him and breaking his jaw. Fortunately Harry survived the accident and continued with his farming activities for many years. Harry was a visionary, far-sighted and hard-working farmer; he was always prepared to try new ways and methods of farming. Farming nowadays is geared to computers and other mechanical and technical methods, requiring various forms of knowledge. During World War II, farming in Western Canada was transformed by the invention and use of combines.

Unfortunately in those days there were no antibiotics, therefore my father Harry died an untimely death due to blood poisoning and tuberculosis in September 1942, during the Second World War, and from that time forward the farm was operated by his wife, Jemima, and her family. However, when her eldest son George married in 1945, George assumed full responsibility for the home farm. Jemima decided to move to Vancouver to retire, where she had several brothers and sisters. She was accompanied by three of her children, Edythe, Betty and Lem, beginning a further chapter in the story of the Burnham family.

Model of a Red River cart used by early pioneers, Indian Head Park, Saskatchewan.

A wooden oxen's yoke used in the 1880s for pulling the Red River carts.

Maternal grandparents in their horse drawn buggy.

Grandfather Thomas Fleming's home built in the 1880s.

Family photo: Grandmother Fleming with daughters Mary, Jemima and Lovina.

CHAPTER 2

Farming in the 1930s

THE BURNHAM FARM STILL remains within the family—like a miracle it has survived the ups and downs of nearly a century, extending from 1903 to the present time, 2000.

I recall as a child, our farm, like all farms in the same region of (south Eastern) Saskatchewan in the 1930s, endured drought, dust storms, tumbleweeds (also known as Russian thistles), and plagues of grasshoppers. The grasshoppers flew from North Dakota and Montana (U.S.A.) by countless millions. You could have a fine looking garden today; however, the grasshoppers were so thick, they could devour the garden over night. You could literally hear the grasshoppers snipping in the garden and fields by night—it sounded much like scissors. The grasshoppers were so thick it was common for them to obscure the sun as they flew from the United States, like dark clouds obscuring the brilliance of the sun. They were so abundant they would get stuck in the radiators of the early cars having to be cleaned out to keep the car from overheating. The government provided poison, which the farmers mixed with sawdust; they spread the poison along the sides of the fields, killing the grasshoppers. It was exceedingly discouraging and disheartening to be a farmer in the 1930s.

Besides grasshoppers, the farmers frequently battled other pests like cutworms attacking the root system of the crops, causing the grain to wither and die. Caterpillars infested everything, eating the leaves of the trees. They made their web-like nests among the branches of the trees. My sister recalled how caterpillars even crept into our home and crawled on the baby carriage. Wheat rust (marquis wheat) ruined the stems of the grain during its formative stage, deforming the kernels and devastating the crops in the 1930s. That specific period in Canada's history is often referred to as the Dirty Thirties, the Hungry Thirties, or the Great Depression.

Besides drought, Canada also experienced a serious economic depression. I vividly recall, as we drove our 1924 Nash from the farm into the village of Summerberry for shopping, or perhaps on the way to church, we frequently had to wait for a freight train to pass before the car could cross the railway tracks. Freight trains sometimes exceeded a mile in length as they passed. As children, one of our favorite pastimes was to count the number of freight cars on the trains; we also counted the number of young and middle-aged men riding on top of the freight cars, which was an extremely dangerous and hazardous mode of transportation. They travelled that way due to the inability to find employment in their own village across the land. They couldn't afford a regular railway ticket on the train, so they "rode the rods" or "the rails," as they were known. Occasionally the riders would accidentally slip off the speedily moving trains, seriously injuring themselves, even severing one or both legs. The men would ordinarily jump off the moving box or freight cars on the outskirts of cities like Regina, Moose Jaw or Saskatoon to prevent being arrested by the local police. It was a sad and difficult time for them. The riders on the trains were further subjected to the indignity of being referred to as "hobos" or "bums" by the general public.

During the thirties we also experienced tremendous dust storms that were almost indescribable as they blew across the broad wide-open prairies. The storms resulted in large numbers of Canadians fleeing to other areas of the land as if they were refugees.

The farm on which I was born and raised was located five and a half miles north of the village of Summerberry. Summerberry was a small village 80 miles east of Regina, established in the early 1880s by some of the early settlers, including the Fleming brothers. The village was located adjacent to the transcontinental railway (c.p.r.), then under construction and completed from coast to coast in 1885. The land was purchased from the Canadian Northwest Land Company. Since the Canadian Pacific Railway was still under construction, it therefore, naturally seemed a logical and fine location to establish a village.

Mrs. Edna Laidlaw, in her article entitled "Summerberry Then and Now," published in the Wolseley Centennial publication 1880–1980 "Bridging the Past," stated "along the path of the rail was a small creek, which was known as Summerberry Creek due to the abundance of berries growing along its banks during the summer. It was a place where a small town sprang up, named after the creek. A certain amount of land was allocated toward making up the town. This was to be the north half of section 7 and the south half of 18-17-8, the 'old highway' or front street was the dividing line between the two sections" (p.85, 1981).

The local church was in the foreground of development across the nation, helping the residents in varied ways. The first Methodist service in the Summerberry district was held in Uncle Sam Fleming's home on August 26, 1883. Later a stone Methodist church was erected in Summerberry in 1903; it unfortunately burned to the ground on November 27, 1949. The Methodist Church had become an integral part of the United Church of Canada on June 10, 1925 through church union.

I personally became an integral part of the United Church of Canada from infancy. Years later I studied for its ministry and served as a missionary in Hong Kong for eighteen years, returning to Canada in 1973 to become one of the ministers of the Chinese United Church in Vancouver for an additional seventeen years until retirement. The church was a vital and essential part of our family life.

Two important public holidays, apart from Christmas and Easter, we celebrated in those days were May 24th or Victoria Day and July 1st. May 24th commemorated Queen Victoria's birthday. There was a saying, which went as follows, "the 24th of May is the Queen's birthday, if we don't get a holiday we'll all run away." Ordinarily we celebrated the day at the Grenfell Fair Ground; people gathered from far and near. There were races for all ages, young and old. They had a competition of cart races (also known as harness racing) drawn by horses, a sport ordinarily reserved for the men in the community, however, Mother wanted to participate in the cart races (harness racing). She owned a beautiful mare called Queen. Mother was extremely fond and proud of Queen; she kept her spic and span at all times and would often use her own hairbrush and comb to help make the horse appear more attractive. Mother often fed Queen sugar cubes if she did well that particular day. One year Mother entered Queen in the cart races. She was mocked and ridiculed by many of her male competitors; however, Mother didn't let it bother her—she entered the race in spite of obvious disapproval. The crowds gathered, the races began and Queen won the cart race. The men lost face when Mother's horse received first prize, which in those days was a beautiful and coveted red ribbon. Her male competitors had little to say after the race. From that time forward, their unexpected defeat at the racecourse encouraged more ladies' participation in the cart races.

July 1st was known as Dominion Day, the day we all celebrated the birthday of Canada. Usually we went to Wolseley or Ellisboro to celebrate. They had races for both children and adults, such as a three-legged race or wheelbarrow race: one person served as the wheelbarrow; the other person lifted both legs of his/her partner. Their arms and body represented the wheelbarrow or the moving part of the wheelbarrow. Wolseley ordinarily featured cart races, attracting large crowds of people from all over the district some of the competitors came from around the province.

Another important occasion celebrated by our people was Thanksgiving Day. We especially thanked God for an abundant, plentiful harvest during the past year, and for his other blessings. A fowl supper was frequently held. The women in the community prepared a delicious harvest Thanksgiving dinner of chicken or turkeys with all the trimmings, including pumpkin pies, delicious pastries etc. After supper, there was a musical programme featuring selections sung by Mrs. McCague and Mrs. Fred Pollock. Both had beautiful voices and were popular singers in the local community.

A natural phenomenon the Prairies experience on a regular basis is a spectacular display of Northern Lights in the heavens. The Northern Lights (aurora borealis) would light up the sky (and still do) in an almost magical manner, especially on a clear cool crisp autumn evening. It was amazing how the sky lit up with streams of light above the northern magnetic pole to the sound of snap, crackle and pop. The lights danced to and fro in the northern hemisphere with coloured streams of lights: a fabulous display, representing every hue and colour in the rainbow. You could stand and appreciate the beautiful, natural display as long as you wished as it danced back and forth in the heavens. Often the display was accompanied by the wailing and howling of coyotes or wolves in the valley and hills, as if they had experienced the loss of one or more of their mates, leaving a strange, eerie, haunting and uneasy feeling in the pit of your stomach.

During my mother's time, Sunday (or the sabbath) was strictly observed. They weren't permitted to prepare food on Sunday and most time was spent worshipping or attending church and Sunday school. The same church choir used to sing for two or more services by different denominations on the same day.

Three years after grandfather Thomas Fleming and his brothers arrived in the Northwest Territories in 1882, the Riel Rebellion (sometimes known as the Northwest Rebellion) broke out, lasting for only a few days in 1885. Grandfather Fleming and his three brothers volunteered their service by helping to transport the munitions and personnel from Swift Current to Battleford and Batoche located about 70 miles north of Saskatoon. On May 14, 1885, the final showdown culminated in the Battle of Batoche.

The Fleming side of our family decided to commemorate our grandparent's arrival on their farm in Western Canada by holding a fiftieth anniversary celebration. They held a family reunion on Stan and Ida Fleming's farm on July 14, 1932, known as "the Fleming Reunion." It was held on the exact site where the farm was established in the spring of 1882. Our grandparents settled on the farm after having travelled to the Northwest Territories from Ontario by train, then by Red River carts or wagons from Brandon, Manitoba, which was the terminal of the railway in 1882. Over 186 family members, adults and children, attended the family reunion. Since no building was large enough on the farm to accommodate all the guests gathered at the same time and place, they rented a huge canvas tent for the occasion. (Note: a second Fleming reunion was held on July 3 and 4, 1982 to commemorate the first century of our grandparents arrival in Western Canada. Around 90 people attended it in Grenfell, Saskatchewan. The social portion of the occasion was held in the Ellis Hall and the Grenfell Museum.

My earliest recollection of the 1932 Fleming reunion was the fact each family brought along their own dishes for the occasion. The dishes were turned upside down on the tables to keep the dust away from an approaching prairie dust storm blowing heavily that day.

During that period the principal source of meat was raising our own birds and animals on the farm. The other source was hunting ducks, geese, grouse and partridges (Hungarian). During the open season for hunting, Father and some of the hired men would hunt ducks and geese on the nearby sloughs, ordinarily using shotguns, providing a wide range of fire as they hunted. Usually they returned home with several dozen ducks or geese. Besides hunting birds, occasionally they returned with a deer (venison), making a change from our limited diet.

My brother George enjoyed hunting jackrabbits for the little money he could make from selling the pelts. One time when it had snowed the night before, as George walked into the coulee to check his trap line, snow accidentally got in the barrel of his .22 rifle. He proceeded to clean off the muzzle of the gun with his other hand. When a branch from a nearby tree accidentally pulled the trigger, the rifle went off, shooting him through the hand. He still carries the scar of his hunting expedition to this day from the accident.

During the 1930s, due to the shortage of fresh fruit, the British Columbian Fruit Growers Association shipped carloads of apples by train to the Prairies for distribution. The apples were a welcome change for all the farmers and their families. It was a most generous gift, since we had little variety of fruit to eat at the time. I recall eating so many apples as a child, I became fed up with them. To this day I cannot eat many apples, due to my experience of the 1930s.

All prairie farmers were extremely resourceful, enabling them to survive. We naturally raised our own cattle, pigs, chickens, ducks and turkeys for sale, slaughtering some of the pigs and cattle for the family's food. The animals were raised for meat. We used to make sausages by using animal intestines as casings, first soaking them in salt. Father had built a smokehouse on the side of a nearby hill only the roof protruded from the hillside. The smoke provided a little extra taste and flavour for the meat.

Some years later, the farmers in our district formed a "beef ring." Each participating farmer slaughtered one of his best year-old animals. The animal was carved up by the farmers like Stan Fleming, and Billy Ferguson; then the farmer delivered the meat to the various members of the beef ring. By using such a method many of the farmers had fresh meat to eat during the summer season. The meat was placed in cotton flour sacks with the family's name on it, then delivered to the homes of the participating farmers on a weekly basis. An additional source of meat for the farmers was fishing in the nearby Qu'Appelle River for suckers, jackfish or yellow perch. Occasionally we used pitchforks to catch the fish in the river (illegal, but many farmers used pitchforks anyway).

After slaughtering pigs the family trimmed off all excess fat. Mother gathered the fat, melted it down and added lye, creating homemade soap for family use. The soap was a dark yellowish amber colour used for cleaning everything, including washing the clothes. Mother usually added bluing to make the bed sheets and work clothes appear much whiter and cleaner.

The family laundry was originally done on an old scrub board. The scrub board consisted of corrugated glass, which formed the upper part of the board. I recall the copper tub washing machine that rocked back and forth; later we used an electric power washing machine with a small motor attached. Later Mother bought a Maytag washing machine. She used her homemade soap for washing the clothes. To begin with a hand-operated wringer was used to wring the excess water from the clothes, then the clothes were hung outside on a clothesline to air and dry.

Father built an icehouse on the farm for the purpose of refrigeration. It was located not far from the house. We used it for storing perishable food during the warmer months of the year. The ice house was about 20 feet long by 15 feet wide and 8 feet high. A large hole was excavated in the ground with boards standing upright preventing the earth from caving in and a wooden-framed structure was placed over the hole. We stored large blocks of ice during the warmer months. The blocks of ice were about 3 feet long, 2 feet wide and 3 feet thick, depending upon the severity of the winter. The blocks of ice were taken from the nearby frozen dam, pulled out by a team of horses, and moved around by large ice tongs. Sawdust was placed on top and between the layers of ice, preserving the ice from melting too rapidly and enabling the preservation of food during the summer months. All perishable food was stored in the icehouse. We also used an icebox in the house itself, where we stored smaller amounts of ice to help preserve lesser quantities of food like milk, cream, butter, meat etc.

I will never forget the way we made delicious homemade ice cream; usually it was made on Sundays as a special treat for the entire family. We felt the homemade ice cream was superior to the ice cream we could purchase from the local grocery store and, of course, much cheaper. It was made by using an ice cream freezer with a mixture of cream, vanilla, eggs and sugar. One person would turn the handle of the freezer, adding chopped ice and salt to pack around the outside of the rotating cylinder until it froze the contents, forming ice cream. We made gallons of ice cream for the family using that method.

One of the first modern communicational gadgets I recall entering the community during the thirties was a version of the telephone. It was a box shaped affair that hung on the wall. A small circular mouthpiece served as the speaker, resembling a tube like affair for speaking into. The phone had two round bells attached that rang whenever someone called. An earphone was connected to a wire placed up to the ear as a receiver. The telephone had a small handle that was turned as you rang the switchboard. A handle was located on the side of the box; if rung it helped draw the switchboard operator's attention in town. The handle was also used for ringing a neighbour or friend. Each family had a code or series of long and short rings, similar to Morse code. One continuous ring drew the attention of all the neighbours on the line, in the event of the cancellation of school due to stormy weather, or perhaps an emergency like a house or barn fire etc. The telephone was a tremendous help in passing along local news and gossip. Some people had the habit of listening in on the telephone conversations of their neighbours. If either of the parties didn't know the answer to a specific query raised, the listener would occasionally butt in to provide the correct answer, if he/she knew the answer to it.

The other instrument of mass communication I recall was the early radio, providing the daily news to the nation and the world. It became a great source of amusement and entertainment for the entire family and general public. I recall we owned a 32-volt Philco radio; often it became noisy on account of static electricity with the approach of an electrical storm.

During the evening the entire family would gather around the radio to listen to the news or programmes such as dramatic presentations of the Green Hornet, Lux Radio Theatre, or the Major Bows talent contest broadcast from New York.

I will never forget when Japan attacked Pearl Harbor, the American president Franklin D. Roosevelt presented a public address by radio and announced the official entry of America into the Second World War.

We also enjoyed listening to stories like the Lone Ranger and Superman, and to comedians such as Amos and Andy, Mert and Marg of the Happy Gang, and famous bands like Guy Lombardo and his Royal Canadians, or Mart Kenny and his Western Canadian Gentlemen. The radio was as important in those days as T V is for families today.

We also owned, and still have on the old home farm, a Thomas A. Edison gramophone (No. 15, patented November 7, 1903); the records were shaped like cylinders. The sound of the records was frequently scratchy, but we valued them highly since it was considered an important and revolutionary invention providing recorded ("canned") music for the home and general public.

During the war (1939–1945) the Canadian government issued ration books with coupons for all families across the nation, introducing rationing of meat, sugar, butter, flour and gasoline for cars. However, food rationing didn't affect farmers as much as it affected residents living in cities and villages, since the farmers had more control over their food source (except for sugar, flour and gasoline). The farmers used purple gas for their trucks or tractors, which was a cheaper grade of fuel than the ordinary gasoline used for automobiles.

The family garden played a vital important and essential role on the farm. We always planted a large garden, growing potatoes, carrots, peas, beans, corn, asparagus, horseradish etc. We also had fruit bushes like gooseberries, raspberry canes, saskatoons, crab apple trees and a reddish coloured plum etc. The only way we could maintain the garden was to water it with large tanks of water drawn from the dam or sloughs. Around the edge of the garden were planted caragana trees to protect the garden and house from the powerful and mighty prairie winds.

During the summer, Mother would bottle (or can) vegetables and fruit, preserving them for use during the long cold winter months. If the slough dried up, we would plant potatoes or vegetables in it; it still had a little more moisture enabling the vegetables to grow larger and better.

Preservation of food was vitally important. For the preservation of hen eggs we used "waterglass," a concentrated solution of sodium silicate that formed a transparent layer, as a preservative for keeping the eggs from spoiling. (Recently, I was at a local city drug store, when an old timer enquired from the druggist, "Do you sell water-glass?" The druggist appeared somewhat mystified so one of the older customers enquired, "Do you know what waterglass is?" His reply was no, so the gentleman said, "Formerly we used it to pre-serve eggs and as a waterproofing agent." Nowadays it's a term that has largely passed out of our present day vocabulary.

We also had a root cellar below the kitchen where we stored vege-tables for the winter months. We especially stored large quantities of potatoes in the basement beneath the house. During the winter the potatoes would frequently sprout. The sprouts had to be removed every so often during the winter. Sometimes lizards would be found living among the potatoes; they varied in length, some nearly 5 inches or more.

We picked wild fruit by the pail from the nearby valleys and coulees, varying according to the kind of spring weather experi-enced during the year. Some of the berries we picked (placing them in cream cans, making excellent pies) were saskatoons, wild cranber-ries, chokecherries, pin cherries, wild strawberries, and raspberries. The entire family assisted in picking the berries, making it an im-portant outing for the family. The neighbours often joined us in picking berries in the coulees (and valleys).

Father raised bees for producing fresh honey and sugar for the family. The honey was delicious; however, raising bees required a special skill. We used to have three or more hives of bees situated near the edge of the garden; they helped to pollinate the flowers. Fa-ther wore specially designed clothes for attending the bees. He used a fine mesh veil placed over his head to protect himself from bee stings and he usually carried along a smoker in one hand to squirt smoke into the bee hives when adding a further layer to the hive for increasing the capacity for storage of honey. The bees sometimes be-came angry; therefore, he squirted smoke into the hive to control them, making the bees somewhat dizzy and confused. Each hive contained wax honeycombs where the bees deposited their honey. They filled up the tiny cells within the honeycombs. After the bees filled the cells we extracted the raw honey from the honeycombs.

The machine used was known as a honey extractor. They also used extremely hot knives to remove the beeswax from the honeycombs, placed the dripping honeycombs into the extractor, and then rapidly turned the handle of the extractor, depositing the liquid honey down the walls of the extractor. The process was usually carried out in our kitchen. It was an interesting and fascinating procedure to observe especially for children. My younger sister Betty and I stood nearby watching the entire procedure. We were only tall enough to look into the extractor as it whirled around; consequently we were covered from head to toe with honey. After the process was completed by the honey extractor, mother gave us a much-needed bath to clean us up again.

Before the days of electricity, we lit our homes with coal oil lamps using wicks. Later we used Aladdin and Coleman lamps, which had tiny mantles for burners. The chimneys of the lamps had to be cleaned on a regular basis since they became covered with black soot and smoke.

Later father installed an electrical power plant in the basement of our home. The 32-volt storage batteries were neatly arranged on shelves in the basement. The system was used for many years, a great improvement over the coal oil and gasoline lamps formerly used for lighting our home.

A few years later, Father installed a wind charger resembling a windmill. It was about forty feet tall, powered solely by wind, situated on a nearby hill not far from the house. It helped generate electricity for the 32-volt storage batteries in the basement, supplementing the power the engine generated. Years later the Saskatchewan Light and Power Corporation was formed, installing a universal system of electricity for the entire province, including cities, towns and the farms themselves.

Our home was heated by a wood-burning furnace in the basement, which heated the water in the radiators located in each room throughout the house. Trees were cut down from the nearby coulees for fuel, which came from the Qu'Appelle Valley near our home.

We had a woodshed, where we stored a considerable amount of wood, located about twenty-five feet from the house. Besides wood we also used some coal (anthracite or lignite) from Drumheller, Alberta. I recall as a child, one of my regular duties was to cut and split wood for the cook stove (McClary) in the kitchen. I piled the wood between the kitchen wall and the stove on a daily basis, so it would be dry and ready for use.

Milking cows was an important task that took place on a daily basis. We milked eight cows twice a day, morning and evening. However, during harvest time, Mother and I shared the responsibility of milking the cows. The fresh milk was run through a machine known as a cream separator, which conveniently separated the cream from the milk. Some of the cream was shipped in metal containers, known as cream-cans, to the creamery in Brandon, Manitoba. The skimmed milk was usually fed to the pigs and turkeys to help them grow faster and plumper.

Mother reserved sufficient fresh cream for our family's use. Some was used for making butter. Originally we used a hand-style churn which had a plunger; the plunger had to be moved rapidly up and down until butter was eventually formed. Later we used an end-over churn, shaped like a barrel, which was placed on a frame and turned. Later Father attached a small motor on it to save the labour of turning the churn. As butter formed in the churn, Mother took it out, placed it in a large wooden butter bowl, kneaded the butter with a wooden ladle and added a little salt to the butter, so it would be a little more tasty. The remaining butter was shaped in a mould; then the butter was either used or sold by the pound to the local grocery store.

During the Second World War it was difficult to obtain hired help, since most men were off to Europe. We obtained help wherever we could get it. I recall we had a real greenhorn of a medical student from McGill University in Montreal; he didn't know the front of a cow from the rear. One day he stood by the open barn door cracking jokes. Mother had already heard enough of his jokes, so she squirted warm milk directly into his mouth to try and silence him for a time. Because of the warm milk, he became as sick as a dog. He never pulled such a trick again while we were milking the cows. When we milked the cows we always sat down beside the cow on a three-legged stool especially used by farmers for milking.

Three times a year, every family across Canada received a copy of Timothy Eaton's or Robert Simpson's Spring, Summer, Fall and Winter catalogues. They were exceedingly popular catalogues mailed across the nation. We obtained most of our clothes and other necessities, such as hot water bottles to keep our beds warm in the winter. You could even buy a mail-order house from Eaton's catalogue. One of our neighbours, Ryle Smith, owned such a house, costing approximately $1,600 to $2,000 dollars. The Smiths were good neighbours of our family. All family members enjoyed looking through the catalogues. We as children especially enjoyed seeing the latest toys on the market and the clothing available in the catalogues, then gave hints to Santa Claus regarding what we would like for Christmas. Most of our toys and other items came through the mail-order catalogues from Winnipeg. Since we lived eighty miles east of Regina, our parents would drive the family to Regina about twice a year to do a little shopping, a memorable occasion for all.

The other important mail-order catalogue I personally enjoyed enormously was the Spring Seed Catalogue, also from Winnipeg. It was beautifully illustrated in colour—most attractive. I regularly ordered packages of McKenzie's flower seeds from the catalogue.

Flower gardening was my hobby. So much so, occasionally I won prizes for my well-kept and planned flower garden. One year, I recall I had over fifty different varieties of flowers in my garden; it was a riot of colour. My garden was located along the side of a nearby ravine adjacent to the house. However, after Father purchased a tractor, instead of using the old steam engine, I received permission to dismantle the water boiler from the old Sawyer-Massey steam engine. I placed it on its side in the ravine, filled the tank with water, and planted water lilies in buckets placed in the boiler. The water lilies bloomed profusely, making the garden more attractive and colourful. I also raised goldfish in the water lily tank.

The local community school I attended was called Rose Lane Public School (built in 1905, closed in 1966); it was situated two and a half miles from our farm. We commuted by horse and buggy. After the first snowfall, we drove a bobsled to school, drawn by a team of horses. Most families did the same thing. The schoolteacher usually lived in our home, which carried mixed blessings.

If it was an extremely cold winter, Mother would place bricks in the oven to heat them, and then wrap the bricks in old newspapers (the Winnipeg Free Press) so they would retain their heat much longer. She placed the bricks at our feet, or in our hands to keep them warm. During the recess periods at school, we usually played softball in the spring and fall. After the snow arrived we took our sleds and went sleigh riding down the nearby hills.

Upon completing my Grade Nine and Ten by correspondence, I went to high school in Summerberry, our nearest village. It was five and a half miles south of our farm. One year I lived in town with my Uncle Will and Aunt Annie (Fleming), the next year with the Jack Bennett family. The school consisted of an elementary school on the ground floor and a high school located on the second floor.

Ours was a typical prairie high school: the principal usually served in a double capacity. As principal and teacher she taught all subjects ranging from grade 9 to 12. It was a tremendous responsibility for her. The principle idea was to help the students become more self-reliant, so as not to be overly dependent upon the teacher or principal.

I was a student in Summerberry High School, originally built in 1906. Miss Madeline Daeschel was the principal. She was the daughter of the local Lutheran pastor from the town of Grenfell. I came to admire her since she was extremely hard working, exceedingly diligent and clever. I wanted to study Latin, thinking perhaps one day I might study medicine. She was already teaching French and German, the required languages within the curriculum. She informed me that since I was her only Latin student, she would teach me after school hours—I gratefully accepted her offer. She was a person who always went the second mile to help a student needing assistance.

Healthwise, from time to time we had the ordinary common aches, pains and children's diseases as others experienced, including minor cuts and bruises. There were a number of homemade remedies we utilized. If we had a chest cold, the old standby was a mustard plaster placed on the chest. If we had a sliver in our finger, Mother would place a poultice made of oatmeal or bread and milk to draw out the foreign particle. Sulfur and molasses were used for measles, flu or other ailments. Another home remedy was to gather wormwood, a silvery-grey coloured plant, ordinarily considered a weed—if it was cut and boiled, you could drink the liquid as a remedy for colds. Cod-liver oil and castor oil were also reliable old standbys. Besides there were the many patent medicines sold by a representative of the Watkins or the Raleigh man who travelled from door to door peddling remedies. However, for more serious illnesses we would inform the local doctor to seek his help, advice and care.

In the days before there were local hospitals in the smaller communities of Saskatchewan, there were a few very dedicated people like Nurse Eva Merrifield. She did her utmost to provide basic medical care in Wolseley and the surrounding communities including the village of Summerberry. Most of our family members were brought into the world by Nurse Merrifield, including myself. She was a saintly sort of person who was always concerned about the family's health and welfare; as a result, Nurse Merrifield spent her entire life serving others. She also did her best providing services for the surrounding communities. Her name was a password in the area of medical health and care, since there was little in the way of professional medical services for the general public, except for extremely dedicated people like Nurse Merrifield. She also operated a small private maternity home out of her own home.

In 1921 Nurse Merrifield graduated as a maternity nurse from the Old Cottage Hospital in Regina, served the local community for some twenty years and attended to the delivery of 860 babies in her maternity home, while others were born in the homes of patients. The general physician in Wolseley was Dr. R. J. Cooke. Dr. Cooke did many of his tonsillectomies in Nurse Merrifield's private hospital. Nurse Merrifield worked long hours—holidays were only a thing she dreamed about. (Courtesy of the *Indian Head-Wolseley News*: July 7, 1982, page 14: a quote from an article written by Virna about Nurse Eva Merrifield.)

The greater medical needs of our community were largely met by Dr. Robert J. Cooke (Senior) from the neighbouring town of Wolseley, who practiced there for some forty-three years. His area was huge, covering Wolseley, Lemberg, Neudorf, Ellisboro, Glenavon, Baring, Montmartre, Summerberry and Sintiluta. He belonged to an era which has since long disappeared—that of the country doctor of horse and buggy days, and later the automobile.

There was no hospital in Wolseley at the time; he tended to his patients in their homes, which meant long drives in all kinds of weather by day or by night. Country drives were often difficult, unpleasant, hazardous and dangerous. (Courtesy of the *Indian Head-Wolseley News*, June 30, 1982, Centennial edition 1882-1982).

Last, but by no means least, I should mention the sanitary aspect of our home, in other words, the toilet or the outhouse, whichever term is preferred. It was the familiar little building all prairie folks are acquainted with, ordinarily located outside, usually located among the caragana trees. Ours was a "two holer:" one small and the other large. The outhouse was about eight feet in height and five feet squared. Ordinarily the toilet paper consisted of old catalogues or newspapers; you could glance through the paper during one's period of meditation. Other forms of toilet paper consisted of paper wrappings placed around the oranges and pears etc. (Note: Modern toilet paper was invented in 1857 by Joseph Gayetty in the U.S.A. It became known as "Gayetty Medicated Paper." In 1857 it cost fifty cents U.S. per 500 sheets. Most likely the cost prevented it from being more widely used. Information derived from the Peoples Almanac, New York, 1975: Courtesy of the Cameron Library, Burnaby, B.C.)

(I hope the foregoing description of life on a prairie farm in the 1930s enables readers to recollect, identify and relate to experiences in rural Western Canada.)

A binder drawn by horses during harvest.

Binders and stookers.

Stook loader and hay rack in action.

Mother examines the grain bin.

A barrel-type butter churn.

Early Post Office boxes used.

An early telephone.

Mary Salak examining some grain.

A local celebration depicting a Sakimay Indian chief, Indian travois and early automobiles near the fairgrounds at Grenfell, Saskatchewan.

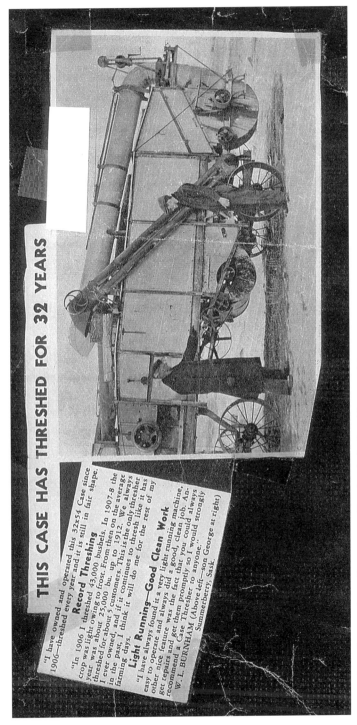

THIS CASE HAS THRESHED FOR 32 YEARS

"I have owned and operated this 32x54 Case since 1906—threshed every year and it is still in fair shape.

Record Threshing

"In 1906 I threshed 43,000 bushels. In 1907-8 the crop was light owing to frost. From then on the average year was about 25,000 bu. up to 1912. We always threshed for about 5 customers. This is the only thresher I ever owned, and if it continues to thresh like it has in the past, I think it will do me for the rest of my farming days.

Light Running—Good Clean Work

"I have always found it a very light running machine, easy to operate and always did a good, clean job. Another nice feature was the fact that you could always get repairs and get them promptly so I would strongly recommend a Case Thresher to anyone."

W. L. BURNHAM (Above left—son George at right)

Summerberry, Sask.

Harry Burnham and son George standing by their threshing machine.

Berry pickers taking a brief break.

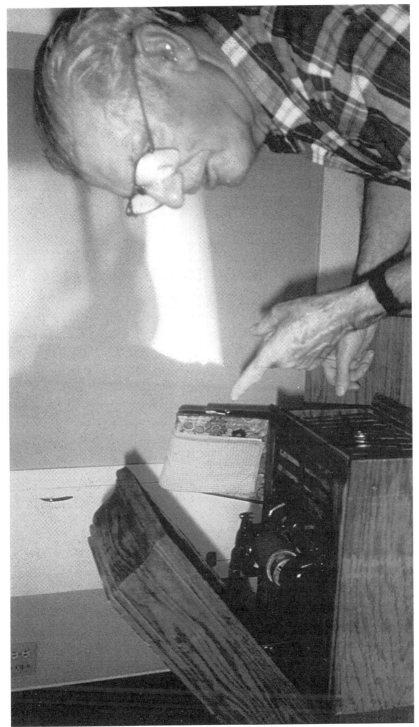

Brother George listening to our old Edison phonograph.

Varying sizes of milk bottles and butter moulds.

A pump organ and oil lamp holder.

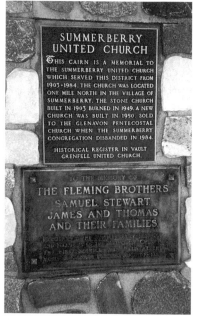

Summerberry United Church cairn.

A typical prairie-style classroom with desks.

RATION
BOOK 1

CARNET DE
RATIONNEMENT 1

Serial Number   VR 392616   No de série

DOMINION OF/DU CANADA

Name
Nom ....
Address
Adresse ....

Age if under 16 .... Age, si au-dessous de 16 ans

ISSUED BY THE WARTIME PRICES AND TRADE BOARD
ÉMIS PAR LA COMMISSION DES PRIX ET DU COMMERCE EN TEMPS DE GUERRE

War-time rationing booklet used in the 1940s.

CLARENCE HOUSE
SW1A 1BA

12th August 1999

Dear Mr. Burnham,

The good wishes expressed in the many
cards and letters received by Queen Elizabeth
The Queen Mother on her birthday are a source of
great pleasure to Her Majesty.

The Queen Mother thanks you most
sincerely for your thoughts for
Her Majesty's 99th birthday, and for all your
kind remarks.

I am also to thank you for the
photographs you sent, taken during
Their Majesties' visit to Canada in 1939, which
brought back many happy memories.

Yours sincerely,

Catriona Leslie

Lady-in-Waiting

The Reverend L. Burnham.

Celebrating the
Queen Mother's
99th birthday.

In 1939 the royal train stopped at Broadview, Saskatchewan to meet local residents and school children.

CHAPTER 3

British Columbia:
A New Beginning

U PON ARRIVING IN VANCOUVER in the fall of 1945, I enrolled at King Edward High School (the corner of 12th Avenue and Oak Street) to study additional subjects to qualify for admission to the University of British Columbia. I remember King Edward High School as a stately looking structure with a fine reputation for helping students. The principal Dr. Ray J. Sanderson and Dr. W. C. Wilson (vice-principal) did their best to help all students enrolling.

Vancouver High School was officially opened on January 5, 1905. It was the first high school in the newly established city of Vancouver (1886) and was renamed King Edward High School in 1908. It served the fledgling city of Vancouver exceedingly well. The attractive looking wooden-framed school was unfortunately levelled to ashes on June 13, 1973. The only remaining portion of the original school is its attractive stone fence that still surrounds the prime property which now belongs to the Vancouver General Hospital. The new King Edward High School successor is located on West Broadway. The school's motto was *Ad summum* (to the highest) and the school's colours were blue and white. A lion symbolizing courage and fortitude was adopted on its shield for all student publications. King Edward High School represented a fine cross-section of Vancouver's student population. The multicultural aspect of the student body especially impressed me, since I was a newcomer to the city of Vancouver from a small prairie town in Saskatchewan. The fiftieth reunion of the class of 1946, from which I graduated, held its reunion on June 21, 1996. Many of us gathered at Heritage Hall, located on

Main Street in Vancouver. A happy time was thoroughly enjoyed by all who attended; it was an experience we will not forget. Naturally, fifty years had changed each of us, but we still maintained the one common bond of graduating from King Edward High School, which made us exceedingly proud and happy. For me, the most valuable lesson I learned from my short period of study at King Edward High School was coming to recognize, acknowledge and accept the multicultural nature of the school in the city of Vancouver. It was an invaluable lesson—enabling me to realize the necessity of accepting other students as brothers and sisters, regardless of language, creed, faith, race or what-have-you—similar to discovering a pearl of great price. For me it became a liberating concept and idea, enabling me to recognize that we are basically the same in our aims and objectives. Each person has a unique and invaluable contribution to make originating from our varied culture and social backgrounds. There is no room today for attitudes of intolerance or feelings of being superior or inferior to one another. This concept of equality and acceptance enabled me to establish a firm foundation for my life's work, both in Canada and Hong Kong, where I lived for some 18 years. Equality is a precious and invaluable gift that remains an integral part of me as an individual. I discovered the world is only what we make it, providing we learn to live, love, and respect each other through living and working together in peace and harmony. We may help transform and change the world into a better, safer, happier more prosperous and peaceful place in which to live.

My first working experience in B.C. was at Smithers, located midway between Prince George and Prince Rupert in the northern part of British Columbia. I was assigned there as a lay pastor by the United Church of Canada. It was only God's grace and my faith that enabled me to respond positively to the many tasks that laid ahead, to survive the individual challenges before me as I began my work as a student. Besides Smithers, I was responsible for travelling to Quick, Evelyn and Telkwa, as lay pastor for those communities. At the time, I was in my early twenties with no practical experience to call upon. The people were exceedingly cooperative and accepting in all aspects in spite of me being a complete "greenhorn." They tolerated my preaching, which I admit was not really up to standard. They also entrusted me to work with their youth in various groups—in fact, the older folk in the community leaned over backwards to encourage me in the many aspects of the church work, providing wise advice and counsel as necessary. Since I had no vehicle of my own, I relied upon various people to help me travel from one town and village to another by car or truck. I used to frequently travel long distances in the caboose of the Canadian National Railway. Locally I did my visitation by horseback. The farmers lent me one of their horses, so I could more conveniently get around. The fact I was born and raised on a farm in Saskatchewan helped me feel quite at home travelling by horse. One of the most annoying problems I faced and eventually overcame was the opening and closing of the heavy tight barbed-wire gates of the former Scandinavian residents leading into their farmyards. I was not accustomed to opening such tight gates .The hospitality of the individual farmers was tremendous; I will never forget the way they would readily accommodate me for the night. The food was plain and varied but always tasty, delicious and nourishing. However, I found the coffee exceedingly strong, especially in the homes of those who came from a Scandinavian background. Often they would place an egg in the coffee pot, for some reason that I never did discover. At the time (1948) there were no TVs or such entertainment. The farmers usually entertained me by telling interesting and absorbing stories concerning their home town, village or city from the country of their origin. I enjoyed listening to their colourful tales and varied experiences as farmers in Norway or Sweden. It was a splendid cultural and educational experience for me. They told how they were practically raised upon skis from childhood, even attending school on skis. They travelled long distances over hills and mountains on their skis to visit friends, attend church or do their shopping; because of that they felt very much at home in British Columbia. The mountainous terrain helped them recall their native land in Norway or Sweden.

One of the major features of Smithers, where I lived for a full year, was the extremely heavy snowfall received each winter. I clearly recall three feet or more of snow would suddenly blanket the area within a few hours. The town of Smithers fifty years ago has since grown into a modern, attractive, beautiful resort city with every modern convenience—a far cry from the way I originally knew it. Smithers is located at the foot of the large and impressive Hudson

Bay Mountain directly opposite the city. A large glacier was a permanent fixture throughout the year. Another range of snow-capped mountains known as the Babine Mountains is located north of Smithers, where many skiers and hunters enjoyed the area. Near the town of Smithers were the communities of Telkwa, Quick, and Evelyn. The Bulkley River gracefully wends its way through the beautiful Bulkley Valley. Beyond Smithers to the northwest are more mountains including the Roche Deboule mountain range, plus the new and old towns of Hazelton. The old town has many colourful and artistically carved totem poles reminding the residents and visitors of their rich Native heritage. The swiftly flowing water of the Skeena River wends its way through the rugged mountains to the Pacific Ocean, to the city of Prince Rupert on the Pacific coast. Prince Rupert is an important grain shipping terminal for Western Canada; it has a first class natural harbour, linking up with Alaska. In July 1996, when Smithers was celebrating its seventy-fifth anniversary, marking the establishment of the city, they kindly invited me to attend the gala celebrations. I had not returned to Smithers for fifty years since I served there as a lay minister in 1947. It was great to revisit Smithers and see the way a quaint little town had grown and flourished over the years, much like a beautiful butterfly. It had transformed and changed from the chrysalis stage to a beautiful attractive city following a brief period of only half a century. I especially enjoyed visiting some of the local people whom I had formerly known. The mayor of Smithers even reminded me of the fact he previously attended one of my youth groups. Likewise, many of the older people still remembered me, such as Jean Kilpatrick, who was in her 90s. My sister Betty and I attended the July 1st celebrations, which consisted of a pancake breakfast, a colourful parade, and an outdoor inter-church worship service held on the school lawn. The mosquitoes and black flies were abundantly present, leaving their unforgettable trademarks. The varied and carefully planned celebrations lasted for a total of nine days. The people of Smithers certainly went all out in their varied celebrations and hospitality to recall bygone days and experiences. After having spent a year at Smithers when I was a student, I returned to Vancouver to attend the University of British Columbia, studying in the Faculty of Arts. The university's student population at the time was a little over

10,000 students. Many classes were held in Quonset huts (semicylindrical-roofed buildings) constructed for World War Two military purposes. Many of the students attending the university formerly served in the Armed Forces during the war. They seized the opportunity to upgrade their educational standard by returning to the university. During the summer of 1948, the United Church of Canada reassigned me to Arrowhead (thirty miles south of Revelstoke—it no longer exists) for additional student work, and Malakwa (west of Revelstoke), situated on the main line of the C.P.R., beside a glacier east of Revelstoke, amid the surrounding towering mountains. It happened 1948 was the year of a major flood that occurred on the Columbia River. At the time, I happened to be living at Malakwa as the flood struck the Columbia River around the end of May. I wanted to return to Arrowhead to rescue some of my possessions. However, all road and rail communications had been suspended due to severe flood conditions. My only alternative was to travel from Revelstoke down the Columbia River to Arrowhead by mail boat. It was rather frightening to contemplate the journey, since ordinarily rapids could be found as one travelled down the Columbia River. However, since the river was in a state of flood, the water completely covered the rapids, which resulted in a fairly pleasant and smooth journey to Arrowhead, providing a totally new perspective of the broad valley under flood conditions. At the time I was living in the C.P.R. station residence. The water rose over forty feet, flooding the entire station floor. There was some eighteen inches of water on the floor and we literally shovelled several inches of silt and muck off the floor, tossing it out the front and back doors of the station. It was necessary to spread lime over the floor to help sweeten and neutralize the smell.

During the summer, I had the opportunity to meet many interesting people. One such person was the only female prospector in the area. She was reputed to be one of the first women graduates from Oxford University. She lived near Beaton in the Arrow Lake region. During her many journeys she ascended the mountains by riding on a donkey, prospecting for minerals. One day as I visited her home, she asked me to open a certain cupboard drawer in the living room. The drawer was filled with numerous samples of minerals she had collected. She requested I select a rock from the drawer, and then asked me "Young man, what are you holding in your hand?" I replied, "Honestly I don't know one rock from the other, since I have never studied geology." She replied "Young man, learn to use your eyes!" I replied, "It appears to me to be a cinder." She replied, "You are correct; it's a cinder of a kind." She claimed it was a meteorite that had fallen from outer space. She then chose still another rock she picked up on the mountaintop and commented, "This rock is radioactive." My friend was one of the most intelligent and highly educated persons living in the community. Besides being a skilled geologist, she always kept her hands busy by crocheting various articles to pass on to her children and grandchildren.

Since autumn had arrived once again, I returned to U.B.C. to continue my studies in the Faculty of Arts, which kept me fully occupied. It happened anthropology was one of my favorite subjects. From my study of anthropology I became extremely interested in the Native people living on the northwest coast of B.C. Therefore, I applied for and accepted employment at Bella Bella for summer work in the R. W. Large Memorial Hospital, a United Church mission hospital, for the summer. Dr. George Darby Sr. was the superintendent of the hospital. Dr. Darby was an excellent mentor and guide. He came to know the Native people intimately after having spent most of his adult life working with them. Dr. Darby frequently explained some of the ancient customs to me of the traditions and habits of the Natives. During the week I worked as the general chore boy in the Bella Bella hospital and on the weekends I was responsible for conducting the worship services and Sunday school within the local church. In order to become accustomed with the villagers and their way of life, frequently I visited many of the church members' homes. I was often requested to conduct funeral services for a villager, if somebody had been killed in an accident or drowned.

The Native people on the Pacific coast occasionally resorted to holding a "potlatch." By holding a potlatch, they were observing a tradition that had unfortunately been banned by the federal government. A potlatch was frequently held by a chief or some wealthy person from a clan such as bear, wolf, beaver, thunderbird, whale etc. At the time they held a large feast. The feast was occasionally held daily for a month or six weeks. The guests were invited to help celebrate the occasion; it included important people from other villages along the coast. They feasted and danced with elaborate mechanically-operated masks placed over their heads, representing a wolf, bear, beaver or a mythical thunderbird, whale etc. They frequently drank liquor, or gambled for the duration of the potlatch until the sponsor of the potlatch became broke. The sponsor presented gifts to the guests like blankets, food, rifles, clocks, trunks, canoes and so on. The potlatch was only considered successful if the sponsor completely squandered all of his earthly wealth; by so doing he gained tremendous "face" and prestige in the presence of all of the village people. At the time the federal government declared the potlatch was an evil custom and a waste of their earthly wealth; therefore they discouraged the Indians from holding potlatches. When I lived in Bella Bella, the government was gradually beginning to have second thoughts concerning the potlatch, its significance and meaning. Some of the villagers secretly showed the nurses and me elaborately carved and artistically painted masks, including colourful red and blue blankets with designs outlined in white buttons. In the fall, I returned to Vancouver to further my studies at the University of B.C., continuing to study anthropology. The experiences I received from firsthand knowledge helped me greatly with my studies at U.B.C.

The following summer I was assigned to still another village called Klemtu, located a few hours north of Bella Bella by fish boat. Adjacent to the village of Klemtu was a J. H. Todd salmon cannery. Many female villagers worked in the cannery during the week. The men worked on their trawlers from Monday to Friday, while their wives worked at processing fish in the cannery. Originally I was only responsible for a handful of elderly folks and children during the week; however, I received permission from the authorities of the United Church of Canada in Vancouver to work in the J. H. Todd cannery for the remainder of the week.

My principal responsibility within the cannery was cooking the fish in large retorts (ovens). The fish were first cleaned, cut and placed in tin cans, sealed, and loaded into the retorts by Chinese labourers. The Chinese assisted by sealing the retort doors for cooking the salmon. When I took over cooking the salmon, it was my first actual working relationship and contact with the Chinese people. We became good friends and mutually appreciated the good working relationships we had. Little did I realize from such a brief working experience that it would later become a lifelong relationship for me. Upon returning to Vancouver, I was a full-time student in theology at Union College of B.C. One of the requirements was to do part-time work under the supervision of a Union (Theological) College staff member. Originally I requested permission to continue working in a Native setting in Vancouver; however, I was informed the United Church had no work with the Natives in the city of Vancouver (1952). My second choice was to work with either a Chinese or Japanese congregation. The United Church promptly appointed me to the Chinese United Church in Chinatown, located on Pender and Dunlevy Avenue in Vancouver. Therefore, I officially became the student assistant to Rev. Chow Ling, specifically to help the youth of the Chinese United Church congregation in Vancouver.

The youth group in the Chinese church met on a regular weekly basis. I held a Bible class besides a weekly gathering each Saturday evening. At the beginning there were approximately twelve members; gradually it expanded with the passage of time. My hope and desire was to help mould the two groups into one. The youth were a combination of those born in Canada and others who came as immigrants from Hong Kong and China. We looked all around to find a positive contribution we could possibly make to the life and work of the local church.

The chancel of the church was greatly in need of a coat of paint therefore, the youth group offered to paint it during the Thanksgiving weekend (1952), making it appear much brighter and attractive: naturally at the same time it made the remainder of the church appear drab and unattractive. Our next project was to paint the interior of the church between Christmas and New Year's Day. All of the youth group happily participated in the project, helping to unite the two groups by bringing them closer together. The parents supplied delicious and tasty Chinese meals. The projects helped infuse new life and meaning into the local church life. My other role in the Chinese United Church was to assist teaching the English language. Rev. Chow Ling, the minister, had already begun operating an exceedingly active night school. At one time there were 450 new immigrants from Hong Kong and China coming to the church five days a week to study English in the evenings. Our church as well as other Protestant churches pioneered in the field of teaching English as a second language, now known as E.S.L. classes, sponsored by the government. It was a tremendous opportunity and challenge, working and witnessing among recent immigrants from China, enabling them to realize the Christian church was interested in their immediate and long-term future in Canada. The vast majority of the teachers were Canadian-born Chinese, helping the immigrants recognize locally born Chinese were interested in assisting the newcomers to adjust to their new home in Canada.

My work with the Chinese at the local community level in Vancouver changed the entire direction and emphasis of my life: volunteering to become a United Church missionary in Hong Kong (1955-1973), where I served for eighteen years before returning permanently to live in Canada. Hong Kong became one of the most exciting and challenging periods of my life. I never regretted the decision and change which took place.

Note references: (**) Reference *From Potlatch to Pulpit*, an autobiography by William Henry Pierce, a Native Indian ordained into the Methodist Church. Published by the Vancouver Bindery Limited, Vancouver, B.C., 1933. Another reference *Up and Down the North Pacific Coast by Canoe and Mission Ship* by Rev. Thomas Crosby, published by the Missionary Society of the Methodist Church. The Young People's Forward Movement Department: Methodist Mission Rooms, Toronto, Ontario, published by Frederick Clarke Stephanson in 1914.

Former Chinese United Church and dormitory on Pender Street, Vancouver, in the 1950s.

During the 1950s, immigrant students eagerly studied English at the Chinese United Church Night School in Vancouver. The minister, Rev. Chow Ling, stands to the right in the middle row.

Chinese United Church bazaar, Vancouver.

Centennial celebration of the Chinese United Church in 1988. The guest speaker was the moderatory of the United Church of Canada, Rev. San Chul Lee.

Rev. James Pan, Richard Kao and Lem Burnham.

CHAPTER 4

Valued Chinese Customs and Traditions

T HE CUSTOMS AND CULTURE as practiced in Hong Kong are obviously Chinese in origin with modifications and variations from place to place and time to time.

The most outstanding of the customs is the celebration of the Lunar New Year, also known as the Spring Festival or Chinese New Year. The New Year always occurs in late January (as in 1998) or February, according to Western calculation. The years rotate in cycles of twelve animals: the rat, ox, tiger, hare, dragon, serpent, horse, goat, monkey, cock, dog and boar, equivalent to zodiac symbols. Each year has its own individual characteristics and significance. Each animal is supposed to exercise some mystical influence over that period of time. The custom possibly originated from around the time of the T'ang Dynasty, which began in 618 A.D. and lasted until 907. A zodiac of twelve is common among most nations in the Far East. All people of Chinese origin are familiar with the year of the animal under which he/she was born.

The lunar New Year is the most joyous and happy time of the entire season. Everyone in Hong Kong observes the Chinese New Year, celebrating a public holiday ranging from three days to one week or even longer in China or other locations in the Orient. At the time of the New Year all business firms cease labour and are closed, except for essential services like the police, hospitals, fire department, public transportation and restaurants.

Another ancient tradition was the use of firecrackers to welcome in the New Year. It is believed the noise and explosion of the fireworks would chase away all evil spirits that may be lingering around the corner; however, in recent years, firecrackers or fireworks have not been so popular due the possibility of injury to the eyes and ears of those using them. The Hong Kong government officially banned the use of firecrackers due to the leftist disturbances in 1966–67, the beginning of the Cultural Revolution in China. The powder used in fireworks was occasionally misdirected into making weapons of destruction. China officially banned the use of fireworks, due to the possibility of causing fire, or injury to the people.

Every home is swept and cleaned until it is spotless and immaculate, eliminating all possible dirt or filth. Younger children wear new clothes if at all possible. Eating is the major and dominant feature of the season including sweets, nuts, fresh fruits and various sweetmeats. Hong Kong always holds special New Year fairs. They are held about ten days previous to New Year's Day. At the fair they sell flowers (plum and peach blossoms, bell flowers and water narcissus) as well as a multitude of other beautiful flowering plants which are in season. The fair sells many kinds of goodies, for children, lovers and all. The fairs are held on the side streets, where the hawkers and vendors unload various kinds of odds and ends including clothes, plants, flower pots, jewellery, toys and hand made articles.

Chinese New Year is a time when special attention is given to children; they wear new clothes and are usually presented with lucky red envelopes (*laisee*) by relatives or friends of the family. The red envelopes are also occasionally presented to unmarried adults. Lucky envelopes (*laisee*) are used for numerous other happy occasions throughout the year as well as certain unhappy events.

Most people, including domestic servants, receive an extra month's wage, or bonus of some kind. All one's debts are supposed to be paid, to begin the New Year free of such encumbrance if possible.

The visitation of relatives and friends is at the head of the list of things that should be done: all public transport is filled to capacity and then some. You can scarcely walk down the sidewalks without accidentally bumping into someone along the way. Familiar and famous sayings written down on red paper splashed with gold concerning the New Year may be purchased from a street vendor, then pasted up on the entrance to the home or elsewhere in a house or place of business. Such sayings or slogans usually convey good wishes for a happy, prosperous and peaceful New Year to all.

One should not talk about unhappy occasions or events during the New Year celebrations, in case they recall unhappy or sad feelings to mind. The Chinese New Year is indeed a very special occasion for all people, regardless of who they may be. Some Westerners living in Hong Kong scheduled a brief break or holiday to bypass some of the hectic celebrations.

The *Ching Ming* festival is an important occasion observed by most people living in Hong Kong. The literal meaning of *Ching Ming* is clear and bright. It has some similarities to the Western observance of Easter.

By the time of *Ching Ming* spring has arrived; winter is at an end. The trees are beginning to bud, like the pussy willows, giving the impression of the resurgence of new life again. The observance of Easter is determined by the lunar calendar; it therefore varies annually. It occurs at a different time every year according to the Western custom of reckoning time.

Both *Ching Ming* and the Christian celebration of Easter are related to the afterlife: Easter emphasizes the belief in an afterlife with the resurrection. *Ching Ming* requires a visit to the ancestral graves, pacifying the spirits hovering around the tombs of the loved ones. The graves of the ancestors must be swept clean, repaired and cleaned or fixed up. The Chinese leave no stone unturned during the period of *Ching Ming*.

Yes, *Ching Ming* has a distinct connection with the departed, but at the same time is a celebration for the revival of life in the season of spring. There is undoubtedly a desire to invoke the aid of the spirits. The tombs of the ancestors are cleaned and repaired; a feast or food offering is carefully laid out on the top of the loved one's grave. For the comfort of the spirits, candles or tapers are also burned, while a bonfire of paper money (hell bank notes) provide the departed a means of softening the hearts of the attendants. Fresh flowers are also taken to the graves of the beloved. The entire cemetery appears to be much like a huge flower garden. Similarly, Christians frequently take along a floral tribute to place on the grave of their loved one. *Ching Ming* is a time for showing respect and love for the ancestors.

The Dragon Boat Festival is a festival marking the beginning of the summer solstice. It is specifically connected with the story of Ch'u Yuan, a virtuous minister of state who lived during the fourth century B.C. He frequently advised the emperor to change his ways about this or that matter; however, it appeared to be a vain and hopeless situation. However, the emperor didn't heed his wise counsel, therefore, Ch'u Yuan took his own life by drowning, hoping to draw the emperor's attention and change his mind. The local fishermen tried their best to preserve Ch'u Yuan's body by making glutinous rice dumplings known as *tsung*, which contain glutinous rice, sweet meat and eggs wrapped up and cooked in dried bamboo leaves. They dropped the small parcels of *tsung* into the river hoping to divert the fishes from devouring Ch'u Yuan's body. From that time onward people began observing what has become known as the Dragon Boat Festival, continuing throughout the ages until today. The dragon boat festival is also observed in Vancouver, B.C. At the time of the festival, boats shaped in the form of dragon are sponsored in an annual competition to attract tourists to the city.

The moon plays a vital and significant role in Chinese life and culture. The moon festival always occurs in the autumn when the moon is at its fullest and brightest. The moon is believed to be at its brightest and fullest on the fifteenth day of the eighth moon. The harvest has already been taken in and the farmers are ready for a celebration. The Chinese believe there is a hare or rabbit who lives on the moon, not a man, as in Western tradition. The moon, of course, is round and shaped much like a drum. Moon cakes are made to honour the occasion. They consist of lotus seeds and/or red melon seeds, plus salted duck eggs. The moon cakes are always placed in square boxes or containers with four cakes per box. They are often presented as gifts to relatives or friends. There is a very well known story relating to the moon cakes, dating back to the Yuan dynasty, when the Mongols ruled China early in the thirteenth century (960 to 1280 A.D.). It was reported each of the cakes had a secret message hidden within, a signal for the Chinese to rise up and overthrow the Mongols from within their borders.

An interesting sidelight and feature of the moon festival is the tradition whereby children buy or make fancy lanterns resembling the moon, rabbits, fish, butterflies etc. They carry the lanterns through the streets with a candle placed inside. They carry the lanterns to the homes of their friends and neighbours as well as through the streets, making it an extremely colourful and romantic celebration.

The concept of *feng shui* is a manifestation of magic, combining the idea of yin (male) and yang (female) elements, which represent light and darkness. In the 12th century A.D. it was elevated to a pseudo-science, and plays a vital role in ancestral worship by finding the proper location of a grave for a loved one, which is equally important for the children and grandchildren as for the deceased. The site of the grave is extremely important for all concerned, the living and the dead—it requires the correct day, time and location for the burial. Many other elements are also involved in the process.

Even though proper disposal of the deceased is the main function of the *feng shui* man, he should also be consulted in the selection of buying or building a house, ancestral hall, or building of a temple etc. The *feng shui* man may even be consulted in the arrangement of an existing home or structure. A bedroom may be changed to a living room, or a partition may be erected to ward off adverse influence. Hong Kong is filled with houses that have mirrors erected to ward off and confuse the evil spirits, deflecting them from influencing the lives of the inhabitants.

The *feng shui* man has a special type of compass that he uses. The geomantic compass is for sale in most Chinese villages and cities. The compass consists of a wooden or baked clay disc about six inches in diameter, with a regular magnetic compass in the centre. The wooden disc is covered with lacquered concentric circles. The central part is where the yin and yang are located. The innermost circle consists of the *pa kua*, or eight trigrams. They denote the evolution of nature and its numerous cycles. The eight lines on the trigrams represent heaven, fire, thunder, wind and water, hills and earth. They are also represented by eight animals:the horse, goat, pheasant, dragon, fowl, swine, dog and ox.

I clearly recall when the Chinese University of Hong Kong was in the process of being established during the 1960s. They had a considerable hassle purchasing the land from the farmers living in the New Territories. The land consisted mostly of hills that had to be levelled for the construction of the university buildings. They encountered many unforeseen problems as they proceeded with the levelling process, such as discovering bones buried in ancient burial urns many years ago. The company contracted to do the work was required to make a public announcement in the local newspapers regarding any unexpected finds, enquiring whether or not the bones belonged to a known ancestor in that specific area of the new territories. If so, relatives were requested to come forth and claim the bones. However, if there was no response they ceremoniously buried the remains with the help of a *feng shui* man to avoid any possible difficulty, bad luck or misfortune in the future.

Yes, the belief in *feng shui* is still very much alive in Hong Kong and other countries of South East Asia where overseas Chinese dwell, as well as in North America in the cities of Vancouver, Toronto, San Francisco etc.

Chinese cuisine is one of the most familiar, well known and loved cuisines enjoyed by countless numbers of people throughout the world. Chinese restaurants are found everywhere in cities, towns and villages; whether large or small they provide some of the tastiest food to be found anywhere. Eating is a matter of primary importance for the Chinese. It is a common practice in the Cantonese dialect to enquire of a friend or acquaintance you meet on the street: "Have you eaten yet?"

If a Chinese friend invites you to their home for a meal, the food is always served in an attractive and eatable form. You needn't cut the food into smaller portions before beginning to enjoy the meal, like you do when eating a Western dinner. The kitchen where the food is prepared is spotlessly clean. You will be provided with a set of chopsticks to eat the meal, since it is firmly believed Chinese food doesn't taste nearly as good if it is eaten with a knife and fork. Likewise the flavouring of every dish has already been carefully prepared, somewhat like a masterpiece of art. Side dishes of ginger, mustard or other flavouring are placed in tiny dishes to the side, just in case they are required.

The varying number of courses of Chinese food could be reckoned in the thousands. Each province has its own food specialties. The four principal styles (or kinds) of Chinese cooking which are usually regarded as the most outstanding in the land, originate from Peking, Shantung, Canton and Szechuan. It is important to realize pork is one of the principal and preferred foods in the diet of the Chinese. However, there are considerable numbers of people living in northwestern China who are followers of the Islamic (Muslim) tradition. They are strictly forbidden from eating pork on religious grounds; therefore, mutton is used as a substitute in place of pork. Rice is a staple food for all people living south of the Yangtze River, while north of the Yangtze River, noodles or spaghetti are more commonly eaten as a substitute for rice.

Circular tables are nearly always used at home or at banquets held in a restaurant, since all the guests are seated an equal distance from the food. A circular rotating piece is frequently placed in the centre of the table, known as a "lazy Susan," making it easier to serve the food, as well as for collecting the dishes while the various courses are being served, keeping the guests from passing each course around the banquet table from guest to guest as in the Western fashion. The host or hostess of the banquet usually has a pre-arranged seating plan prepared for the convenience of the guests. Ordinarily the guest list is written on a card placed in the centre of the table so everyone realizes the seating arrangement in advance, finding his/her place at the table.

Symbolism in Chinese art is most essential and of utmost significance in Chinese homes. Representations of the Chinese characters for good luck, happiness and longevity are considered the three principal ingredients for living a fruitful, long and happy life. The concepts are symbolized by using the individual written characters for the words, or by having porcelain statues vividly and visually conveying the idea.

The use of the bat for good luck and happiness is a play on sounds: *pin fook* is similar to the word meaning happiness, blessing or benediction. The bat always conveys a good meaning in the Chinese language. The design of five bats in a circular form represents the five blessings, which are old age, wealth, health, love of virtue, and natural death. In the Western tradition the bat conveys the opposite meaning, like when we say he/she has "bats in the belfry."

Floral designs, often referred to as the "three friends," are the plum, the pine and the bamboo. The pine, being evergreen, is regarded is an emblem of longevity, and of friends who remain faithful in constant adversity.

Another flower much loved is the peony, a symbol for riches and nobility.

The symbolic meaning of the lotus is derived from its connection with Buddhism. The seedpod, blossom and bud represent the past, present, and future. Its leaves and roots represent steadfastness in the family, essential requirements in a land where the family is of primary importance.

The dragon originally was a sign representing imperial China, specifically the emperor or male element, while the phoenix symbolizes the empress or female element. Today both the dragon and the phoenix are used on wedding invitations, and as decorations for restaurants at the time of wedding banquets.

The customs and traditions of China have been the subject of numerous books throughout the years. The author is aware of the limitations of this chapter—it leaves volumes unspoken; however, it does provide basic ideas and concepts which, if a person is interested, may be researched further by the reader to his/her personal satisfaction and benefit.

Picturesque and attractive Chinese junks in Hong Kong in 1958.

Hong Kong Hop Yat Church on Bonham Road.

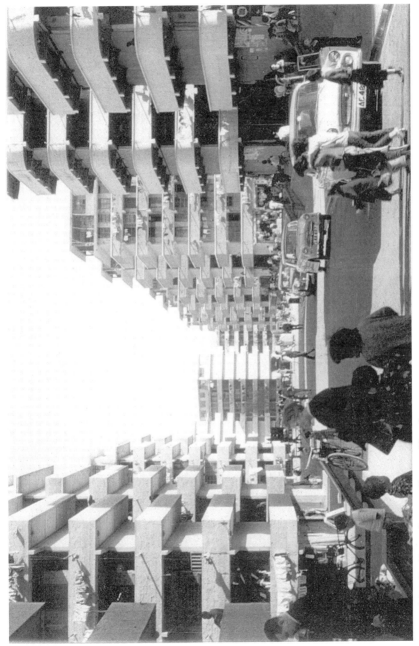

Wong Tai Sin Resettlement Estate, Kowloon.

Outdoor library in the Wong Tai Sin Resettlement Estate, Kowloon, Hong Kong.

The author with children in Chuk Yuen squatter area.

A Chuk Yuen area family being interviewed.

Early refugee squatter area in Kowloon.

The devastation and destruction by typhoon Wanda, September, 1962.

Children enjoying a drink of milk.

Hong Kong typhoon shelter for smaller boats.

Burial urns located on a Kowloon hillside.

Congregational photo at Mui-Woh.

Participants in the Rennie's Mill Christmas pageant, 1957.

ASIAN CHURCH WOMEN'S CONFERENCE NOV. 15-30, 1958 HONG KONG

In Commemoration of the 75th Anniversary of the Founding of the China Congregational Church
in Hongkong and the Ordination of new Deacon and Deaconesses   November 16th, 1958

中華基督教會公理堂開基七十五週年紀念暨接立新執事典禮   一九五八年十一月十六日

CHAPTER 5

Appreciation of Chinese Medicine

AFTER LIVING IN HONG KONG for some eighteen years, I had the privilege of gaining knowledge and understanding of Chinese medical skills as practiced in Hong Kong and China. The knowledge consisted of a combination of first-hand experience and theory, but due to my personal ignorance, I was uncertain regarding many of their skills as used for thousands of years. The lack of understanding was purely due to my own ignorance of Chinese philosophy and way of life. However, my understanding of Chinese medicine gradually increased until I decided to venture into the unknown by gaining first hand experience. During the years, I learned so much from my Chinese colleagues and friends, whose ancestors practiced their medical skills for countless generations. While I was in Hong Kong I lived in a Chinese home environment and thus more readily came to recognize and accept Chinese medicine. I discovered the way it has so many unique features, which have proven beneficial and helpful to countless numbers of people for generations. In view of that I asked myself, if their practices have benefited so many people, why shouldn't they also help a person like me?

I will now illustrate what I mean using practical illustrations. One day in Hong Kong I was returning to work; I needed to climb three flights of stairs, since there was no elevator in the building. Upon reaching the first level, I continued up the stairs. Unexpectedly, something happened to one of my legs, and I suddenly lost my balance, falling backwards on the landing. When I got up I realized I had injured my leg. It was extremely painful and sore, however, I continued on the way to my office.

During the afternoon, I had an important meeting to attend at a nearby hotel. The manager, who was a good friend of mine, enquired why I was limping. I told him what had happened. Immediately he replied, "You should see a doctor," but added, "a doctor of Western medicine is of no use for that sort of problem." Without my permission, he immediately contacted his friend, a practitioner of Chinese medicine. He made an appointment for me to see the doctor the next day at 9:00 a.m. He added, "I will personally accompany you to his office on Hong Kong Island." I was somewhat annoyed he hadn't consulted me before making the appointment. However, I realized if I turned down his offer of assistance, he would possibly lose face with his friend, therefore, I consented to go along with him to see the doctor.

The next day we went together to the doctor's office on Hong Kong Island. His office was small and clean, but exceedingly crowded. After being introduced, the doctor requested me to be seated, then pushed up my trouser leg and felt my leg with both hands. He said, "You have decidedly torn a ligament in your leg." He massaged my leg for some time. It was extremely painful as he massaged the calf of my leg for several minutes. Finally he said, "You wait here until I get medicine to put on your leg." He went to a stainless steel vat in another corner of the same room, returned with some black smelly looking goulash made of herbs and Chinese wine, placed the medicine on my leg and then bandaged it. The herbs had been heated, so it felt quite comfortable along with the bandage, but it had a very strong smell—it seemed almost as if I was a walking brewery. The doctor instructed me to leave the bandage on my leg for twenty-four hours, then cut off the bandage and my leg should feel fine. I thanked him and left his office.

Frankly speaking I was exceedingly skeptical regarding my leg feeling well after a one-time treatment. However, I accepted his word, and returned to my office. The other passengers on the bus and ferry began staring at me since they could smell my leg. At the office I reported the incident to our general secretary. He enquired, "What happened to you?" since he detected the smell of Chinese medicine. I replied, "Yesterday I injured my leg going upstairs," explaining how I went to see a doctor of Chinese medicine. He replied, "You have done the correct thing, since a doctor of Chinese medicine is much better than a doctor of Western medicine for that kind of injury." Later the same day, I returned home to the family with whom I was living and they too agreed I had done the correct thing. I was encouraged and comforted by their positive response. I could hardly wait for 24 hours to expire when I would cut off the bandage, since it had become much like a cast. The doctor was correct; my leg felt normal once again. I was extremely pleased, impressed and appreciative; my doubt was now replaced by belief. Ever since the incident occurred, I have had no further problems with my leg.

Sometime later, I contracted a bad strain of Asian flu in Hong Kong. It was quite severe, accompanied by an exceedingly high fever. The family with whom I was living had previously come down with the flu. It was now my turn. Our maidservant said, yes, you certainly have the flu, which was evident by the way my pyjamas were soaking wet with sweat. I called my doctor (of Western medicine) and he said to take some aspirin. However, nothing resulted from the aspirins; my temperature still remained high. The maidservant said: if I prepare some Chinese herbal medicine, will you take it? I replied, yes. She went to the kitchen to prepare the herbal mixture for several hours. Eventually she returned to my room with a bowl full of black uninviting-looking medicine and requested I drink it, while she stood there watching me. The medicine was as bitter as gall. I told her she could leave and I would drink the medicine. She replied, no, you will only pour the medicine down the toilet. You take it now in front of me, which I did. It was so bitter and unpleasant tasting, I didn't really wish to finish the bowl of medicine, but she insisted I drink every drop of it. In about two hours time, I could literally feel my temperature begin to recede and before long I felt greatly improved. Now I became convinced of the merit of certain kinds of Chinese herbal medicine.

My sister living in Vancouver had a severe case of osteoarthritis which was beginning to cripple her so much she could hardly walk without the aid of two canes. A friend of hers, who helped with the housework, suggested she go and see a Chinese acupuncturist, who had helped her with various ailments. Betty went to see the acupuncturist; immediately he began treatment and requested another member of the staff massage her once weekly. She was required to take a certain mixture of Chinese herbs as well as do regular exercises. She boiled the herbs for three hours, and began drinking the liquid on a daily basis. It was extremely bitter; however, she persisted in taking it, in spite of the poor taste. After several months of treatment, she felt decidedly better; her arthritis was making progress. After one year's treatment she was like a new person— her arthritis had been arrested and she could once again walk normally.

Somewhat later my sister developed a bad earache and went to an ear specialist. He requested she have an x-ray, which she did. Several months later she hadn't heard the results from the x-ray, so she contacted the doctor again. He looked up his record and was very upset; he told her to immediately see a certain neurologist. After the neurologist looked at the x-ray, he requested she go in for an appointment. The neurologist informed Betty the x-ray revealed she had an aneurysm of the brain; therefore, an operation would be required. The doctor explained the various implications and dangers of having such an operation, such as the possibility of having a stroke etc. He claimed the procedure would require shaving off her hair and opening her skull so the aneurysm could be removed. However, the neurologist requested she first have an MRI (magnetic resonance imaging) x-ray as soon as possible. The MRI was taken and the neurologist requested she return to his office for the results. Betty asked me to accompany her to hear the results, which I did. The doctor asked us to be seated and opened the conversation by saying, "Betty, I have good news for you. You no longer have an aneurysm in the brain." We were both extremely happy about the good news. I told the doctor, "You know, doctor, I formerly worked in Hong Kong for many years, and believe in certain kinds of Chinese medical treatment such as acupuncture and Chinese massage." The doctor became noticeably irritated and upset. He replied, "I don't want to hear any more about the matter," and wouldn't listen any further. We thanked him for his time, saying goodbye, but he wouldn't even reply.

The above illustration reveals how biased and ignorant the specific neurologist was regarding acupuncture and Chinese massage. In this day and age, he seems to be living in the dark ages with his own biases. He believes Western medicine is far superior, providing all the answers. It is my frank and personal opinion the Chinese have much to teach us from their thousands of years of medical practice and experience. The medical profession in the Western world needs to be more humble and willing to learn from the Oriental experience, not just shut others out of their minds, ignoring them altogether, as if they never existed. Later we were told by a well-informed medical friend that the neurologist was biased and unable to recognize any possible merit in Chinese medicine. It is sad and unbelievable to realize, in our day and age, there are still certain medical practitioners in Canada unwilling to learn from other people and countries for the long-term benefit of their clients. My sister was informed by a doctor friend that it was the acupuncture and massage that dissolved her aneurysm; therefore no operation was necessary. In my humble opinion, no one method or way is absolutely correct to the complete exclusion of all others. Such an attitude needs to be critically questioned, when it comes to eliminating something that varies from the usual practice. For me it is not an either/or situation but both and one may complement the other.

In January 1991 I had a stroke affecting the entire left side of my body, including my left arm, hand and leg. I received the finest medical treatment in both St. Paul's and Holy Family hospitals in Vancouver, B.C. They did all they could to help me, for which I am most grateful and appreciative. I was hospitalized nearly five months. They helped me to get back on my feet, even though I still need to walk with a four-pointed cane. I have recovered to the extent that I am able to do everything I used to do as a retired United Church minister, such as preach in the church from time to time; conduct weddings and funerals; drive my car; operate my computer, write and publish a book. I still take an active part in social affairs and activities like the British Columbia Stroke Association, the Canadian Society for Asian Arts, the Pacific Interfaith Citizenship Association of B.C. and many other organizations and activities.

It is most important stroke victims do not withdraw from the community in which they live, but keep actively involved in daily life. Having a stroke is not the end of the world, but only the beginning of a new phase or aspect of life. Being involved in the community means we are still able to make a positive contribution to society. If we withdraw from the world we are only injuring and hurting ourselves and our family members. Being involved shows we still have a contribution to make to society and are trying to be good examples by encouraging other stroke victims like ourselves. It is a tremendous challenge filled with opportunities to serve the society in which we live, rather than become burdens upon our family and community. Naturally it depends upon the severity of the stroke and its limiting disabilities, but there is a wide variation of disability. We should do our best to improve ourselves by not giving up. We must have a daily routine of physical activities. Such activities will enable us to be active in our home, and in outdoor interests, weather permitting.

In the fall of 1997 the same acupuncturist who helped my sister claimed he felt he could help me, even though nearly seven years had already expired since my stroke (January 1991). I began acupuncture treatments, a totally new experience for me. Acupuncture uses a special type of needle to help stimulate the nerves. They also use electricity to further help stimulate the nerves. It has helped my left leg: my foot used to swing to one side when I walked—now the foot goes straight ahead. The treatment is decidedly helping me. In my opinion, it is a form of treatment that should be more widely recognized and promoted by the medical profession in B.C. and across Canada.

The second part of this chapter is a summary of the history of Chinese medical science, to illustrate the long and honoured tradition of Chinese medicine. The information largely derives from a book written in both Chinese and English by Professor Chan Yuen Chen, living in Hong Kong. His title is *History of Chinese Medical Science*. The book was published in Hong Kong in 1968; it is most informative and enlightening, written by a person obviously familiar with the details of his subject and illustrated with pictures.

Professor Chen indicates that history of Chinese medical science dates back to the very beginning of the life history of the Chinese people. Its entire development covers a period of well over five thousand years. From the ruins of ancient towns, the relics of ancient men, sculptures, paintings and other products of art, and discoveries of archaeologists, we can invariably find things related to the great Chinese art of medicine. From the writings of philosophers, religionists, historians, geographers or men of letters, we can also trace out and find material of immense value to this branch of study. The author of the volume, a Chinese medical practitioner by profession for forty years, had devoted much of his available time to the collection of pictures of all the facts that have close connection with the progress of Chinese medicine and the lives of celebrated Chinese medical scholars. (From the preface to *History of Chinese Medical Science,* illustrated with pictures by Professor C. Y. Chen, published in Hong Kong in 1968).

Professor Chen explains through his introduction a few of the most remarkable examples as follows.

1. Surgery and Anesthetics:

The discovery of surgery marked a new era in the history of Western medicine. When in 1847 the British doctor Sir James Young Simpson discovered the application of anesthetics, surgery registered a great stride in its development. This was therefore considered a great event in the history of medicine during the last (19th) century. Yet anesthetics were already employed by Chinese practitioners towards the end of the Han dynasty in the second century A.D. It was recorded that Hua To, a famous surgeon of the Han dynasty, performed an operation on the arm of general Kuan Yu by first giving him a "narcotic soup," which was an anesthetic taken orally. The use of such anesthetics was recorded in medical treatises published in later centuries.

2. Application of mineral products and chemical compounds:

Native mining methods were long known to the Chinese who also had considerable knowledge in geology and mineralogy. Many mineral products have been used by the Chinese for medical purposes. Among the commoner ones are cinnabar, loadstone, red and white arsenic, amethyst, talc, gypsum, saltpeter, borax, mercury, alum, calomel etc. Application of these mineral products for treatment of diseases was recorded in Pen Tsao Ching, a Chinese classic of medicine attributed to the legendary emperor Shen Ning, although it was later found to be actually written in the period of the three kingdoms, about 200 A.D. Like the alchemists in Europe, the Chinese medical men and philosophers made a series of experiments in the refining processes of mercury, cinnabar, or calomel in their attempts at the production of pills of elixir.

The use of arsenic and calomel for venereal diseases was also practised in very early times. In 1521 the "casebook of a doctor" by Wang Shih-Shan recorded the use of calomel for treatment of venereal diseases. In the reign of Chung Ching of the Ming dynasty (about 1630) in his "secret prescriptions for the treatment of venereal diseases" referred to the effective use of arsenic as the "use of poison against poison."

3. The application of herbs for medical treatments:

"Modern medicine uses to a great extent rutin for the treatment of high blood pressure. However, such well known Chinese drugs as mulberry epiphytes, huai flower (Sophora japonica), carthamus, tinctorius, the cratoegus cuneata, the tu chung bark (Eucommia ulmoides) all contain rutin. Of these the huai flower has long been recorded in Chinese medical treatises as an effective drug for bringing down blood pressure."

"Again in the treatment of the enlargement of thyroid gland (the Chinese name for the disease is yin (a goitre), medical circles all over the world now prescribe iodine drugs. As early as the 7th century. Chinese doctors had used for the treatment of goitre such vegetable drugs as sea-weeds, kelp, aresch and laver. It has lately been established that these vegetable products contain much iodine. Thus the Chinese have been using iodine for more than 1,000 years.

In the more than 700 Chinese drugs in common use by doctors, more than 100 of them have had their curative properties confirmed by modern medical science."

4. Chinese process similar to that for producing penicillin:

"The invention of penicillin startled the whole world. I venture to say, however, that there is a Chinese prescription that has a similar chemical process as that of this world-famous drug. The Chinese people used the brine of salted vegetables for the treatment of "ulcer of the lung", which is the formation of pus on the lung or the various streptococcal diseases.

The manufacture of this brine of salted vegetables is carried out by putting vegetables in earthen pots, allowing them to rot and to have an outgrowth of fur, which at first is green and long, and produces chlorine gas. The vegetable is buried underground for at least three years, when it is turned into liquid, called brine of salted vegetables. I am not familiar with the exact chemical processes, but from various scientific books I understand the rotting vegetable produces streptomycetes, and that same process was followed in the initial experiments on the production of penicillin.

Unfortunately the Chinese herbalists only know the prescription, but do not appreciate it is a great invention and hence have not carried out any detailed research on it. There are, however, still numerous great inventions of mineral outcrops among Chinese drugs, which await research and development by future medical scientists."

5. Acupuncture and treatment of fractures and injuries:

In Chinese medicine there is the practice of acupuncture, which is most effective for the treatment of diseases of the nervous system. Invented in China, acupuncture is also practised in Japan and France (and many other nations today including Canada.)

There is also a system in the treatment of bodily injuries special to Chinese medicine. Fractures of bones are first restored to the proper positions, and bandaged properly to prevent their further dislocation. An experienced doctor can even restore broken bones to proper places and use a permanent bandage for months when the broken pieces will be rejoined to the other parts, and normally restored. Chinese doctors of this special branch of medicine do not advocate the amputation of legs or arms, which they consider contrary to nature, taking an entirely different view of Western doctors who formerly favoured amputation at the first instance. Now however, Western doctors also employ the system of the use of plaster of Paris cast, and the basic principle is thus similar to that of the Chinese doctors. But the Chinese system, in addition to the use of bandages, also requires the administration of drugs orally.

"In the field of surgery, the Chinese surgeons are behind Western surgeons in the art of performing many operations. But they also possess a special quality. In Western surgery, when a wound heals, the doctor only looks after disinfection, and does little to promote the healing process which takes its natural course."

"Chinese doctors administer oral drugs to speed up the elimination of pus and the growth of new tissues, supplemented by medicine for application over the wounds, principally powdered which are very effective in promoting the healing of the wounds. This difference between Chinese and Western surgery is worthy of attention."

Generally speaking, it may be stated that Chinese medicine at a very early date registered important achievements in the identification, classification and treatment of various diseases. The discoveries well in advance of Western medicine.

"As a Chinese doctor myself, I might be taken to have the inclination of exaggerating the accomplishments of Chinese medicine. It is true, however, that while historical discoveries in Chinese medicine have been colossal, there has been in recent times little progress in the development of the original discoveries. Marco Polo brought gunpowder from China to Europe, but European armaments today are much superior to those of China. The Chinese were original inventors, like the discovery of ores, but did not do much to improve their metallurgical processes."

"I hope the future will surpass the past, and that Chinese medicine will continue to make important contributions to medical science by more inventions and new discoveries in medicine. Scientists, I hope will dig in the field of Chinese medicine which has numerous veins and inexhaustible deposits."

It is my sincere hope the foregoing information will enable readers to have a greater and more sympathetic understanding of Chinese medical science in our day and age. I hope it may also help dispel some of the misunderstanding that has arisen by practitioners of Western medicine. Yes, I believe it is not a matter of discarding one for the other, but may help us to realize the Chinese concept of medicine has considerable validity for our day and generation.

Principle reference: *History of Chinese Medical Science*, illustrated with pictures by Professor C.Y.Chen: published in Hong Kong 1968 (bilingual).

CHAPTER 6

Transportation in Hong Kong

T RANSPORTATION IN HONG KONG is a multi-faceted subject consisting of a combination of ancient and modern means fused together into a single unit and system.

In the fall of 1955 when I left Vancouver by train for San Francisco and transferred to a Norwegian bound freighter for Hong Kong, requiring nearly six weeks before arriving at my destination, it was somewhat similar to the proverbial expression of taking "a slow boat to China." The first glimpse of my future home came as I sighted a colourful host of boats on the distant horizon known as "Chinese junks." It left a deep and lasting impression upon me as I spotted the junks on the distant horizon. The junks were gracefully sailing off the southeastern coast of China. The wind filled their majestic, colourful and picturesque sails to capacity, similar to huge oriental fans. It was somewhat like a page from a storybook, sailing vessels were still commonly used. Before long dozens upon dozens of the wind-driven vessels (junks) were clearly visible as the freighter approached the southeastern coast of China drawing nearer to the beautiful and famed natural harbour of Hong Kong.

Before long tiny sampans (small boats) converged upon the freighter as it prepared to anchor in the harbour at a nearby bouy. The ship first required clearance from the Medical and Health Department of Hong Kong; followed by a similar clearance from customs and immigration officers who boarded the vessel. Before long a large number of merchants hurriedly swarmed up the gangplank boarding the freighter. The merchants displayed their colourful and varied wares upon the deck of the ship, ranging all the way from jade to ivory, costume jewellery, embroidery work, lace tablecloths, etc. Tailors likewise came fully prepared to take on the spot measurements for shirts and suits. It was necessary for all passengers to understand the meaning of the warning "buyer beware," and realize if they weren't careful, they could be easily rooked or cheated.

The system of communication which had been established many years ago enabled the cities of Hong Kong and Kowloon to be linked together. Ferry services operated between Kowloon and Victoria City on Hong Kong Island and were developed in 1890. Victoria City had expanded lengthwise along the northern coast of Hong Kong Island. By 1904 a tramway was constructed to East Point and Shaukiwan on Hong Kong Island.

Hong Kong eventually developed an amazing network of local shipping services. The most familiar and popular being the "star ferry," a reasonably priced and fully reliable form of passenger service, designed to serve the general public crossing the harbour, a distance of nearly one mile, it required only ten minutes for the "star ferry" to make its crossing to Tsimshatsui on the southern tip of the Kowloon peninsula to Hong Kong Island, landing near the central district of Hong Kong. The ferries transport their passengers on a first and second class basis. The upper level of the ferry is known as first class, while the lower level is known as third class. First class designed to shelter its passengers from the hot sub-tropical sun and the elements like wind and rain. The ferry provides a spectacular view of the picturesque and famed natural harbour of Hong Kong whether day or night. Anyone transporting goods such as large crates of chickens, ducks, geese, quail, etc. carried in large circular baskets were required to travel third class similar to steerage, while passengers travelling Hong Kong third class were more readily exposed to the elements and inclement weather or an approaching typhoon. Many passengers prefer travelling third class, a little cheaper, but not as protected from the elements. Passengers transporting bulky cargoes moved them by the aid of a bamboo pole, placed over his/her shoulder, a method still in common use in Hong Kong, were required to pay a modest fee for their load.

A parallel ferry system known as the "Yaumati ferry" located on Jordan road in Kowloon, known as "the vehicular ferry," was designed to transport vehicles like automobiles lorries (trucks), bicycles and their passengers. The construction of the Cross Harbour Tunnel years later resulted in the company losing a certain amount of business, however, was still utilized by the general public. All public announcements were made over a loudspeaker on the vehicular ferry informing passengers, neither smoking nor spitting were allowed on the decks of the ferry. Still another announcement prominently posted on the ferries, requested passengers to "beware of pickpockets."

The "Yaumati ferry" was conveniently built near the passenger ferry, travelling from Kowloon to the outer islands of Hong Kong's territory, Lantau Island, Hong Kong's largest island and Cheung Chau (known for fishing) consisted of a constant hustle and bustle of people while the vehicles could be heard drawing closer to the terminal where the public pier is located.

The bus and tram system of Hong Kong had their terminals near the ferries for the convenience of the general public. It must be mentioned all transportation drives on the left hand side of the road in Hong Kong similar to Britain. A tradition handed down from the British when Hong Kong, was originally established as a crown colony in 1841, during the reign of Queen Victoria.

Most local buses are double-deckers, the lower deck is known as third class. A slight difference occurs in the fare structure depending upon where the passenger plans to travel by bus. Passengers travelling a further distance may prefer to travel on the upper deck of the bus, having a better view, while at the same time receiving more fresh air.

Most automobiles/lorries (trucks) used in Hong Kong originate from the United Kingdom (Britain), since they don't require adjustments to the steering gear of the vehicles. All buses are designed for left hand traffic as in the United Kingdom. However, there are still other vehicles in Hong Kong originating from Japan, Germany, France, America, etc. American made vehicles on the whole are too large for Hong Kong's limited road system, since driving and parking large American-style vehicles require more space, therefore, not as practical nor popular. Air conditioned vehicles are common, due to the hot sub-tropical weather conditions. It is more economical to import automobile/lorry (truck) repairs from Britain where the vehicles were manufactured.

In 1888 "the peak tram," a funicular cable car was established on Hong Kong Island, providing transportation between the central district of Hong Kong Island and the peak, ordinarily referred to as "the cable car" operated on a system of two parallel cables, one ascending and the other descending, the weight of the individual cars help balance each other travelling up and down. The peak tram is one of the most famous and popular tourist attractions on Hong Kong Island transporting its passengers to the peak for a panoramic and scenic view of Hong Kong's splendid natural harbour. A fine road system was also established linking the two areas of the island with each other. From the main terminal on the peak, a cement sidewalk was constructed encircling the entire upper part of the island (360 degrees) providing a splendid and breathtaking view of the surrounding scenery including Hong Kong's harbour, Kowloon and Hong Kong along with its many (235) islands. A fine panoramic view of the South China Sea may be seen in the distance, leading towards Hong Kong's natural harbour.

Bicycles provide an essential and important mode of travel in Hong Kong as well as for many nations of Asia. Wherever you turn there are bicycles, a fact that is especially true for Beijing, the capital of China. You can scarcely cross the streets of Beijing without being run over by bicycles (first hand experience).

Bicycles not only carry the rider, but are used for transporting tremendous loads in Hong Kong. One Sunday morning I recall seeing a bicycle loaded with fourteen large baskets stacked within each other, carried on the rear end of a single bicycle in Kowloon, wending its way through the crowded streets of a resettlement area. It was also common to see three or four live pigs loaded into a special type of woven basket, transporting their load to Yuen Long or other villages in the new territories. Within the city you frequently see older people carrying birdcages with birds in the cages loaded on a bicycle travelling to a park or restaurant for a brief outing. The above illustrates the way bicycles have varied uses in Hong Kong and China. Besides the ordinary bicycle, you may also see three-wheeled bicycles (tricycles) popular with the stores delivering their groceries and other goods.

Upon my arrival in Hong Kong (1955), sedan chairs were gradually becoming a fading chapter of Chinese custom and tradition, which formerly existed on Hong Kong Island. The last of the sedan chairs disappeared from the scene in 1965, they were used by a few wealthier clients transporting their passengers up a mountain, or from Queens Road central to Upper Albert road. In old China sedan chairs were used by the imperial family and wealthier clients as a special means of transportation. The sedan chair had a seat situated between two poles carried either by two (or four men) known as bearers, one (or two) bearers walked in front, while other bearers brought up the rear. Sedan chairs were also used to a limited extent on Lantau Island for transporting passengers up the mountain to their summer homes.

Nowadays rickshaws are only used for a tourist attraction. The rickshaw being a light two-wheeled covered vehicle drawn by a man literally pulling it. A few rickshaws may still be seen near the Star Ferry Terminal, used mostly by tourists.

The Kowloon-Canton railway was originally established in the year 1912. Its terminal is located adjacent to the Star Ferry in Kowloon. Years later it was transferred to the Hung-Him area in Kowloon. The British sector of the Kowloon-Canton railway travelled from the southern tip of the Kowloon peninsula to the Chinese frontier at Sham Chun where it linked up with the railway in China. The southern bank of the Sham Chun river formed part of the International Boundary of Hong Kong adjacent to Kwangtung province in southern China. From 1949 (the year of China's so-called liberation) passengers travelled back and forth were required to change trains at the border between Hong Kong and China, the passengers were required to walk 300 yards between the two terminals. Mail and goods travelled in wagonloads, however, it travelled without trans-shipment. The distance between Shum Chun at the Chinese border to Kowloon was only 22 miles.

The development of civil aviation in Hong Kong was the beginning of a new era which helped Hong Kong become what it is today. The first flight by an aircraft in Hong Kong occurred in 1911, however, it wasn't until 20 years later air travel began to flourish and bloom showing evidence of growth and development. During the Japanese occupation of Hong Kong from Christmas day 1941 to August 1945, Hong Kong literally died due to the Japanese occupation. The only practical contribution the Japanese made during their occupation of Hong Kong was an airstrip, designed purely for military purposes. Following the end of the Pacific conflict in 1945, the British returned to Hong Kong to help reconstruct the colony along with its air field.

Due to the mountainous terrain of Hong Kong, it was difficult to find a proper site for a new airport, the decision to modernize, update and develop the existing site by extensive reclamation of land. Work on the project began in 1956. In a remarkable feat of engineering a promontory 7,800 feet long and 800 feet wide was reclaimed from the waters off Kowloon Bay. The extensive removal of hills was carried out by means of countless labourers carrying small baskets of rock and earth on their backs. They continually dumped the rocks and debris into the sea providing a safe approach from the landward end. The new runway, 8,340 feet long, accommodating aircraft up to 400,000 pounds, was opened in 1958, suitable for use by more modern types of aircraft.

A modern terminal building, one of the most advanced in the far east, came into being in November 1962. It operates a "two level" system, having arriving passengers processed on the ground floor while departing passengers on the first floor. Modern shops, bars and a restaurant catered to the needs of passengers and visitors, including a spacious waving bay (gallery), which offered a clear view of arriving and departing aircraft.

Hong Kong relies heavily upon the industry of tourism, given the geographical centrality of its location in the Pacific region of Asia. It became recognized the existing airport (opened in 1962) would be completely inadequate before the turn of the century, therefore it was necessary to visualize, conceptualize, and begin construction of an ultra-modern airport with all its infrastructure.

The annual 1993 "Hong Kong report" states "an airport core development (ACP) programme has been designed to provide these facilities in ten core projects which will build a base for economic expansion into the next century. Hong Kong's key role as a centre for international and regional aviation will be enhanced by a new modern airport located away from centres of urban population and capable of operating round-the-clock. Associated infrastructure development will relieve serious traffic congestion, open up new land for urban development and for further expansion of port facilities. New space will be provided for recreational activities and there will be overall environmental benefit." The 1993 report continues "the programme comprises: of an airport at Chek Lap Kok off northern Lantau to replace Kai Tak in 1997; six road and rail projects, including extensive tunnels and bridges, stretching from the central district, along the west side of Kowloon, across Tsing Yi and Ma Wan and the north Lantau coast; two major land reclamations in west Kowloon and central: and a new town on north Lantau." (Hong Kong 1993 year book, page 233).

Due to the increasing strain on Hong Kong's transportation system within the city because of an ever increasing population, the government decided it was urgent something should be done as soon as possible to help relieve the situation. In view of the decision, a mass transit system was established in 1979. The mass transit railway system (MTR) would greatly help relieve some of the burden of public transport to the present day.

In accordance with the agreement between London and Beijing, Hong Kong was to be returned as agreed to the People's Republic of China on June 30th 1997.

In 1979 a mass transit railway was constructed in Hong Kong of which 80% was completed in 1979. The first stage of Mass Transit Railway (MTR) was completed in 1980.

In an exceedingly informative and enlightened report entitled "Hong Kong's Return to China . . . and Western Tunnel Company" from the article "Building a New Gateway to China," by John J. Kosowatz, December 1997, pages 102 and 104, approximately 335 words, indicated the following:

"Hong Kong's return to China in July (1997) sparked widespread speculation. People around the world offered their predictions as to how this tiny bastion of raw, unfetterred capitalism would change once enveloped by the last great venue of communism. Despite the range of opinions voiced, however, most agreed that one thing would remain the same: Hong Kong would maintain its status as the major gateway to China. (Copyright December 1997 by *Scientific American Inc*. All rights reserved. (approval 16 august 2000) by Linda Hertz.

One reason Hong Kong will continue to serve as an entry point to the mainland is the airport core program, an ambitious $21 billion infrastructure project due for completion next year (1998). Only in mercantile Hong Kong could a job of this magnitude be conceived, approved and financed, bid and largely completed in seven short years. The scope of work is enormous. Indeed, the airport core program is the largest public works upgrade ever undertaken.

It centers on building what will be the world's largest airport on Chek Lap Kok off Lantau Island, 25 kilometers west of Hong Kong's central business district. It also calls for 34 kilometers of new highways and railway lines, two massive bridges and two submerged crossings of Victoria Harbor to connect Chek Lap Kok to Hong Kong proper. In addition, contractors are erecting a new town, called Tung Chung, near Lantau to house at least 200,000 people, most of whom will work at the airport at Chek Lap Kok."

"City planners first proposed the construction in the late 1980s, because Hong Kong was fast becoming one of the globe's busiest destinations. The existing airport, Kai Tak, could not be expanded because of its location in the middle of Kowloon: this district is highly congested, and airplanes must make harrowing approaches directly over buildings there. So, in 1989, the government approved plans for a new facility. A year later it formed the new airport projects coordination office, or NAPCO, which serves as the design and construction manager for the project's owners: the local government, airport authority of Hong Kong, the mass transit railway corporation and western tunnel company . . . "

(Special thanks and appreciation to *Scientific American*, December 1997 granting permission to use this direct quotation from pages 102 and 104 of its article "Building a New Gateway to China" by John J. Kosowatz.)

The foregoing being an overview of the tremendous challenge and development of Hong Kong's enlightened transportation system from 1841 to 1998. Hong Kong has every right to be proud of its progress and unparalleled accomplishments. May the years ahead be a living and dynamic tribute to the hard work and vision for the future which lies before them.

CHAPTER 7

Housing and Water

Housing in Hong Kong is nothing less than a modern miracle deserving our attention. It was a mammoth task almost beyond imagination and description. The war in the Pacific ended in August 1945. It created innumerable and unbelievable problems for the residents of Hong Kong in all respects; among the most urgent problems was the housing situation. Many of Hong Kong's former residents hurriedly left the colony during the Pacific War to live in China due to the Japanese occupation of Hong Kong. They returned following the conclusion of the conflict in the Pacific. In the fall of 1945 many hoped to resume something of their former life style in Hong Kong. However, they had adjustments and changes beyond imagination, with seemingly endless problems to face; such as accommodating a fantastic influx of refugees leaving Kwangtung (neighbouring) province of China to live in Hong Kong. The political struggle between the nationalist forces of Chiang Kai Shek and the communist forces of Mao Tse Tung compounded the problems. The Chinese communist forces proved to be better organized and stronger; they occupied the entire continent of China by October 1949. Many residents in China were exceedingly concerned how a communist system could possibly adversely affect their lives; therefore, they voted with their feet to begin life once again in Hong Kong.

During the period of Japanese occupation of Hong Kong from Christmas Day, 1941 until the time of the liberation at the end of the war in August 1945, absolutely nothing had been done to promote better housing for the local residents of the colony. Life was so wretched and unbearable that literally thousands upon thousands of its residents fled to Macau and China to protect their families and participate in the war effort to assist in defeating Japan. Following the war, Hong Kong was left in a state of decay and shambles. It had been used by the Japanese war machine to promote its own aggressive and expansive policy in the Pacific. The single contribution Japan made to life in Hong Kong was the construction of a new airfield for the use of Japan's warplanes.

Likewise, Hong Kong's natural harbour was filled with bombed and sunken ship hulls. The harbour was utilized mainly as a point of rendezvous for the Japanese navy promoting its imperialistic and ambitious plan to dominate the entire continent of Asia.

Literally nothing had been done by the Japanese to repair or replace bombed out housing in Hong Kong. The roads had also deteriorated plus the sewage system making life exceedingly miserable and unbearable. The British colonial government had begun exploring the possibility of building a tunnel to improve transportation between Hong Kong Island and Kowloon on the mainland. The construction of the Tai Lam Chung reservoir was also adopted to help provide a more constant and adequate supply of water.

The construction of the new 200-bed Tsan Yuk maternity hospital was begun; its foundation stone was laid in 1952.

The entry of China into the Korean conflict in the 1950s resulted in tight international restrictions being laid upon international trade with China; within a few months Hong Kong had experienced nearly a total loss of trade with China, upon which it had always depended as its principle source of income. The commencement of a building programme for the resettlement of refugees and squatters became one of the largest and most swiftly organized poor man's housing schemes ever launched, even though Hong Kong was nearly completely robbed of its trade with China. The colony immediately switched its energy to production and manufacturing. The change occurred almost overnight: it was so rapid, Hong Kong was frequently falsely accused of placing "Made in Hong Kong" on goods produced elsewhere. The extraordinary transformation from an entrepot to a manufacturing economy soon became advanced and continued to proceed.

When I arrived in Hong Kong during the autumn of 1955 most buildings were only two or three storeys high, except for the Hong Kong Shanghai bank and the Bank of China buildings, both were located in the central district of Hong Kong Island, besides a few other businesses on the island and on the Kowloon Peninsula.

Squatter huts were constructed from any leftover pieces of wood, plywood, cardboard or tin. They were hastily erected on the sides of the mountains and slopes of nearby hills of both Hong Kong Island and Kowloon, providing a substandard type of shelter for the families concerned. The squatter areas had no running water in the primitive huts for cooking or cleansing purposes. There was no privacy whatsoever for individual families. Diseases like tuberculosis were rampant, spreading rapidly due to overcrowded conditions. Squatter huts sprang up, providing only basic shelter for countless numbers of people arriving on a daily basis in Hong Kong from China. The sewage system was practically non-existent, having open sewers that stunk. Water had to be piped into the areas whenever possible; otherwise water was carried in by the bucketful. Tremendous lineups for water could be readily seen; disputes frequently broke out concerning whose turn came first, yours or mine. If a heavy wind, rain or typhoon occurred, the water came tumbling down the hills, literally pouring over the slopes and damaging, destroying and wrecking many of the flimsy structures erected. Another major hazard was fire, which broke out frequently, any time of the day or night, burning all huts within that specific area to the ground and leaving the residents destitute and homeless by the hundreds of thousands. The residents fled for their lives losing all their meagre belongings. They had to begin life all over again; it was indeed a continual battle and struggle for existence.

All of Hong Kong's buildings had flat roofs; therefore, frequently squatters would erect a makeshift shelter on the flat roof of an older building, providing temporary cover for the family. If the makeshift hut on the roof accidentally caught fire, it usually destroyed the entire structure with it. Hong Kong's fire department was forever rushing here or there to fight fires in the squatter areas. The entrance to the squatter areas was ordinarily narrow and inaccessible, increasing the problems and difficulties for the fire department and their equipment. It was simply amazing how most residents miraculously escaped unharmed; they had been used to fleeing, sometimes receiving minor or superficial burns. If a school or church hall happened to be located nearby, the fire victims were temporarily moved to such locations until the emergency department of the social welfare department of the Hong Kong government could provide alternative accommodation. All victims were temporarily provided with food and clothing to help meet their immediate and temporal requirements.

Squatter areas sprang up here, there and all over the colony, some of the most familiar being Wong Tai Sin and Chuk Yuen, located in Kowloon adjacent to Kai Tak airport.

In 1954, with the estimated population of 2,400,000 rapidly increasing, plus a high birth rate, Hong Kong had a housing problem as difficult as any country in the world, despite the most vigorous action on part of the Hong Kong government. It appeared like remaining one of the colony's chief internal problems for many years to come.

In 1955, the most obvious and spectacular progress was made by continuing the programme of resettling squatters in multi-storey buildings, in which another 30,000 people were housed. The total population of the resettlement areas increased by 42,000, bringing the population of the areas to 153,000. The resettlement programme had been on an accelerated basis since early 1954, at which time there were more than 40,000 people homeless as a result of a series of disastrous fires in the squatter areas. The decision was taken to break away from earlier ideas, which envisaged resettlement in terms of cottage development, and go for multi-storey buildings. A special department of government was created to deal solely with resettlement problems.

The resettlement buildings were planned and erected by government and were originally designed in the shape of a capital H. Each building was seven storeys high, with no lifts or elevators. The individual family room measured 10 by 12 feet in size; in that space they cooked, ate, slept and lived out their everyday lives. The only partitions in the rooms were curtains placed there by the families themselves, otherwise no privacy whatsoever was available within the room.

The washrooms or toilets were shared by all other residents on a communal basis. The washrooms were located at the "bar" of the individual H-style buildings on all seven floors. The families washed their clothes and hung them out on bamboo poles from the narrow balconies of the buildings. Many people referred to the clothes in the Cantonese dialect as "the flags of ten thousand nations"—descriptive of the colour and variation of the clothes. An average of 2,500 people lived in each H-style building, which was far from ideal but considerably better than living in small squatter huts on the side of a hill or mountain, constantly subject to the elements of rain, flood, wind or fire. The H-style resettlement buildings were built parallel to each other in the resettlement areas. The flat roof tops of the buildings were frequently converted into privately operated daycare centres for children, or kindergartens, chapels, libraries etc., operated by churches and voluntary agencies. The din, hum, buzz and noise pollution of the many buildings varied during the evenings, was always present. On a very hot evening, many people slept outside of their assigned location on a small balcony to try and cool off.

The ground floors of the resettlement buildings were always reserved for individual shops and stores. The shops included a variety of goods such as groceries, rice, fresh fruit, vegetables, meat, eggs, poultry etc. Others sold newspapers, ancestral shrines, incense, dry goods, enamelled pots, pans, dishes etc. Space was often utilized for producing artificial flowers, toys and other items.

Apart from the direct government involvement of creating better housing conditions, various independent bodies, assisted wholly or in part by the government, made notable contributions toward dealing with the urgent problem.

The Housing Authority was set up in 1954; it consisted of all members of the urban council, ex officio, along with not more than three others appointed by the governor. It announced plans for two housing schemes: the first of those off Java Road, North Point accommodating 16,000 people in 1,975 flats. The second was in Cadogan Street and housed 4,800 people in 640 flats. Both were for families in the lower income groups of the white-collar class.

The Hong Kong Housing Society, another independent body, started its activities in 1952 with the construction of 270 flats in 5-storey blocks accommodating 1,420 people. The society's funds were obtained on loan at interest from the colony's developmental fund, and grants for site formation were obtained from Colonial Development and Welfare. In 1955 it completed a cottage resettlement at Ma Tau Chung for 1,000 people whose total earning capacity was less than $350 H.K. per month. It also began a scheme at Hung Hom, which when completed accommodated 8,000 people in 6-storey blocks of flats. The first block, housing 900, was completed during the year. The estate included 24 shops and a school.

Upon the British reoccupation of Hong Kong following the Pacific war. The old immigration restrictions were not enforced as far as travelers from the mainland were concerned, and many thousands of people, impelled by the chaotic conditions in China at the time, flooded into Hong Kong seeking, in the main, better opportunities and economic security. Hong Kong began to accept the implications of a population some 25% greater than what might be regarded as its normal capacity. However, the worse was to come. By the end of 1949, China's civil war had spread to the southern provinces. This, and rapid consolidation of the new regime, resulted in a fresh influx, greater than Hong Kong had ever known. This time they were mainly political refugees. By May 1950 there was an increase in population of some 700,000 from this cause alone and in addition to economic increase between the end of the Pacific war and the capture of Canton by the communists. Restrictions on entry from China were inevitable. On this occasion, a quota system was applied and a rough balance was struck between those entering and leaving the colony at the border. By February 1956 it was thought that the position might have stabilized itself, in the sense that either no more Chinese wished to enter the colony permanently or that new immigrants would be naturally balanced by those who, having sheltered in the colony since the closing stages of the civil war, were now prepared to return to China. All restrictions were relaxed for a trial period of seven months. There was, however, no stability. The seven months showed an adverse balance of at least 56,000 permanent immigrants—a rate of immigration in excess of the colony's high natural increase. The quota system was, therefore, reimposed early in September 1956.

In the Shek Kip Mei fire of December 25, 1953, over 50,000 persons lost their homes. This constituted a crisis of the first order, for not only did government have on its hand a relief programme that was beyond imagination, but it was faced with a wholesale reappraisal of existing policy which was no longer a practical proposition in terms of available land. Three immediate decisions were taken which formed the basis of a new policy with marked success. The decisions were first, that the land cleared by the fire should be used to the maximum practical intensity for the resettlement of the fire victim; second, that the government would itself build and finance the resettlement buildings; and third, that government would make itself responsible for the provision of food for the homeless until they could be resettled in permanent buildings.

It will be appreciated these three decisions constituted a radical departure from every aspect of the policy which had been applied before, and in particular that they implied that government assumed direct responsibility for the squatters in their moment of extreme need, and that government would, from now on itself enter the field of resettlement using public funds and its own constructional resources. There is no doubt that these decisions were not taken without full appreciation of the implications or without many misgivings. But they were taken is no doubt that they were right. Their effect was to place upon a community still suffering, with some indignation, from the economic effects of the China embargo, as vast new burden that would not be lightened for many years to come. Hong Kong had entered upon many major public works since the war. A $125 million reservoir was nearing completion; a $10 million airport was under construction; a $50 million hospital had begun, and reclamations totalling $30 million were constructed to provide land for industry, housing, for open spaces and for civic purposes. (H.K. Annual Report 1956, pages 20–21).

CHAPTER 8

A Journey to Remember

Britain, Turkey,
Iran and Hong Kong

A FTER HAVING STUDIED social work (1960–61) at the University of British Columbia in Vancouver, I returned to Hong Kong, travelling via the United Kingdom and across Asia. I was granted permission to remain nearly three months in Britain observing the work and witness of the church in various industrial areas throughout England and Scotland. I finally returned to Hong Kong after brief stopovers in Turkey and Iran, passed over the towering mountain peaks of Afghanistan to India and Thailand before arriving back in Hong Kong.

My itinerary in Britain was prearranged by Rev. Stephen Hopkinson, General Secretary of the South London Industrial Mission in London (s.l.i.m.). I flew to the United Kingdom by British Overseas Air Line (b.o.a.c.). I travelled via Toronto, Montreal, Prestwick, then on to London, England. It was a smooth journey all the way from Canada to Scotland. The plane landed at Prestwick Airport, Scotland, where it picked up many students on their way to study in London.

Suddenly the weather changed, flying between Prestwick and London. It became extremely rough, and many of the students became air sick. Until that time, I had believed air sickness was entirely a figment of a person's imagination, however, I was forced to alter my theory radically before landing at London's Heathrow airport, since I became deathly sick like many of the students. My friend who met me at the airport noticed my face appeared unusually white, as if I had seen a ghost. He enquired, "Whatever happened to you?" I replied, "Nothing more than a theory blown to pieces." Up until then I firmly believed air and seasickness were purely a matter of the imagination; now I knew otherwise.

Originally I was invited to reside at the home of Rev. S. Hopkinson, General Secretary of s.l.i.m., the organization which sponsored my visit in Britain. Unexpectedly they had friends arrive from Paris to visit the family so Rev. Hopkinson arranged for me to live at Lambeth Palace, the London residence of the Archbishop of Canterbury, on the opposite side of the Thames River from the British Houses of Parliament. I was thrilled by the alternative arrangements made for my accommodation, since the archbishop had only recently opened a portion of his palace to visiting clergy and laypeople from other lands.

Lambeth Palace is an extremely interesting and historic building erected many centuries ago (circa 1495) for the exclusive use of the Archbishop of Canterbury and his family. A stately stone fence surrounds the palace grounds. At the entrance of the grounds is the gatehouse where a watchman guards the palace. He granted permission to all seeking admission to the grounds. The gateman was a retired London bobby, knowledgeable about the background of Lambeth Palace. When he realized I was interested in its history and existing surroundings, he related many interesting and absorbing stories. When off duty, the guard personally guided me around a number of interesting buildings, pointing out many historic points of interest and significance including the palace garden, the beautiful medieval-style chapel, the spacious residence of the archbishop, and the former religious prison. I climbed up Morton's tower for a panoramic bird's-eye view of London. Whenever I left or returned to the palace, I was required to ring the doorbell at the guardhouse to obtain permission.

Lambeth Palace overlooks the busy throbbing Thames River with ships and barges constantly travelling up and down the river. I enjoyed walking along the famed embankment adjacent to the Thames, appreciating its beautiful gardens and surrounding scenery and its numerous activities. Frequently I crossed Westminster Bridge (completed in 1750) near the Parliament buildings with Big Ben marking the time. I enjoyed listening to Big Ben's melodic chimes, a sound recognized by all b.b.c. radio listeners from around the world. I enjoyed visiting many interesting monuments, such as Queen Boadicea, the warrior queen from Roman times, riding in her stately chariot at the end of the bridge; famed Westminster Abbey where all of Britain's royal family are crowned and Abraham Lincoln, well-known president of the United States. Many of Britain's most famous poets (such as Chaucer and Shakespeare), artists, musicians (Handel), scientists and other geniuses are recognized, all within walking distance of Trafalgar Square and its graceful guardian lions and host of pigeons. The National Gallery, the central area of London including St. Paul's Cathedral, Buckingham Palace and its long wide mall, St. James' Palace and its guards wearing their distinguished tall black fur hats and red uniform; guards mounted on beautiful black horses etc. are a few of the more famous and familiar sights appreciated and enjoyed by all visitors to London.

Martin Baker from the staff of the South London Industrial Mission made arrangements and plans for me during my stay in London and other locations. I was impressed by the detailed plans he prepared long in advance of my arrival in Britain. Martin arranged for me to meet Janice Lacey, the interchurch person responsible for interchurch aid, and Ms. Proud from the National Council of Social Services.

My first field trip was to Stevenage, about 30 miles north of London, a new town established by the British government to move some of its industry from the crowded and congested city of London. At the time Stevenage only had a population of around 30,000 people. I was taken to visit the Le Roi shirt factory, hiring some 100 employees, mostly women. Stevenage was neatly laid out with modern streets, an attractive shopping area, a new Anglican church known as St. George's built to help meet the spiritual needs of the working people living in Stevenage.

One day while in London, I walked to St. Paul's Cathedral, designed and built by Sir Christopher Wren (1632-1723). St. Paul's Cathedral with its stately and beautiful old dome is one of the most outstanding landmarks of London. It needs to be seen to be fully appreciated. I walked up its stairway to the Whispering Gallery, climbed as high as I could go to the base of the bronze cross crowning the top of the cathedral, and waited my turn to ascend the stairway to obtain a fleeting glimpse of the enormity of London. It is the 365 feet from the pavement to the top of the cross. Words fail to describe the beauty of the cathedral with its stained glass windows, a sight that nearly defies description. Holman Hunt's famous painting of Jesus knocking at the heart of Christians hangs in the cathedral. In the crypt were the remains of people like Sir Christopher Wren, the Duke of Wellington, Lord Horatio Nelson, Sir John A. Macdonald of Canadian fame et cetera.

I worshipped in famous Westminster Abbey (opposite the Houses of Parliament), with its lofty arches and magnificent and beautiful rose-stained glass windows. The church was begun in 1065 by Edward the Confessor and added onto by others throughout the years. All British monarchs were crowned there. It is the final resting place for many famous people, and is filled with tombs and memorials scattered throughout. It is the final resting place of the famous missionary to Africa, Dr. David Livingstone, who died May 1, 1873. His heart was buried by his friends in Africa, as a symbol of his love and devotion for the people of Africa, while his mortal remains were interred beneath the principle aisle leading in to Westminster Abbey. I vividly recall the beautiful strains of organ music vibrantly filling each corner of Westminster Abbey, along with the cathedral choir and its mellow and angelic voices, uplifting one's heart and soul during the worship service. You fully realize you are sitting in the presence of many of Britain's greatest men and women spanning the centuries.

Another day I was driven by car from London to Wolverhampton, over 100 miles northwest of London. It was a lovely ride through the rolling Midlands; beautiful, typically picturesque English countryside. We crossed over Roman roads and arrived at St. George's Hostel in Wolverhampton. The following day we visited the headmaster of a technical school in Wolverhampton and attended lectures held at St. George's parish by the educational committee on such topics as "Modern Industrial Problems."

I was driven to Lichfield where we visited the beautiful and noted Lichfield Cathedral erected around 700 A.D. Most of its statues suffered tremendously at the hands of Oliver Cromwell, who wrecked and defaced them. The cathedral has three tall spires (each 258 feet). Its marvellous stained glass windows are of Flemish origin. Lichfield was also the home of Dr. Samuel Johnson (1709–1784), British lexicographer, critic and poet.

From Wolverhampton I was driven to Trysull to see the former Trysull workhouse used during the British industrial revolution. While visiting the area, we were informed that the Secretary General of the United Nations, Dag Hammarskjöld had just been killed in an air crash in Rhodesia, Africa.

Outside of Wolverhampton, they drove me to Winson Green Prison. I was shown through the prison by the chaplain, who explained something of the British prison system to me. Back in Wolverhampton we went to the Eveready Company, which has over 1700 employees. They showed me the principal steps of how they produce Eveready batteries.

Later I boarded a train to Rugby, passing through Birmingham, and continued on to Rugby, resided at William Temple College. From Rugby, friends drove me to the city of Coventry for a short visit. Coventry suffered terribly at the hands of Nazi Germany during the intensive bombings of the city during World War Two. The highlight was a visit to the former Coventry Cathedral, which was completely destroyed during the war. The cathedral was Coventry's pride and joy, the spiritual powerhouse and centre of the people's lives, encouraging them in times of grave crisis.

Coventry Cathedral was completed in 1500 A.D. On the night of Thursday, November 14, 1940, the city of Coventry suffered a severe German air raid, and during the course of bombing, the cathedral was destroyed by fire bombs. Two months later, in January 1941, the altar and a charred cross were set up in the ruined sanctuary.

The altar is made from stones of the ruins; Holy Communion is celebrated there every Easter and Whitsunday. The charred cross is made from half-burnt beams of wood which fell from the roof during the evening the building was destroyed by bombs.

A cross was also made from three large nails which bound the roof beams together. The Coventry cross of nails has become famous throughout the world.

The words "Father, forgive," inscribed on the wall above the altar, recall the crucifixion of Jesus, when they were come to the place which is called Calvary. There they crucified him and the malefactors, one on the right hand, and the other on the left. Jesus said, "Father, forgive them; for they know not what they do." (Luke 24: 33,34)

FATHER, FORGIVE

All have sinned, and come short of the glory of God.
From St. Paul's letter to the Romans)

The hatred which divides nation from nation,
Race from race, class from class,
Father, forgive.
The covetous desires of men and nations to
Possess what is not their own,
Father, forgive.
The greed which exploits the labours of men,
Lays waste the earth,
Father, forgive.
Our envy of the welfare and happiness of others,
Father, forgive.
Our indifference to the plight of the homeless
And the refugee,
Father, forgive.
The lust which uses for ignoble ends
The bodies of men and women,
Father, forgive.
The pride which leads us to trust
In ourselves, and not in God,
Father, forgive.

Be kind one to another, tenderhearted,
Forgiving one another, as God in Christ forgave you.
(St. Paul's letter to the Ephesians)

(Note: the foregoing quotation originated from a pamphlet in Coventry
Cathedral).

A new ultramodern cathedral in Coventry adjacent to the
burnt-out one was in the process of being constructed and was dedicated in 1962. The spirit of Coventry could never be wiped out by the
threat of tyranny and war. It lives on to this day as a living testimony
to the resurrection of Jesus Christ that first Easter morning nearly
2,000 years ago.

My next destination was William Temple College in Rugby, dedicated in the name of the former archbishop William Temple (1881–1944), Archbishop of Canterbury (1942–1944). He was an outspoken advocate of social reform and crusaded against usury, slums, dishonesty and the aberrations of the profit motive. He was also a leader in the reform of church structures and in the ecumenical movement (*Cambridge Encyclopedia*, 1992).

In September 1961 I had the privilege and honour of spending time living and studying briefly at William Temple College, Rugby. The following is a brief quotation from the college report covering the period 1955–1960.

The college was founded and continues within the tradition of the Church of England: nevertheless all are welcome, whether Christian or not. Often our faith is set forth in relation to contemporary religions and current philosophical debate. We do not seek to promote any sectarian views or group activities, either within or outside the church. The aim is to enable Christians to understand better and to be loyal to their several traditions while appreciating the contributions of other communions in the life of the whole church. There have been members of courses from every Christian tradition: Orthodox and Roman, Anglican and Presbyterian, Lutheran, Reformed and Independent, the Society of Friends and the Salvation Army . . . .

For our work we have needed sound scholarship in all the subjects of our courses and especially from those engaged in scientific and technical studies we have turned to William Temple's friends and others in the universities, in the educational world, in social administration, in industry and commerce and in organized churches. They have responded most generously. Some are Christians and some are not but all have been concerned, as we have been, honestly to seek the truth, courageously to make decision and to act upon the convictions to which their thinking has led them.

Longer and shorter courses are also presented like the following: courses on responsibility in industry (short and long courses), weekend conferences for those interested in personnel management on "decision-making," mid-week courses for members of trades unions; mid-week courses for senior executives in industry, commerce and the social services on the meeting of cultures in the Middle West today etc. (*Report from William Temple College for the years* 1955-1960)

After leaving Rugby, my destination was Manchester, a city built and centered on industry; industry became its heart and soul. Manchester was a city open to new ideas and ways and rapidly expanding in every respect. Cotton was used in the mid-seventeenth century and the organization of industry became more advanced. Manchester became especially known for its linen, cotton and small wares, woolen cloths called Manchester cottons, bays and silken goods.

An advantage enjoyed by Manchester was its readiness to receive new ideas and the demonstration of new skills by foreigners. There was apparently no opposition to the introduction of the Dutch loom in the late 17th century. During the eighteenth century the most important changes were in the expansion of trade and industry. This century saw the construction of the major canals, the most famous being the Bridgewater Canal built to bring coal from the Bridgewater mines at Worsley direct to Manchester. The first exchange was opened in 1729, the first bank in 1771. Canals remained a vital means of transport up to the 1850s when railway competition began to make its influence felt. In the nineteenth century even greater improvements followed with the improved road making methods of Thomas Telford and J. L. Macadam.

Entering into the twentieth century Manchester continued with less dependence on textiles and heavy engineering. During two great wars the Manchester area had the largest concentration of industry for the war effort with the greatest variety of products. These included steam power plant, turbines, railway axles, motor vehicles etc. Put in a nutshell, Manchester became one the most important and advanced industrial cities of Britain.

I returned to London to attend the annual meeting of the South London Industrial Mission, held in "Mansion House," the official residence of the lord mayor of London. Mansion House was built by George Dance the Elder (1739–53). It is a magnificent structure surrounded by much beauty, pomp and ceremony. I went to Mansion House with Martin Baker from the South London Industrial Mission. We were driven to Mansion House by taxi, where a red carpet was literally laid out for all guests attending the meeting to walk upon.

The official business meeting was held in the "Long Parlour," a splendid room with marvellous carpets on the floor and intricately woven tapestries hanging on the walls. The general meeting was held in "The Egyptian Room," a large elaborate room with magnificent chandeliers used for the lighting, along with other beautiful decorations. I had the rare privilege and honour of being one of four guest speakers at the meeting. The lord mayor of London presided over the meeting and introduced each speaker. It was an occasion and event to remember. The British certainly know how to present such gatherings with pomp and ceremony.

Following the annual meeting I was scheduled to leave London for Nottingham and Sheffield. The next day was taken to observe an English steel factory, and I was shown some of the huge blast furnaces. Later I attended a group discussion on labour problems associated with technical change. The following day Margaret Kane accompanied me to the training centre for the coalmines, and later drove me to the steel works. It was fascinating seeing the red-hot blast furnaces and molten sheets being flattened out and pounded into shape.

My next destination was travelling from Sheffield to Glasgow, Scotland by train. Before I boarded the train in Sheffield, the senior chaplain showed me around the various departments of the British railway system there. After lunch I boarded the train for Glasgow, passing through some beautiful countryside including the Pennine mountains. The train stopped for a short time at Carlyle. On the train in the same compartment as me was a gentleman known as Jim Wilson who was exceedingly kind; he explained in detail the passing countryside and scenery. Just before arriving by train in Glasgow around 8:00 p.m. Jim invited me to go home with him and stay with his family for the weekend.

The Wilsons were the personification of kindness. Their daughter Alison was studying medicine at Glasgow University. She guided me around the city of Glasgow including the university, and the cathedral of St. Mungo, dating back to 1136 A.D. In the cathedral they have an old hourglass near the pulpit so the minister wouldn't be too long winded (great idea). We visited the National Art Museum and Gallery, and went where we could receive splendid views of Glasgow. Since it was Saturday, the Wilson family drove me on a tour of many interesting places such as Port Glasgow, Greenock where the inventor James Watt, designer of the steam engine and the metric unit of power, was born (1736–1819). We drove to where we could see the Atlantic Ocean on the distant horizon. Further off could also be seen "Paddy's Milestone," which was a rock guiding the ships on their way to Ireland, besides the place where curling rocks originated.

The following day was Sunday, the Wilsons kindly drove me to Kilmarnock, Prestwick (the airport), and to Alloway in Ayr where Scotland's favorite poet and son Robert Burns was born. We visited his home, stopped at Alloway to see the beautiful stone bridge where Burns wrote "Tam O'Shanter." In the poem, Tam O'Shanter's old horse, Meg, lost her tail by the witch etc. We continued on to the village of Brig a' doon. However, the actual destination for the day was Culzean Castle, overlooking the sea. The former American president Dwight D. Eisenhower was presented with a flat in Culzean Castle in gratitude for his contribution to freedom during the Second World War.

The Scottish people are among the most kindly, friendly and hospitable people I have ever met; they went out of their way to help me feel at home. From Glasgow I continued on my way to Edinburgh, the capital of Scotland, about one hour and a half's train ride from Glasgow. Unfortunately, I only had part of a day in Edinburgh, sufficient time only for a fleeting view of the city. My tour included a visit to Edinburgh Castle, St. Margaret's Chapel, the museum, St. Giles' Cathedral where Robert Louis Stevenson (1850–1894) is honoured by a memorial tablet. He was born in Edinburgh, but died at Vailima, Samoa. We also went through John Knox's (reformer) home and the National Art Gallery with its splendid masterpieces. Later the same day, I boarded an evening train in Edinburgh, arriving at London's King's Cross station the following morning.

During my final visit to London, it was a matter of winding up and completing my journey in Britain before returning to Hong Kong. On Sunday November 12th, I attended the Remembrance Day service on Whitehall Street where the cenotaph is situated. It was a beautiful clear sunny morning to mark the occasion. Huge crowds gathered along the side of Whitehall near the cenotaph, remembering their loved ones killed during the two world wars, including regiments from the army, navy and air force. The Queen's own guards were smartly dressed in bright red tunics with black trousers and tall black fur hats, adding to the colour and pageantry. Members of the St. John's Ambulance Corps were out in force. They were kept exceedingly busy reviving members from the various units who fainted due to the heat of the sun. On the stroke of 11:00 a.m. precisely, Big Ben marked the time beginning two minutes' silence, followed by bugles echoing the familiar sound of reveille, followed by a ceremonial wreath-laying service concluding the occasion.

Two days later on November 14, 1961, I boarded a British Overseas airliner bound for Istanbul, Turkey where I had planned a short visit. After arriving at London's Heathrow airport for check in, I unexpectedly met Rev. E. O. Janes from the London Missionary Society (L.M.S), whom I formerly knew quite well from Hong Kong and London, preparing to travel on the same flight as me. Rev. Janes and others were travelling to India to participate in the World Council of Churches conference in New Delhi, India (November 1961). It's a small world, isn't it? Imagine accidentally meeting the delegates on their way to India at London's Heathrow airport!

The airliner I travelled on flew to Turkey, Iran and India, the same route as my friend. The plane left London around 11:00 A.M., landed one and a half hours later at Zurich, Switzerland's international airport, continued its flight over Zagreb and Belgrade, Yugoslavia at 33,000 feet, and arrived at Istanbul, my destination, by 6:45 p.m., local time. I resided at the Park Hotel, a moderately priced hotel and ate supper consisting of dolma (rice and vegetables).

The following morning I walked along one of the main streets of Istanbul, doing some window shopping. The streets were narrow and made of cobblestones.

During the afternoon, I took a Thomas Cook tour. Stopping at the outstanding and famous Topkapi Serglio from 1468, a former palace of the sultans, we were shown through the palace kitchen with its many domes and chimneys. It formerly employed over 1,000 cooks. The kitchen was later converted into the present day museum. The Topkapi Serglio, formerly the administrative centre for the Ottoman Empire, contained an unforgettable collection of Chinese blue and white porcelain, reputed to be the largest collection of

Chinese porcelain outside of China—I don't doubt it. The collection is an integral part of the Topkapi palace and literally filled the shelves from floor to ceiling. We also went to the Sultan's Treasury, containing amazing exhibits of a fabulous collection of jewels like emeralds, rubies, diamonds etc., including the Topkapi dagger with its jewel-encrusted handle. Many of the jewels were sewn onto garments; the throne and its cushion were also decorated with pearls, other precious stones, and inlaid mother-of-pearl. It was unbelievable seeing the wealth amassed by the sultans (rulers) of bygone days.

After leaving the palace, the next stop was at the Justinian Reservoir, reserved for use by the imperial gardens and palaces. The dimensions of the underground reservoir were huge (230 by 459 feet, divided by 12 rows of 28 pillars); it was constructed so no enemy could cut off their water supply. The final point of interest for the day was the Grand Oriental Bazaar, completely covered and selling everything from jewellery to carpets.

During my second day in Istanbul I joined still another Cook's Tour of Turkey; the destination was the Black Sea. The bus crossed the Galatia Bridge to the old city of Istanbul or "the Golden Horn." We had a splendid view of the harbour, which at the time was filled with oil tankers and freighters plus a host of smaller craft. We transferred to a ferry; when it blew its shrill whistle, we had to cover our ears. Standing on the deck of the ferry, we received a marvellous view of the European coastline, including the Galatia Bridge, which stood out firm and clear.

It was a beautiful bright day, which enhanced our sightseeing tour. The ferry we rode upon continued to the Bosphorus Sea. We observed the remains of numerous palaces and mosques. Eventually the ferry passed a large castle called Rumeli Hisar, marking the closest point between Asia and Europe. By 1452 A.D., Mehmet landed on the European side of the Bosphorus. There he built Rumeli Hisar, an extremely historic place since it was from there the first cannon-balls were fired across the channel from Asia to Europe, utilizing the Chinese invention of gunpowder and marking the commencement of the Ottoman conquest, and the subsequent downfall of Constantinople, the end of the Roman Empire.

During my last day in Istanbul I went for a further tour of the old city, stopped at Theodosius' Obelisk made in Egypt between

1504–1450 B.C. The obelisk originated from Karnak (Egypt); it was taken to Istanbul in 390 A.D. The obelisk was cut from one long piece of syenite porphyr, with Egyptian hieroglyphics beautifully engraved on it. It is ten metres high and nearly 3,500 years old, located in the centre of Istanbul. Nearby is the Sultan Ahmet's mosque, more commonly known as "the Blue Mosque," built between 1609 and 1619 A.D. A magnificent structure, the mosque is the only one of its kind to have six minarets, besides "a cascade of domes and half domes." The mosque measures 210 by 236 feet. The interior of the mosque has 20,000 strikingly blue tiles from which it derives its name, as well as a painted dome, making it a most impressive and important centre for Muslim worship.

Near by is the Hagia Sofia or Sancta Sofia (Church of the Holy Wisdom), which had its early beginning in 325 A.D. from the reign of the emperor Constantine (the first Roman emperor converted to Christianity). It was the largest church in Christendom for one thousand years. Following the Turkish conquest its beautiful mosaics were covered with plaster, since Islam prohibits displaying images. During the 1930s Ataturk (symbol of modern Turkey) declared Sancta Sofia as a museum. Its minarets were added after Sancta Sofia was converted into a mosque. Sancta Sofia burned down twice, but was rebuilt each time. The present structure was completed in 548 A.D., following a triumphal march through the Hippodrome in front of the blue mosque. The emperor at the time entered the basilica of Sancta Sofia, and cried out "Glory be to God, who has found me worthy of this work, I have outstripped thee, oh Solomon." On May 29, 1453 A.D. Constantinople fell to Mehmet II Fatih, who entered Sancta Sofia and ordered it converted into a mosque.

My final tour of Turkey was a drive to Asia Minor. I crossed the Bosphorus by ferry to Scutari and climbed Tchamlidja Hill, obtaining an outstanding and picturesque view of the sea of Marmara, Prince's Islands (formerly the site of monasteries and a haven for pirates), the Bosphorus Sea and the Golden Horn, including the city of Istanbul.

I said my personal farewell to Turkey and continued on my way to Iran by B.O.A.C., leaving Istanbul for Teheran, Iran by 7:30 p.m.

The plane arrived at Mehrabad Airport (aerodrome) by 11:30 p.m., a four hour flight from Turkey. I checked into the Maysun Hotel on Zahedi (Fisherabad) Avenue, in downtown Teheran.

My first day in Teheran was quiet and relaxing. I went to the B.O.A.C. office to confirm my ongoing flight from Teheran to Hong Kong in a few days time. While at the airline office, I met Brian MacKay from Calgary, Alberta. He had just spent seven months in Iran and planned to stop in Hong Kong for a brief time. Brian was preparing to leave Teheran for Hong Kong and Canada the evening of the day we met. We had a pleasant visit and agreed to meet at Ferdowsi Square to exchange information with each other. He clued me in regarding Iran, while I did the same for him concerning Hong Kong. Brian took me to some nearby shops in Teheran providing me with many useful hints. We had lunch together, did more shopping, and took a taxi to the home of Reuben and Irma Batoon, missionary friends of Brian's from the Philippines.

The next day was Sunday, so I went to the nearby English-speaking community church in Teheran. It happened to be American Thanksgiving Sunday, a most suitable occasion. While at church, I met Reuben and Irma Batoon once again. They introduced me to friends within the church; among them were Mr. and Mrs. Robert Y. Bucher, social workers for one of the English speaking churches in Iran.

The following day I took a guided tour. The first stop was the University of Teheran, a modern university with over 11,000 students (1961) in attendance. The buildings were strikingly Western in architecture. From there we drove past the senate building, ultra-modern in appearance, however, it was closed due to a dispute over recent election results. Nearby we passed the palace of His Majesty Mohammad Reza, the Shah of Iran, which appeared to be heavily guarded.

The highlight of the tour was a visit to the Gulistan Palace. The palace served as the official residence of the Qajar kings for centuries. In 1925 Reza Shah, the founder of the Pahlavi dynasty, decided to live and work in surroundings not associated with the fun-loving and easygoing Qajars. Subsequently the Marble Palace came into being. The most famous palace in Teheran, it is now used only for state occasions, and is also known as the Gulistan Palace.

The attractive looking building stands in the midst of a fable-like Persian garden, with a mirror-studded and arched entrance that is most attractive. A series of great vaulted rooms opened onto court-yards with large pools surrounded by plane, poplar and cypress trees—it contained some of the most priceless treasures of Iran, if not the world.

Among the treasures was the famous Peacock Throne, brought by Nader Shah, the conqueror from Delhi. In 1739, following the conquest of the subcontinent, he turned that vast country back to the grateful king he had defeated as a gesture of generosity. Within the palace were many beautiful Persian rugs covering the floors. Large attractive and colourful chandeliers were evident. There was a display of gifts presented many years ago by rulers like Napoleon Bonaparte, George II and Queen Victoria from Britain, and others, many of the gifts being porcelain items and clocks.

The most unforgettable exhibit in the palace was the Peacock Throne, a symbol of national greatness. It is protected by the same spirit of reverence as a church or sacred vessels of a temple. It is inlaid with mother-of-pearl and studded with precious gems and stones. The exterior of the palace was artistically decorated with multicol-oured tiles, genuine works of art.

From the royal palace we visited the Seahsalor mosque built in 1831 A.D., used for religious instruction, as well as containing a fa-mous and outstanding library.

The final point of interest was the ethnological museum, display-ing a fascinating and interesting collection of beautiful clothes and costumes from bygone days, illustrating the richness and diversity of Persian life throughout the centuries.

Another day I visited the American school, Reuben Batoon showed me around the school and invited me to speak to the grade 9 to 12 students. Robert Bucher, the social worker whom I had met at the community church on Sunday, drove me to the Bethel School, a finishing school for privileged girls, where I was introduced to the staff and had tea with them. Next we drove to the Alborz Founda-tion, an institution for helping Iranian students studying English; it also served as a cultural centre with a religious emphasis. The final visit for the day was to a municipality-sponsored foundation for the care and training of children; it was exceedingly impressive.

Thursday was celebrated by the American community in Teheran as Thanksgiving Day. I also observed the first snowfall of the season upon the peaks of the mountains not far from Teheran. A special Thanksgiving Day service was held in the community chapel; the Honourable Brenn read the scripture and Stuart W. Rockwell from the American Embassy read the President's Proclamation. Major John C. Hayden delivered the Thanksgiving message. Later in the day about forty American Presbyterian mission staff gathered for a Thanksgiving dinner, having turkey with all the trimmings. They invited me to participate in their festivities; following dinner we had a singsong and played games.

The day following Thanksgiving (Friday, 1961) was observed as a Muslim holiday. I was invited by friends from the Presbyterian mission to go on a picnic with them. There were three carloads of us who drove to the outskirts of Teheran for a picnic. It was extremely interesting seeing the outskirts of the city with snow-capped mountains in the background. We had an excellent view of Mount Damavand, often referred to as the Mount Fuji of Iran. We drove to an Iranian friend's home, located in a rural setting. The roads were narrow and rough. They parked their vehicles; then we hiked through a narrow passageway in the hill to their friend's home. Afterwards we walked through some small Iranian villages into the mountains. The hills were mostly barren with little or no vegetation on them. We walked halfway up one of the snow-covered mountains, which was rugged, with a very cold wind blowing between the hills. I wore two sweaters but really felt the cold. My trousers were suitable for the tropics and the cold wind whistled through them. I didn't expect such a difference in temperature when I went on the journey, but managed to endure it.

Lunch consisted of locally made bread eaten by the slab; it was hot and delicious. We ate wieners and hamburgers, a typical American-style picnic lunch, and sang familiar songs around the camp fire, then returned to Teheran. I had a short rest in the hotel, and then drove to the airport departing from Teheran around midnight for New Delhi, India. My memories of Iran are vivid and extremely pleasant. I made many new friends while on my visit to the country; it resulted in a satisfying and worthwhile experience.

The B.O.A.C. flight from Teheran was smooth and uneventful.

The route flew via Afghanistan and northern India. The weather was clear and bright; the moon and stars shone brilliantly. It took about 3 hours and 20 minutes before touching down at the New Delhi Airport. The captain announced the plane would be delayed at New Delhi for a few hours due to an instrument problem. We didn't leave again until 7:30 a.m. The flight crossed northern India to Calcutta, across Burma to Bangkok, Thailand, where the temperature was in the 80s. The plane remained only half an hour at Bangkok airport before it flew directly to Hong Kong. In Hong Kong I was met by some of our United Church mission folks. It was wonderful to return to familiar territory once again, concluding an unforgettable "journey to remember."

Note: My visit to Iran took place before the revolution that overturned the monarchy. Many changes have come about since; the situation is completely different today. Mohammed Reza, the last Shah of Iran, fled on January 16, 1979, then moved from one country to another. The Shah eventually died in Egypt in 1980. The Ayatollah Khomeini returned from exile to Iran on February 1, 1979.

中华人民共和国
The Great Wall of China

颁

此证书颁发给 *Lem Buturham*
This is to certify that

攀登长城日期 *July 4th, 1987*
did climb the Great Wall on

颁发者: 中国国家旅游局
Issued by
China National Tourism Administration

八达岭长城管理处主任签字
(Signed)
Manager of Badaling Great Wall Administration Office

证 书
Certificate

A "Great Wall Certificate" from 1987.

Standing on the Great Wall of China, 1987.

"Temple of Heaven," Beijing, China.

Our tour group who visited China in 1987. Taken in front of the "Nine Dragon Wall" within the palace grounds.

A view of Kweilin, China, taken from Mt. Fubo.

Enjoying a boat ride on the Yangtsze River.

Chinese river boats on the Yangtsze River.

Visiting a church in Hankow in 1987.

Panda bears relaxing in a zoo.

CHAPTER 9

Journeys to China

CHINA IS INDEED a land of culture and tremendous beauty. Its culture extends for well over 5,000 years, while its beauty is legendary. Due to the political situation and climate existing in China during the 1960s when I was living in Hong Kong, it was not possible for me to travel to China. The closest I could hope to get to China was Lok Ma Chau, the border crossing point where I frequently accompanied visitors while taking them on a tour to the New Territories in Hong Kong. Often visitors would request me to drive them to a place where they could at least peek into China at Lok Ma Chau, near Castle Peak where Chinese agricultural products were transferred on a daily basis from the People's Republic of China to the busy throbbing markets of Hong Kong. I parked my car on a nearby hill overlooking the beautiful and picturesque emerald green rice paddies of China, a splendid agricultural region of Kwangtung province. Often I asked myself, would I ever be allowed to visit China in the near future? A purely rhetorical question, there seemed to be no answer, however, ten years later, after I had returned to live in Canada, permission was finally granted for me to obtain a tourist visa to visit the People's Republic of China.

In May 1966 (the Cultural Revolution began May 1966 and lasted until 1976), I placed in my application along with two friends from New Zealand and Canada for a three-day visit to Canton. At the time we didn't realize it was the beginning of Mao Tse Tung's (Mao Zedong's) Cultural Revolution. We placed our application through the China travel service office in Kowloon. They accepted my passport, withholding it for about six weeks while they thoroughly investigated my background. Weeks later I received a telephone call from the China travel service office in Kowloon requesting me to pick up my passport, which I did. When I examined my passport, I noticed no visa had been granted so enquired why since I was very disappointed. The clerk replied, "Mr. Burnham, don't be disappointed, failure is the mother of success," in other words, apply again at a more appropriate time and date. Later I discovered I was considered a potentially dangerous person, perhaps even a spy. My other friend received a similar reply. Only our friend from New Zealand received a visa and was permitted to travel to Canton. Since no change was forthcoming, we had to accept the reply and leave it in their hands. Their decision was final.

I never again tried until after Mao Tse Tung died in Beijing on September 8, 1976; even then I waited for further passage of time. In 1980 I tried my luck once again for a tour of China and Southeast Asia. This time I placed my application through the Japan Airline office in New York. My application for travel to China was accepted and approved.

PART I

My first journey to China began from San Francisco on June 28, 1980 where I met Mike Johns and his friend Sheila Mah from Vancouver; they were on the same tour to China and Southeast Asia. We met Linda Leong, the airline's guide, and other members travelling on the same tour. The 747 jet was filled to capacity; it was an eleven-hour flight crossing the Pacific from San Francisco to Narita airport in Tokyo, Japan. We spent the night at the Nikko hotel adjacent to the airport. My roommate for the tour was Roger Chen a young man from New York; we became good friends, and were quite compatible. The next day our flight flew to Osaka, Japan, then continued via Shanghai to Beijing, a three and a half hour journey, arriving at Beijing airport about 3:00 p.m.. The temperature was a comfortable 73 degrees. The highway from the airport to Beijing was picturesque with beautiful trees lining both sides of the road. We resided at the Chien Men Hotel, converted money into Chinese currency (yuen), then relaxed. The hotel was old but clean and comfortable.

The following morning I arose early with expectancy and anticipation observing many people outside, near the courtyard of the hotel exercising, doing *tai chi chuan* in a slow and polished fashion, which is an ancient Chinese art. At precisely 8:30 a.m. our tour bus was loaded and headed north out of Beijing on our first official tour of my long awaited China visit, to the historic Ming tombs dating from 1409 to 1644. It seemed as if history's time machine had stopped and we were transported back several centuries. Standing sedately were 24 huge stone animals besides carvings of four men. Some of the animals were standing, others kneeling, included elephants, camels (Bactrian with 2 humps), horses and mythical beasts like the unicorn neatly lined up on both sides leading to the tombs. We passed through a large red gateway leading to the sacred route to the tombs of thirteen Ming emperors. They also displayed artifacts from within the tombs. Tourists could be seen everywhere having their photographs taken to place in their family albums at home.

The next point of interest was further north of Beijing: the Great Wall of China. I had to pinch myself to realize it was a reality, as I stood at the foot of the greatest wall ever built. No, it wasn't a figment of my imagination, the Great Wall of China is a massive structure built to keep out the hostile armies of the Mongols from entering China many years ago. Construction of the wall began during the period of the warring states 403–221 B.C.; separate and individual sections were built in strategic locations. China's emperor Qin Shi Huangdi (221–206 B.C.) ordered the stone wall be joined into a continuous rampart; it was a combination of bricks, stones and earth known as the Great Wall of China. The Great Wall stretches over the northern portion of China for 3,750 miles (nearly the width of Canada), crossing coastal plains, mountain ranges and the Gobi desert to the west. The wall is about 45 miles northwest of Beijing, capital of present day China. It may be of interest to know the average measurement of the wall is about 25 feet high by 15 feet wide and claims to be the only man-made structure which may be seen from the moon. Located at Badaling, the Great Wall is still the highlight for all visitors to modern China in our day and generation.

Ascending the Great Wall of China was an exhilarating, exhausting and emotional experience, requiring endless energy to climb the wall. It brought so many thoughts to mind. Besides the visual beauty of the wall wending and snaking its way across China's endless mountain ranges, it has served as an inspiration to countless observers throughout generations like historians, artists and poets. Its influence is beyond measure: songs and poetry have been composed to inspire and unify the nation; stamps have been issued to spread the wall's fame, beauty and notoriety around the world. There seems to be no end to its influence. I have had the privilege of seeing and walking upon Emperor Hadrian's wall, built 122–8 A.D. by the Romans to protect northern England from invaders; it shrinks into complete obscurity when compared to the Great Wall of China. The Great Wall of China is in a separate category by itself, unique in all respects. There is no similar monument anywhere in the world equivalent in stature compared to China's Great Wall.

Beijing, the capital of the People's Republic of China, is a beautiful, fascinating and attractive city. At the centre of the city is the massive Tiananmen Square, the largest of its kind in the world, covering over 100 acres. All important mass rallies have been held there since the establishment of the People's Republic of China on October 1, 1949, including the infamous and notorious demonstrations of June 1989.

Adjacent to Tiananmen Square is the Great Hall of the People; the assembly hall accommodates 10,000 people. Nearby is a 118-foot granite structure known as Monument to the People's Heroes. The square itself accommodates at least one million people. The Mao Tse Tung (Mao Zedong) Memorial Hall dwarfs all structures. The mausoleum stands over 100 feet high, covering some 200,000 square feet. Waiting in line to pass through the structure may be seen a host of local and foreign guests, patiently waiting to file past the body of the great helmsman, Mao Tse Tung, preserved in a crystal sarcophagus. People from across China may be seen paying their respect. It was so quiet in the hall you could nearly hear a pin drop. Before being allowed to enter the mausoleum everyone was politely instructed by the guides there was to be no talking, photos, or smoking. It was a solemn occasion for all visitors, adults and children alike. Within the mausoleum there is a huge statue of Chairman Mao, along with a mammoth picture of the Great Wall of China in the background, symbolizing the unification of the nation. It was an occasion that left an indelible imprint upon our mind—a sense of awe, similar to visiting a sacred site or temple. We all received the message loud and clear.

The "Forbidden City" is almost adjacent spreads over some 250 acres, protected by a 25 foot wall with a water-filled moat. There are only four gates allowing access to the palace grounds. The Forbidden City itself exceeds five centuries in age. They claim it took 200,000 workers thirteen years to construct the palace from 1407 to 1420 A.D.. During the intervening years since, construction, invaders and fire have had their toll. Most of the buildings are now replicas of the original palace buildings.

The present day complex of buildings within the Forbidden City consists of six major palaces along with many buildings of lesser importance, besides the Imperial Gardens with pine and cypress trees several centuries old, planted during the Ming Dynasty. Some twenty-four dynasties of the Ming and Ching (Qing) formerly dwelt within the Forbidden Palace, living in complete splendour and solitude with their wives, concubines, ministers and thousands of artisans in the palace's 900 rooms.

Today the Forbidden Palace is open to the general public, known as the Palace Museum. The emperor of China was figuratively believed to have lived at the centre of the universe. It is one of the most important sights of Beijing. The palace is the former residence of the various emperors of China. Upon entering the palace grounds may be seen a pair of magnificent Ming Dynasty lions made of bronze, gilded with gold. The lions are majestically sitting there guarding the Forbidden City from all evil and harm. In the centre may be seen a tremendous marble stairway leading to the Hall of Supreme Harmony, the major focal point of the Imperial Palace, built primarily for ceremonial occasions. The imperial throne is located within the Hall of Supreme Harmony. A magnificent marble staircase, consisting of carved five-toed dragons, symbolizes the imperial dragon ascending the stairway. The emperor was carried up the marble stairway in a sedan chair with pomp and ceremony. All of the palace buildings (70) were magnificently decorated by skilled artisans. Within the Imperial Gardens may be seen an artistically decorated tile wall with nine dragons depicted in relief.

Volumes have been written describing the beauty and artistry of the Forbidden City. Space doesn't permit further detailed description, however, this provides a brief glimpse of what may be seen by today's visitors.

Nearby is an exceedingly important structure known as the Temple of Heaven, beautifully and gracefully elevated on a foundation of marble. The Temple of Heaven was the place where the emperor offered prayers for good harvests. A huge marble stairway leads up to the temple.

The Temple of Heaven gracefully sits upon a large white marble terrace, circular in shape. The temple itself is entirely constructed of wood, without a single nail in the five-centuries-old wooden structure (3 tiers). Beautiful cobalt blue tiles encircle the roof; the dark blue tiles have dragons flying through the clouds, symbolizing heaven. Dragons and phoenix are gilded, representing the positive and negative (ying and yang) influences in life, encompassing and surrounding the temple. The interior is exceedingly beautiful and attractive, containing a circular vaulted domed ceiling painted in gold, green, red and white. The emperor offered his prayers for good harvests within the temple. The temple also housed the sacred ceremonial tablets. Due to its perfect proportions, the Temple of Heaven has frequently been called "the most beautiful single creation in all China."

The tour took us through the Summer Palace where the emperor and his family lived from April to September. The Summer Palace is adjacent to beautiful Lake Kunming. The palace grounds and surrounding buildings are kept spick and span. A long corridor skirts by the side of the palace. There are some 5,000 scenic paintings along the walls and ceiling of the hall's corridors, built to shade and protect the emperor from the fierce blazing rays of the scorching summer sun. Spanning Lake Kunming from the side, is the artistic and graceful Jade Belt Bridge which has seven arches making up the span. High upon a nearby hill is the famous and colourful Buddhist temple overlooking the Summer Palace grounds from above. The opera house was exclusively erected for private use by the imperial family, constructed within the palace grounds. Operas were frequently enacted for the entertainment of the imperial household. Located on the shore of Lake Kunming is a garish-looking stone boat, constructed by the Empress Dowager. The boat is a fine illustration of how funds were sometimes wastefully squandered by the imperial family; the funds were originally designated for the establishment of a Chinese navy.

While exploring the many cultural points and interests of Beijing and its historic monuments, our next destination of the tour was Heilongjiang Province, which in the Manchu language means "place for drying nets" (the Chinese characters literally mean "black dragon river"), the most north easterly province of China. During World War II it was known as Manchuria, its closest neighbours being Russia to the north, and Korea to the south. The Russian influence in China became prominent from 1896 as they negotiated the building of a railway passing through Harbin to Vladivostok in eastern Siberia. The railway was completed in 1904; it was followed by various Russian demands, concessions and pressures upon China.

In many ways Heilongjiang province in China is somewhat similar to the Prairie provinces of Canada, being quite flat, with hot summers (110 degrees Fahrenheit the day I arrived) and extremely cold winters. It is blessed with many natural mineral resources including oil and gas.

Harbin is the capital of Heilongjiang, the political centre of the province. Harbin is located on the Songhua river near the border between China and Russia. Heilongjiang was the first province in China to become a socialist state in 1949.

Our tour group lived in the International Hotel in Harbin, somewhat antiquated in many respects, but at the time (1980) very few tourists visited the city, Harbin being the province's centre for industry.

Our initial tour was to visit a workers' commune located about forty minutes from Harbin City. The cadre in charge provided a detailed account of the products the commune could produce. He provided a general lecture. All participants in the tour were required to wear a special type of rubber shoes, besides a white hat and coat as we visited a chicken farm, so we would not pass on any disease to the fowl. We also visited the home of a commune worker, who accompanied us around the fields and greenhouses for which he was responsible. He provided an informative and educational experience for all concerned.

Upon returning from the commune to Harbin City, we stopped at the zoo, visited the pandas and saw large Manchurian tigers famous throughout China. During the p.m. the tour included a splendid musical performance provided by the students from nearby schools.

They danced and sang Korean and Chinese folk songs. During the evening, we were invited to attend a splendid acrobatic show held in a local auditorium.

The following day we visited a high school in Harbin, and were welcomed by the principal and teachers from the school. The classes were extremely crowded: 48 to 58 students per classroom. We visited classes in chemistry, mathematics, and English.

Our final day in Harbin was Sunday. We were taken up the Sungari river by boat. The boat visited Sun Island, along with a group of Italian engineers travelling on the same tour. They had been invited to Heilongjiang to assist the Chinese government to explore some of the province's natural resources. We were shown through a convalescent hospital for the working people. While visiting the hospital, they demonstrated acupuncture and other kinds of Chinese medical treatments. It was evident Dr. Norman Bethune, a former Canadian surgeon who served China during the early days of the revolution, was considered one of China's medical giants and heroes. His statue is prominently displayed throughout Harbin City. It was an extremely informative and educational tour. From the hospital we went to the Children's Park. Children were responsible for operating the entire railway system throughout the park, serving as engineers, conductors etc. During the afternoon we were escorted to the central railway station in Harbin and left for Changchun.

It was a three and a half hour train journey travelling from Harbin to Changchun in Jilin province. The city of Changchun is an industrial city. They guided us through an automobile factory so we could observe an assembly-line process; it provided a bird's-eye view of the record and background of the factory. The finished product was a truck, driven off the end of the assembly line. The factory also had established a kindergarten for the children of workers. The children danced and sang, providing an exceedingly professional performance.

We visited the Changchun Film Studio, and were taken to the prop room to see antique vases and furniture exclusively used for film production. We were also invited to be present for filming one of their productions.

The following day we were driven to Kirin University, an administrative representative of the university explained the background of the university, took us to the university library to see a display of ancient Chinese books made from bamboo strips, including a display of oracle bones, the oldest extant form of Chinese writing in existence. It was a fascinating tour for all interested in the history and background of Chinese calligraphy. From the library we visited the modern language department of the university, where they teach English, Japanese and Russian. We were separated into numerous interest groups of three and four people, so we could ask questions if desired.

Later we visited an embroidery factory, which employs 500 labourers. It was fascinating to see how they were trained to produce such an excellent quality of embroidery targeted for the export market. Many of the employees used Pfaff sewing machines. Their work was extremely fine and dainty. We also visited the Children's Palace for an illustrated lecture to observe the way they were trained in the art of ballet and sculpture. They begin training the children at a tender age while their body structures were more flexible.

The final tour of Changchun in Jilin province was to the former palace of the last emperor of China. Aisin-gioro Pu Yi was the child emperor of China for three years (1908–1911), he was replaced by Dr. Sun Yat Sen's Republic of China. In 1932 Pu Yi was appointed puppet emperor (Manchukuo) of Japan until 1945, the end of the Second World War with the collapse of Japan's empire. His palace in Changchun was a simple but modest palace; it was converted into a museum. They constructed a special air raid shelter for the protection of the emperor living in the palace building during wartime. The former emperor Pu Yi became interested and skillful in painting tigers. Many of his paintings decorate the walls in the palace, leaving a deep impression upon all of us. Pu Yi became a talented artist.

When the tour of Changchun in Jilin province was completed, we were driven to the Changchun airport; at the time (1980) it was a brand new airport. We left Changchun by a propeller aircraft, landing briefly at Shengyang, and continuing onward to Beijing for a three hour flight, however, since it was already 10:00 p.m. when the flight arrived at Beijing airport, they assigned us to a local Beijing hotel.

The next morning we were driven to Beijing International Airport, and provided with a box lunch before boarding the plane. By

12:45 p.m. the plane left Beijing airport for Canton in Gwangdong (Kwangtung) province in southern China, adjacent to Hong Kong. We were all snugly packed into a Russian plane much like sardines with little room to stretch our legs, since Caucasians tend to be larger than many Orientals. If a passenger had to go to the washroom, all those seated in the same row had to rise and let him/her go past, the same was done as he returned to his seat. It was a two and a half hour direct flight from Beijing to Canton, a distance of approximately 1,200 miles. The flight was smooth with no turbulence or tropical depressions occurring on the way. We made the best of the situation, landing at White Cloud Airport in Canton.

A China travel service representative met the plane in Canton, checking us into a local hotel. By 4:30 p.m. the travel agency arranged for a brief tour of Canton city. During the evening we prepared to travel the following day to Hong Kong by train.

On July 11, 1980, after passing through the required procedures in Canton, we were cleared by China's immigration and customs. The train departed Canton precisely at 8:30 a.m.. It was a beautiful sunny morning for the three-hour train journey to Hong Kong. We saw farmers busily engaged in harvesting their rice crops. Both southern China and Hong Kong harvest three crops of rice per year. The distance between Canton and Hong Kong is about 90 miles. The train was not required to stop at Lowu or Shumchun near the Chinese border, but proceeded directly to Hong Kong. It was much like returning home for me, since I formerly lived there for some eighteen years. The tour remained in Hong Kong for two additional days, and then continued our journey through Southeast Asia via Singapore, Malaysia and Thailand, then back to North America.

PART II

My second journey to China commenced July 31, 1982. At the time I prearranged to meet my friends Angus and Annie Mew from Vancouver in Hong Kong. All arrangements were made through the China travel service office in Hong Kong. There were twenty people on the tour. We met for the first time at the Kowloon-Canton railway station in Hung Hom Kowloon on August 4th. The tour included twelve from Northern Ireland, besides eight from Canada, France and Japan.

The train departed Kowloon at 1:00 p.m. and passed through the New Territories of Hong Kong on its way to the People's Republic of China. We crossed the border from Hong Kong into Kwangtung (Guangdong) province of China. The scenery was exceedingly picturesque. The rice fields were in process of being harvested, while other farming activities such as ploughing by means of the water buffalo were proceeding. The train arrived in Canton by 4:00 p.m; a China travel service agent met the train and escorted us on a short visit to the Sun Yat Sen Memorial Hall in Canton (Dr. Sun Yat Sen was the founder of the Republic of China in 1911). By 7:00 p.m. we boarded a direct flight to Beijing, requiring two hours and forty minutes flying time before arriving.

We were accommodated in a Beijing hotel. The next day Miss Wu our guide accompanied us on a tour of Beijing city, including many places of historic interest like the Tiananmen Square, Mao Tse Tung's mausoleum, the Palace Museum, the Summer Palace, and the zoo. (Note: These sights previously described in detail in Part I of this chapter.) The next morning we boarded a train to visit the Great Wall of China. It was a crystal clear day as we toured the Great Wall; an unforgettable sight and experience. Later we visited the Ming tombs where thirteen of the Ming emperors were buried.

From Beijing we flew westward to Lanzhou, the capital city of Kansu (Gansu) province, a two hour flight over varied terrain including mountains, plains and part of the Gobi desert. Lanzhou airport is located 70 kilometres (43.5 miles) from the city on the Yellow River. Lanzhou was formerly an important military garrison. The morning following our arrival at Lanzhou, we were driven by bus to the famous White Pagoda, built during the Yuan Dynasty, totally destroyed due to a severe earthquake several centuries later, then rebuilt during the Ming Dynasty. It was a brisk climb to the White Pagoda Hill Park on the northern bank of the Yellow River, a rewarding experience where we received a splendid view of Lanzhou from the adjacent park.

When we visited Lanzhou in Gansu province (1982) there was a severe shortage of accommodation for foreign guests to the city. For that reason we were billeted inside a military garrison, requiring us to present our passports upon entering or leaving the garrison. The garrison was operated in a strict military fashion; before the troops retired in the evening a bugler played Taps, while in the morning another bugler echoed forth reveille, "You've got to get up in the morning." It seemed strange hearing such music being played within a socialist state like China, a reminder we were visiting under very special circumstances.

Historically Lanzhou (in Gansu province) was a place where dissidents were frequently banished from Beijing. We were told how a former son of a Ming emperor was banished to Lanzhou; it was far enough away from Beijing to be considered safe from any person desiring to upset the status quo. The isolation of the Gobi Desert and the rugged terrain spoke louder than words.

Lanzhou is adjacent to the Yellow River. Placing it in a category by itself, the historic Yellow River is long, broad and frequently floods its banks. The water in the river is a yellowish colour, derived from the soil skirting the riverbanks. The Yellow River is 5,000 kilometres (3106.9 miles) in length flowing through mountain passes, deserts, steppes and plateaus. It affects the entire life of the Chinese nation as it wends and snakes its way across the land.

The following morning we left Lanzhou by train, we were driven to the station and departed at 11:30 a.m. for our destination, Dunhuang, a 28-hour rail journey through Gansu province. The tour group was accommodated in a single railway car; we were each assigned to upper or lower berths. However, the portion of the train we were travelling on was air conditioned and comfortable. It was blistering hot as we crossed through part of the Gobi Desert. I recall as we were eating supper in the dining car during our first day, the temperature reached 110 degrees Fahrenheit. The train was passing through the Gansu corridor, where we could clearly observe the beautiful towering snowcapped mountains of Ching Hai (Qinghai province) in all its majesty, glory and splendour. What a tremendous contrast of weather during one single day!

Travelling from Lanzhou by train provided us with a fine opportunity to see the surrounding scenery from the train, like stooks of golden-coloured grain standing in the fields adjacent to the Yellow River as we left Lanzhou, similar to the fields you see crossing the Canadian prairies in the fall. Before long a sharp contrast began to appear, ranging from valleys with shepherds tending their flocks to sand dunes stretching for countless miles. During the afternoon we saw in the distance the most westerly gate (Jiayuguan gate and fort built in the 14th century) and a portion of the Great Wall of China. The sand of the Gobi Desert varied in colour, drawing my attention as we passed through it. In some places the sand was a light sandy colour, while in other areas it appeared a greyish volcanic colour, quite different from the sand found in the Sahara Desert in North Africa or the Arabian Desert.

By 2:30 p.m. the following day the train pulled into the local railway station where we got off only to be informed we couldn't stay at the hotel we were booked for that evening, since another tour group decided to remain a day longer and occupied our rooms. In view of the totally unexpected situation we were transferred to an ordinary local bus travelling through the desert in still another direction. They promptly transferred us to a bus which bounced on its way over the rough uneven road. The windows of the bus were opened as wide as possible and off we went. I was seated near the rear of the bus. The hot desert wind and dust particles entered one side and blew out the other; one hour and a half later we finally reached our destination. The hotel assigned was somewhat old and primitive, indoor toilets were completely nonexistent in the hotel, but located in another area a considerable distance from the hotel near a pathway leading through a nearby field. It happened I had to go to the toilet during the middle of the night, so picked up my flashlight and headed for the outdoor washroom among the fields. It was a crisp cool clear evening in the desert. As I looked skyward I received a marvellous view of the Big Dipper, since there was little air pollution in the desert. The Big Dipper stood out such as I had never seen before, similar to seven huge lanterns hanging in the sky. An amazing and fantastic sight to behold, I have never forgotten the sight to this day.

We arose at 5:00 a.m., while the stars were still shining large, bright and beautiful in the sky. We packed our bags, ate an early breakfast and began the final part of the ride by bus through the desert to Dunhuang, our destination in Western Kansu (Gansu) province. The road continued to travel through seemingly endless desert. We stopped at one of the ancient watchtowers built by the roadside. Constructed during the Ming Dynasty, the tower was built to help guide travellers like us on the old silk route by night. Huge flaming torches were perched on the top of the towers to guide travellers as they passed through the desert. The mountains were entirely barren, similar to the surface of the moon. Before long another range of hills came into view, we had been journeying along part of the former "Silk Road," arriving at our destination, Dunhuang by 9:00 a.m..

A colourful pagoda-like structure clearly marked the entrance to the caves. We were taken to the Dunhuang Research Centre, where a staff member provided us with a historical background of the caves. We officially began by a visit to the Mogao Grottoes of Dunhuang. The grottoes extend for some 1,600 metres from north to south. The earliest grotto dates back to 366 A.D.. Four hundred and ninety caves were carved and painted over a period of 1,600 years.

The guide commenced showing us through the caves and told of a remarkable incident happening during the Cultural Revolution (1966–1976). A group of zealous Red Guards decided the teachings of Mao Tse Tung should be strictly adhered to and followed—Mao claimed all old teaching and thought should be destroyed. The guards arrived at the entrance of the caves and planned to wreck and destroy the paintings and statues within the caves. However, as they entered the caves one of the leaders was extremely impressed: he noticed a sign indicating the cave in which they were standing had been painted during the Tang Dynasty (618–905 A.D.). It suddenly dawned upon him the long history involved, so he turned to the others and said, "This is part of our heritage and tradition; we should preserve not destroy." The Red Guards immediately left the caves, threw their banners into a nearby ditch, and left the caves unscathed.

Dunhuang's caves are world-famous; many of our tour members who originated from Northern Ireland had especially travelled to China to research and study the famous caves of Dunhuang.

I have been to Rome and through St. Peter's Church in the Vatican, a treasury of Christian art and tradition. Talented artists like Leonardo da Vinci, Michelangelo, Raphael and others all left their mark of distinction upon the art of St. Peter's, a masterpiece of Christian art and tradition. Similarly, the Mogao caves of Dunhuang are masterpieces of Buddhist art and tradition, equivalent in my opinion to St. Peter's in Rome. Most of Dunhuang's artists were unknown; their paintings and artistry in the caves cover Buddhist art and customs in China from its inception. Most of the artists were monks who lost their eyesight accomplishing their task, due to insufficient lighting within the caves, but they continued to paint. The paintings were completed nearly 2,000 years ago, and are still in amazing condition due to the hot dry desert conditions prevailing within the caves. The caves had been completely unknown in the West until the latter part of the 19th century when they were accidentally rediscovered.

Buddhism is the principal religion of China. The founder of Buddhism lived from 563 to 483 B.C. (80 years). Buddhism is a tradition of thought and practice originating from India over 2,500 years ago. It is a worldwide religion. Buddha (Siddhartha Gautama) was considered one of a series of enlightened beings. The teachings of Buddha may be summarized in "the four noble truths," the last of which affirms the existence of a path leading to the universal experience of suffering. The central tenet of Buddhism is the law of karma, by which good and evil deeds result in an appropriate reward or punishment by a succession of rebirths. Through a proper understanding of this condition and by obedience to the right path, human beings may break the chain of karma. The Buddha's path of deliverance is through mortality (*sila*), meditation and wisdom, as set out in the "eightfold path." The goal is *nirvana*, meaning "the blowing out" of the fires of all desire, total absorption of the self into the infinite. All Buddhas are greatly revered, and a place of special importance is accorded to Gautama. (Cambridge Encyclopedia, Cambridge University Press, 1990)

With its golden sand and blue skies, the Silk Road is an age-old witness to China's contacts with the lands of the Middle East. Along this caravan route, many cultures of Eurasia have met and merged into one another—the cultures of the Chinese, the Indians, the Persians and the Greeks, the last having reached the east with the Macedonian conquests. Mankind's commanding achievements were strewn along this road and one of these, the glory of northwest China, is the art of the Mogao Grottoes at Dunhuang.

The Mogao Grottoes, commonly called the cave temples of the thousand Buddhas, are the largest group of rock cut temples in China. According to the tablet, restoration of the Mogao Grottoes, erected by Li Huairang in 698 A.D., began in 366 A.D., and by the time of the Tang Dynasty there were over a thousand caves and niches. In Mogao today, 492 grottoes are extant, dating from the sixteen states period (309–439 A.D.) . . .With over 45,000 square metres of murals, more than 2,000 statues, and five timber structures belonging to the Tang and Sung periods, this group of grottoes is the world's largest treasure house of ancient Buddhist art. In building these caves, the craftsmen of ancient China had assimilated some of the best features of traditional and foreign art over a thousand years, created the unique art of Dunhuang with its distinctive Chinese characteristics and styles of different periods.

(Extract from *Dunhuang's Mogao Grotto Art*, preface by Chang Shuhong, compiled by the Institute for Cultural Relics, The Art Treasures of Dunhuang, joint publishing company, Hong Kong Lee Publishers Group, Incorporated, New York, 1981)

The murals of Dunhuang may be divided into two categories. One consists of pictures depicting single or multiple sequences from Buddhist scriptures, while the other consists of single pictures of Buddhist deities. The skill with which the murals were painted is truly remarkable and imaginative; they trace the life of Buddha from youth through to adulthood including his many works of kindness and love, depicting the way he interacted with others. The visitor receives a splendid view of life in those days through the colourful painting on the walls, far advance of the times.

The sculptures are remarkable, ranging from tiny altarpieces to huge massive figures, including the sleeping Buddha over 30 feet in length plus a seated Buddha, and a large statue of Kwan Yin, the goddess of love. The imagination used in creating such figures 2,000 years ago illustrates how people in those times were desirous of transmitting their thoughts in a visual manner for future genera-tions to study and comprehend.

Photography is not permitted within the caves, which I personally agree with, since over the passage of time the colours of the wall paintings could be adversely affected by photo flashes. However, I received permission to make a tape recording of the background and history of the caves, provided by the local tourist guide.

The following day we were driven by two small buses and taken back to the railway station at Anxi. We left Dunhuang by bus at 6:30

a.m., a distance of 130 kilometres. It was a rough, rocky road with many potholes and bumps. The road travelled over began from Lhasa, Tibet, and thus was frequented by many large trucks. It was an exceedingly long, arduous and slow journey.

Along the road we passed a large herd of camels, and stopped briefly to photograph them. The sunrise of the desert is exceedingly colourful. However, before arriving at the Anxi railway station, the bus driver, who was serving a double shift that morning, became somewhat weary. He was driving eastwards facing the bright desert morning sun. We noticed his head begin to nod; it worried us for our personal safety on the bus. In view of the problem, we insisted he periodically stop for a brief break, taking time to have a rest and smoke. To begin with, he was somewhat annoyed and denied his weariness—he informed us he had driven the road for many years, and had never yet gone to sleep. Eventually the road improved. Finally we arrived safely at Anxi railway station by 9:30 a.m.. At 10:00 a.m. we boarded the train on its return from Dunhuang to Lanzhou, requiring another 28 hours travel time, a distance of about 1069 kilometres. What a tremendous relief to be back on the train after having experienced the bus trip through the desert earlier in the morning.

My friends and I relaxed on the train. My feet had become sore from walking in sandals with little in the way of arch supports; I developed cracks and sores on the soles of my feet due to the constant dry weather. I caught up on some of my reading, and had a much needed rest while on the train. The twenty members of our tour group visited with each other on the train comparing notes and personal impressions. Our national guide, Ms. Wu, was exceedingly friendly and interested in learning all she could about the countries we originated from, seeking our impressions about life in China. The scenery was the same, desert, desert and still more desert. It was exciting to see vegetation off and on as the train gradually approached the Yellow River, one of China's principle lifelines. Our meals on the train were adequate, but due to the constant heat our appetites were suppressed. The train arrived in Lanzhou the next day 28 hours after departing Anxi. A local China Travel service representative awaited the train's arrival and accompanied us to our hotel to freshen up following the long train journey.

Later the local guide took us to visit the famous Kansu (Gansu) Provincial Museum, located in downtown Lanzhou. We spent time viewing exhibits of early painted pottery from the Yang-Shao culture, dating from around 4000 to 2000 B.C.. We were also shown a most impressive display of miniature bronze chariots with mounted horsemen from Wu-wei, Kansu, from the eastern Han period. In Gansu, over 200 miniature figurines and chariots were unearthed, including the famous bronze statue of a horse sometimes referred to as the bronze flying horse, dating from the 2nd century A.D.

The following day we flew from Lanzhou to Sian (Shanxi province) by a four-propeller plane, requiring a one-hour flight. We lived in the Chang On Hotel, opened the day of our arrival in Sian. Shortly after our arrival in Sian we were taken to the Banpo Museum one of the earliest known agriculture sites near the Yellow River. Banpo is considered by many to be next in importance to the terracotta soldiers. Banpo is situated on the outskirts of the city of Sian.

The oldest Yang-Shao culture appears to have been occupied from 4500 B.C. until 3750 B.C. The ancient Banpo site was discovered in 1953 located on the eastern bank of the Chan River. The Banpo ruins are divided into three areas; a residential area, a pottery-manufacturing area and a cemetery. These areas include remains of 45 houses and other buildings, over 200 storage cellars, six pottery kilns, and 250 graves (including 73 for children). The earlier homes were half-underground, in contrast to later houses which stood on ground level having a wooden framework. Some homes were round, others square, with their doors facing southwards. The main building materials were made of wood for the framework plus mud mixed with straw for the walls. It is reputed as the earliest known agricultural village in China.

The day before our departure from Sian was one of the most meaningful, purposeful and exciting days of our visit to the People's Republic of China. We were driven to the tomb of the Emperor Qin Shihuang and his accompanying army of terracotta soldiers. The history of Sian is inextricably linked to the First Emperor of the united Chinese people. In the third century B.C. China was split into five independent and warring states. In 246 B.C., at the age of 13 Ying Zheng ascended the throne of the state of Chin and assumed the title of Shi Huang or "first emperor." One by one Qin defeated the other states, until the last fell in 222 B.C. The emperor united the country, standardized currency and written script. He also burned books and was a cruel tyrant, secretive and suspicious, during his last days fearing assassination and searching for the elixir of immortality. His tyrannical rule lasted until his death in 210 B.C.

When Qin Shihuang ascended the throne of Qin construction of his final resting place began immediately. Qin Shihuang's tomb is still covered by a huge mound of earth that has not yet been excavated, according to the historical records of Sima Qian, the famous historian of the first century B.C. He related how the tomb contains palaces and pavilions filled with rare gems and other treasures and are equipped with crossbows which automatically shoot all intruders, the ceiling inlaid with pearls to simulate the sun, stars and moon. Gold and silver were cast in the form of geese and ducks were arranged on the floor, precious stones were carved into pines. The walls of the tomb are said to be lined with plates of bronze to keep out underground water. Mercury pumped in to create images of flowing rivers and surging oceans. At the end of the internment rites, the artisans who worked on the inside and the palace maids who had no children were said to have been forced to remain in the underground palace—buried alive so that none of its secrets could be revealed.

In 1974, peasants digging a well about 1500 metres east of the tomb uncovered one of the greatest archeological sites in the world. Excavation of the underground vault of earth and timber revealed thousands of life sized "terracotta warriors" with their horses in battle formation—a whole army would follow its emperor into immortality. In 1976 two other vaults were discovered close to the first one; each of the vaults were refilled with soil after evacuation. The first and largest pit has been covered with a roof to become a huge exhibition hall.

The underground vault measures about 210 metres east to west and about 60 metres north to south. The bottom of the pit varies from five to seven metres below ground level. Walls were built running east to west at intervals of three metres, forming corridors on floors laid with grey brick, are arranged the terracotta figures. Pillars and beams once supported a roof.

The 6,000 terracotta figures of soldiers and horses face eastward in a rectangular battle array. The vanguard appears to be three rows of 210 crossbow and longbow bearers who stand at the east most end of the army. Close behind is the main force of armoured soldiers holding spears, dagger axes and long shaft weapons, accompanied by 35 horse-drawn chariots. Every figure differs in facial features and expressions. The horsemen are seen wearing tight-sleeved outer robes, short coats of chain mail and wind proof caps. The archers have bodies and limbs positioned in strict accordance with an ancient book on the art of war.

Many figures originally held real weapons of the day; over 10,000 pieces have been sorted out to date including bronze swords worn by the figures and other senior officers. Surface treatment made the swords resistant to rust and corrosion so that after being buried for more than 2,000 years they were still sharp. Arrowheads are made of a lethal metal alloy containing a high percentage of lead.

The second vault excavated in 1976 but refilled, contained about 1,000 figures. The third vault contained only 68 soldiers and one war chariot and appeared to be the command post for the soldiers in the other vaults presumably the soldiers represent the army command which was meant to protect the necropolis. These are probably just a beginning, and excavation of the entire complex and the tomb itself could take decades.

No photographs of the terracotta soldiers were permitted, if you take a photo and are discovered then the film will immediately be confiscated. The rule is enforced to prevent any possible damage that may be caused by electronic flashes.

After returning from visiting the terracotta soldiers we stopped for a short time at the Huaqing Pool, situated at the foot of Lishan about 30 kilometres from Sian. Water from the hot springs is funnelled in a multitude of public bathhouses.

On December 12, 1936 Chiang Kai Shek was captured by his own generals in his pyjamas and dressing gown on the snow-covered mountains of Lishan. The site was formerly a villa of the Tang emperors, but now serves as a regular tourist stop, nearby is the location where the Emperor Qin was buried. You can clearly see a huge mound where his grave is located, but still left untouched yet.

Our final visit was to the Shanxi Provincial Museum, located in a former Confucian temple, where we saw many of the forest of stele carvings. The most fascinating for me was a stone tablet commemorating the origin of the Nestorian faith, the first evidence Christianity had entered China during the Tang Dynasty (7th century A.D.). The story of the Nestorian Church was engraved on a stone tablet in 781 A.D. The tablet rests on the back of a large stone turtle written in Chinese characters and Syrian script, the tablet indicates Christian monasteries were built in different areas of China and a Christian literature had also been established. This was the first evidence of Christianity officially having entered China. The emperor T'ai Tsung (the Mongol emperor) said "build a monastery for these men and for twenty-one monks at my expense," he also claimed "and let them preach their way wherever they wish in China." The stele was engraved in 781 A.D. a Christian literature was also developed. (Source: *Forward Through the Ages* by Basil Mathews; Friendship Press, New York, 1951. pp. 64–65)

The next morning (Sunday, August 15,1982) we boarded a China airline jet prop flying from Sian (Shanxi) to Canton in (Guangdong province) southern China. It was another lovely clear morning; fortunately I was assigned to a window seat. Flying time required exactly two hours. I had a splendid view while passing over the broad expansive Yangtsze River in central China. The plane arrived on time at White Cloud Airport by 9:00 a.m.; we were directly escorted to the White Cloud Hotel in Canton.

Upon arrival at the hotel and after having been assigned my room, I requested a staff member call a taxi for me. I was eager to attend church. The taxi drove me to one of the few Protestant churches still open for public worship known as Tung-shan church. Most churches were closed during the disturbing period of the Cultural Revolution (1966–1986).

I arrived at Tung-shan church before 11:00 a.m.; I was informed however that the service wouldn't begin until 12:00 noon, their usual worship time. In view of being one hour early, it gave me an opportunity to visit with the minister Rev. Lee Tak Fai, the elderly minister in charge of the church. Since I am also a minister, I knew he no doubt had many other matters that still needed attending to, so excused myself and sat in the main sanctuary of the church under a large electric fan to cool off. It was an exceedingly hot humid day. Before long a gentleman came and sat next to me a Mr. Yu Shang Ti, he was exceedingly friendly, a member of Tung Shan church. He enquired, "Why do you speak Cantonese?" I informed him I was formerly a Canadian missionary working with the church in Hong Kong, therefore, learned to speak Cantonese to communicate with the people. We had a friendly visit with each other from our first acquaintance.

The service began promptly at 12:00 noon it lasted one hour, having about 1,000 people in attendance, since it was a large church. It was a splendid service, the sacred music made me feel quite at home, the kind of music and service I was used to in both Hong Kong and Canada. We were given a copy of the order of service. A choir of 20 members mostly young people sang beautifully and with such clarity, sincerity and enthusiasm. Rev. Lee Tak Fai's sermon topic was "Exploring Again, Choice, Obedience and Sacrifice;" it was a challenging message. The service lasted for one hour. Following the service Mr. Yu Shang Ti invited me to have lunch with him; we travelled on a local city bus. We ate a delicious lunch of soup noodles. Mr. Yu accompanied me back to my hotel. He wanted his family to meet me; therefore, he invited me to have supper at his home. I happily accepted his kind invitation. About 4:00 p.m. Mr. Yu's son and daughter called around to accompany me to their home. We walked, since their home was near the hotel where I was staying. The Yu family had a basement flat with no windows. It was exceedingly hot inside; however, they had an electric fan to alleviate the situation.

We ate about 6:00 p.m.; Mr. and Mrs. Yu, their son and daughter (in their teens), plus an uncle and myself ate supper together. The Yu family live in a modest dwelling in Canton with no windows, similar to a basement suite, clean and tidy. We sat on stools placed around a circular table. It was a most informal and friendly occasion. Supper consisted of soup, rice, chicken and vegetables. It was most delicious and we had plenty to eat.

During the meal they queried me regarding my life in Hong Kong and Canada. During the course of our conversation I mentioned I formerly taught English at Pui Ying Middle School in Hong Kong. Mr. Yu was most interested, since he had attended Pui Ying Middle School in Canton. He enquired whether I knew an Australian by the name of Rev. Hedley Bunton. I replied, yes, we were good friends in Hong Kong; he had already retired and was living in Australia. Next he asked if I ever knew a Rev. Ching Ming Lee, formerly of Canton. Again I replied, yes, he immigrated to the U.S.A. and is now retired and living in San Francisco. We were both astonished about having mutual friends, who formerly lived in China. I couldn't help but think to myself, this is not just a coincidence, it must be through the guidance of the Holy Spirit enabling us to meet each other!!

Mr. Yu also enquired what I used to work at in Hong Kong during China's Cultural Revolution (1966). I informed him it was not an easy time to live in Hong Kong, since some of the Red Guards spread terrorism and planted bombs, causing fear. I asked him what life was like in Canton. He informed me that he and his family had a difficult time. One day Red Guards entered his home, seized the family Bible, tore it to pieces and burned it in front of them. He asked me if I could possibly send them a Chinese Bible from Hong Kong to China. I promised to do so. A Chinese friend of mine personally delivered the Bible to his home. Following the delivery of the Bible, Mr. Yu wrote a beautiful letter expressing his appreciation and thanks to me for the Bible. It was gratifying to receive his letter.

Before we parted we agreed to correspond with each other; he would write me in Chinese, and I would reply in English. Mr. Yu was formerly a teacher so he could easily read English. We began to correspond with each other.

The following day our tour group left Canton for Hong Kong by train at 8:30 a.m.. We arrived in Hong Kong by noon hour. It was pouring rain at the time of our arrival since a typhoon had just passed through Hong Kong. It was a wonderful feeling to return to Hong Kong again to see my friends.

Before leaving the Orient, I was invited to accompany my former colleagues from the Church of Christ in China, Hong Kong Council to the Portuguese colony of Macau (a Portuguese colony since 1557). The occasion was to celebrate the 175th anniversary of Dr. Robert Morrison's 1807 arrival as a missionary in China. Dr. Morrison was the first Protestant missionary to China. He lived in Macau many years. Macau was where he translated the Bible into the Chinese language and compiled the first Chinese-English dictionary. The Church of Christ in China Hong Kong Council held a formal

Thanksgiving service in Chi-to church in Macau. Rev. Ching Ming Lee preached a splendid sermon tracing the courage of Dr. Robert Morrison during his pioneering days. The church was filled to capacity. Following the service we visited the old Protestant cemetery in Macau where Rev. Morrison, his wife Mary and an infant son were all buried. It was an inspiring occasion for all. Later the same day we returned by a chartered vessel to Hong Kong, concluding my second visit to China, Hong Kong and Macau, then back again to Canada.

PART III

A journey with a difference, this time I led a tour to China. The journey began from Vancouver International Airport, a direct flight crossing the Pacific to Shanghai, China, arriving June 25, 1987. It required nearly eleven hours flying time. We required about one hour for clearing all immigration and custom procedures. There was a regrettable incident I have not forgotten; most members of our tour were overseas Chinese travelling on Canadian passports. One member had the exit permit from China removed from her passport. Naturally she was upset and disturbed. Since I was the group leader I became involved; I informed Mr. Wu Wen Jen, the national guide but he replied, it's your problem not mine, so I approached the immigration official at the Shanghai airport concerning the problem. He declared his innocence by using his hands in sign language. However, since one group member informed me an immigration official had removed the exit permit from her passport, then placed the permit in his pocket, I requested he remove the paper from his pocket which he did. He smoothed and straightened out the permit and returned it to her passport. His face turned red with embarrassment. I thanked him, then we continued on our way, no further questions being asked.

We were bussed from the airport to downtown Shanghai, a 45 minute drive to the Mansion Hotel, an older style hotel, however, it was quite adequate and comfortable, overlooking the Huangpu River.

Our first day in Shanghai, we were driven along the *bund* (an Anglo-Indian word for embankment). Shanghai has a population of approximately 12 million plus people, the largest city in China.

Politically, Shanghai is one of the most important cities of China, located on the Huangpu River. The city has had a chequered past. We saw many foreign ships from various countries anchored along the 37-mile-long waterfront.

Early in the morning, as I peered out of my bedroom window overlooking the Huangpu river, there was a tremendous hustle and bustle, including a variety of shaped vessels and barges plying the busy river—most picturesque and exciting. All of the tour members were filled with a genuine feeling of anticipation and excitement, including myself. The traffic was rapidly hurrying here and there by all manner and description of vehicles; especially evident were bicycles. We visited the famous Garden of Happiness (Yue Wo Yuen), a lovely garden built in 1577 A.D. by a city official who wanted to create an idyllic spot for his parents' old age. It was a marvellously constructed garden, hidden by high walls with dragons and other motifs upon it. The garden consisted of a zigzag style bridge, surrounded by pavilions and pools well stocked with carp. After lunch at the Park Hotel we visited a commune, in the form of a housing project; how typical it is questionable (!). Adjacent to the housing project was a training centre, plus an arts and craft shop. We also visited a kindergarten, and a medical clinic where they demonstrated acupuncture. Our final stop of the day was the Shanghai Museum, which contains a splendid set of graduated bells (arranged according to size), ornaments, ceramics, including terracotta figures from Sian. We returned to the Mansion Hotel, going to the 18th floor to obtain a splendid view of the Huangpu River, including the bustling city of Shanghai.

The next day our tour took us to the Jade Buddha Temple, a large and extremely active temple, built between 1911 and 1918. The temple had about 70 active priests. It houses a 1.9 metre (6.23 feet) seated white Buddha, the material having originated from Burma. The Buddha is heavily encrusted with jewels. There was also a smaller reclining Buddha in the temple. In an adjacent room were three gold-plated Buddhas. The fragrance of incense was strong and pungent throughout the temple. From the temple we were driven to the railway station to journey from Shanghai to Suzhou requiring only forty minutes.

Suzhou's (Jiangsu province) history dates back around 2,500

years. Suzhou is strategically situated on a major trading route. Suzhou formerly flourished as a major shipping and grain storage centre. It's also especially noted throughout China for its beautiful women. Marco Polo visited there in 1276 A.D. praising Suzhou's fame and beauty. Suzhou is known for its rockery and gardens that are indeed awe-inspiring. We had the privilege of visiting the Lingering Garden, covering many acres.

Silk is one of Suzhou's major claims to fame. We were guided through a large silk factory, observing how silk is produced from the cocoon to its major product on the market. We visited an embroidery research institute, where they produce double-sided woven pictures of cats, dogs, goldfish etc. The employees are exceedingly skillful with their hands; however, it places a heavy strain upon their eyes. The final products are magnificent.

The next important juncture of the tour was Nanjing, a four-hour train journey from Suzhou. It was picturesque travelling by train; we could see rice fields everywhere. Gradually the land began to roll and eventually became quite hilly. It was interesting to see the way the farms are tilled with water buffalo working in the fields, similar to those of Kwangtung province in southern China.

The first thing we saw upon arriving at Nanking was the famous Yangtsze River Bridge, most impressive, since the bridge spans the wide and mighty Yangtsze River. It is one of the early outstanding achievements by the Chinese communists. The bridge was officially opened on December 23, 1968. It's a two-decker bridge with a 4500-metre roadway on the upper level, plus a 6700-metre-long railway below, making it one of the longest bridges in China.

From the Yangtsze River Bridge we were driven to Xuan Wu Lake, escorted around a portion of the lake, then returned to the entrance of the park to visit the pandas. We were also driven to an interesting exhibition of bonsai plants, an ancient art originating in China. The trees are dwarfed by cutting back the roots of the young plants at a very tender age.

Sunday morning we drove through the city of Nanjing with its magnificent tree-lined streets providing shade and shelter, then walked up to Dr. Sun Yat Sen's mausoleum located upon the Ziji (purple) mountains, an eastern suburb of Nanjing. There are 392 granite steps leading up to the mausoleum. The memorial hall is most interesting and attractive with its white walls and dark cobalt blue tiled roof. Within the mausoleum is a statue of Dr. Sun Yat Sen seated under a domed structure. Dr. Sun Yat Sen established the Republic of China on October 10, 1911 by deposing the Ching, the last Dynasty of China. The mausoleum commands an outstanding view of the surrounding countryside. A constant stream of visitors (local and foreign) goes to the site to visit the mausoleum. Inscribed upon the walls are the three principles for leading the people into a new age as prepared by Dr. Sun Yat Sen: "nationalism, democracy and livelihood."

Next we were escorted to the Ming Dynasty drum tower in Nanjing where we received a splendid view of the city. We were driven around to an ancient Confucian temple built in the traditional Chinese style of architecture with artistically shaped rooves, stopped at the Zhonghua Gate, which has four story gates, observed a former Ming Dynasty garrison adequate for accommodating some 3,000 soldiers. Besides stopping at the Nanjing Theological Seminary, the principle training centre for the Protestant churches in the People's Republic of China, the Rev. Chen Zemin, the vice-principal, spoke to us about the work of the seminary and its theological training. He showed us around their buildings.

Upon leaving Nanjing we flew to Hangzhou (Zhejiang province), requiring 45 minutes flying time, aboard an older style two-engine Russian-built jet airliner (pot-bellied style), which accommodated only thirty-six passengers. While we were walking from the plane to the airline terminal, an interesting and unexpected piece of music was played over the loudspeaker system, "God be with you until we meet again." Before landing we obtained an excellent view of the world famous grand canal of China as the plane approached Hangzhou Airport. We were met by a China Travel Service agent.

The following morning we walked from the Wang Hu Hotel to commence travelling on a private sightseeing launch around the lake, which is legendary. First we were driven to the second longest island, known as Three Pools Mirroring the Moon, taking many photographs of the famous and scenic area containing numerous beautiful and artistic pavilions. The well-known poet So Tung Po was inspired by the lake's famed beauty to write many of his poems.

Hangzhou is bounded to the south by the Qiantang River and to the west by hills. Between the hills and the urban area is the large and famous West Lake. North of the city and south of the river are the exceedingly fertile planes of Jiangnan. We also visited the famous Six Harmonies Pagoda perched high upon the top of Yuelu Hill. The pagoda was built in 970 A.D., and named after the six codes of Buddhism. The pagoda was originally built to serve as a lighthouse, it's believed to possess certain magical powers, plus being able to halt the tidal bore, that thunders up the Qiantang River during the middle of September each year.

The noted Italian merchant Marco Polo, explorer of the 13th century, described Hangzhou as one of the finest and most splendid cities in the world. Hangzhou actually sprung into prominence during the Song (Sung) Dynasty.

One of the most famous of Hangzhou's industries is the silk industry; therefore, we visited a famous silk and silk printing complex. It's a real education to observe how the silk worms are raised to maturity by letting the young worms gorge themselves upon mulberry leaves. When the larva reach maturity they weave themselves a cocoon, the cocoons are soaked in hot water to kill the living larva. The silk is extracted by unwinding the silk from the cocoons then processing the silk. The raw silk is dyed the required colour and woven into large bolts of material, being sold commercially upon the open market.

The final point of interest before leaving Hangzhou was a visit to Lingyin Pagoda (Soul's Retreat), they have a 33.6 metre tall temple building with a 19.6 metre tall Buddha in the temple. We likewise visited and photographed some of the ancient stone carvings located on the slopes of the hills, drove to a large bonsai garden where many dwarfed and minature plants may be found. We visited the botantical garden especially to see a beautiful bamboo grove with many different varieties and types of bamboo.

The remaining point of direct interest was an informal visit to a large Protestant church in Hangzhou. One of the ministers of the church, being a former graduate from Princeton University in the U.S.A. in 1947, the minister spoke flawless English, both ministers Rev. Cai and Rev. Wong knew Dr. Peter Wong and Dr. Andy Roy, mutual friends of mine from Hong Kong.

We were driven to the Hangzhou airport where we flew from

Hangzhou (Zhejiang province) to Xian (Sian), located in Shanxi province, by a Russian Aleutian airliner, requiring an hour and forty five minutes flying time before arriving at our destination Xian (Sian).

Following our arrival in Xian we visited the Shaansi Provincial Museum within an ancient Confucian temple; they have an amazing and astonishing collection of stone steles ranging all the way from the Han to the Ching Dynasties, including the world renowned Nestorian Tablet resting on the back of a large stone turtle dating from the 7th century A.D. It's a rare piece of early Christian history marking the first attempt to spread Christianity in China, besides other steles recording early Chinese literature from the Han to the Ching Dynasties.

The same day we drove outside of Xian (Sian) city to the Huaqing Hotspring, the site where the Xian (Sian) incident occurred, when Chiang Kai Shek was captured (December 12, 1936) trying to escape in his pyjamas and dressing gown on the slopes of a snow-covered mountain. It's a beautiful location with willows and a variety of shrubs and flowering plants surrounding it. Our next destination was the site of the terracotta soldiers, the Qin army vault museum where over 6,000 buried terracotta soldiers (in 1974) were discovered guarding the grave of the Chin Dynasty emperor (described in some detail in part II of this chapter).

A portion of the journey took us from Hangzhou (Zhejiang province) to Beijing (Peking) the capital of the People's Republic of China, requiring only one hour and twenty minutes flying time from Hangzhou. We resided at the Wah-Dou hotel. The tour drove us to see the ancient astronomical observatory, once mounted upon the battlements of a watchtower, formerly part of the old city walls of Beijing. The observatory dates to the period of Kublai Khan. The great Khan and the later Ming and Ching emperors relied heavily upon astrologers before making vital decisions. The observatory was built from 1437 to 1446 A.D., on the roof are located astronomical instruments designed by the Jesuits. The Jesuits (early Roman Catholic priests) who made their way to China in 1601 when Matteo Ricci along with his colleagues were permitted to cooperate work with Chinese scientists.

From the observatory we were driven to the Temple of Heaven. It was a beautiful hot sunny day for commencing our journey to

Beijing; the sun shone and brilliantly reflected the dark rich cobalt blue coloured tiles on the roof (already described in Parts I and II of this chapter).

The next day we were driven by bus to the Great Wall of China, about 75 kilometres (46.5 miles) from Beijing, however, on the way were included a few points concerning farming in China. It required nearly two hours before reaching our destination the Great Wall of China. Weather wise it was a perfect day for such a journey, climbing the Great Wall was somewhat strenuous, nevertheless, the view from the top of the wall is spectacular and rewarding as you see the winding, twisting wall snaking its way endlessly over the rugged mountains (additional details found in part I and II of this chapter). Later in the day we left the Great Wall for the Ming tombs and visited a new international golf club centre recently opened. During the visit to the Ming tombs we descended into the spacious burial chambers to see some of the many burial objects. Unfortunately a few group members experienced claustrophobia so we had to leave the tombs.

The following day was spent in Beijing, travelling on the circle route of the subway. The subway is clean and efficient, built in recent years. Most of the day was used exploring the fascinating and historic sights of the Forbidden City; erected during the Ming era in 1604 A.D. the palace has 999 rooms within it. (See parts I and II of this chapter for further details.) The palace is divided into two parts. The outer palace for business, while the inner portion included palace residential courts etc. The Hall of Supreme Harmony is one of the most stately buildings within the complex. The Hall Of Complete Harmony was used by the emperor to receive his ministers. The antique furniture within the palace is something to admire and remember, especially the numerous clocks like the huge water clock; plus many smaller clocks were donated by world leaders like Queen Victoria and Emperor Napoleon Bonaparte. From there we were taken to the Summer Palace where many imperial banquets were served. We also had a boat ride; strolled along the picturesque hallway that has some 5,000 beautifully painted scenes.

The final portion of the journey in China was flying from Beijing to Chongqing (Chungking), Sichuan (Szechuan) province in Western China, bordering Tibet. The flight required two hours and twenty minutes flying time before arriving at our destination

Chongqing (Chungking). The plane passed over many rugged mountain ranges and rivers on its way. It was especially interesting and exciting for me, since I recall the way many former missionary friends in China referred to Sichuan province in glowing terms.

Chongqing (Chungking) is vastly different from other cities we visited in China. Chongqing is built on the side of hills; the roads are narrow with many trucks, buses and other vehicles, very few bicycles could be seen, but numerous motorbikes due to the mountainous terrain. We also visited the zoo to see the pandas, golden monkeys and Chinese tigers. We visited an institute that specialized in producing wooden carvings, besides meeting many outstanding artists. During the tour of the city, we crossed a bridge in Chongqing spaning the mighty Yangtsze River. Since our group included some Canadian farmers, therefore, the tour concentrated on farming in west China. We visited a dairy farm (many of the cattle black and white originated from Canada). We observed farmers making cement encasements by using moulds. One of the farmers guided us around his farm and escorted us through his house. We saw how they produced bricks including placing the bricks in kilns. The farmers mixed their cement by the help of their water buffaloes. Our final visit for the day was the Sichuan Institute of Fine Arts, a famous institute in the province, they produced sculptures, paintings, decorated porcelain and lacquer ware. The tour provided a splendid opportunity for observing the way life is lived in Western China.

The following morning we were driven from the Chungking Hotel where we resided to the pier where we boarded the M.V. Xiling (Siling) commencing the journey down the Yangtsze River (Changjiang). We made our individual farewells to Chungking. The M.V. Xiling (Siling) was clean and comfortable. By 9:40 a.m., all passengers (132) were requested to gather in the dining room of the ship for a brief period of orientation. They provided an outline of the journey travelling down the Yangtsze River (Changjiang) including relevant facts and figures about M.V. Xiling (Siling). The water of the Yangtsze River (Changjiang) is a dark yellowish brown colour. A short movie provided a historic background of the Yangtsze River, including the three gorges and other noted places of interest. The Yangtsze River (Changjiang) is 6,380 km long the equivalent of 3,964.5 miles in length. From the river may be seen range upon range of green verdant mountains, beside grotesque peaks and beautiful landscape. Within the gorges are a multitude of shoals and rapids, gorges within gorges. The beautiful scenery along the route has been the topic of praise by scholars and writers throughout the ages; its scenery is unique both at home and abroad.

The Xiling Gorge streches from Nanjin-Guan in Yichang, Hubei in the east to the Guandu ferry, eastern Sichuan, a total length of 120 kilometres (74.56 miles) the longest of the three gorges, it is known for its shoals and rapids making navigation extremely hazardous. We passed by Shibao where we had tea and taken ashore to board a bus going to a silk weaving factory. We returned to our ship one hour later. The ship was anchored for the night in the middle of the harbour of the Yangtsze River. The ship departed Wanxian at 7:30 a.m. It passed the temple of Cheung-Fei on the right side of the Yangtsze River. The scenery was breathtaking. It entered the first gorge known as the Qutang Gorge, passed the Emperor's Temple and Bellows Gorge on the way downstream. Stopped at Wushan by 11:00 a.m., then transferred to several smaller motor boats known as "willow leaf boats" going up the Daling River to see the three smaller gorges. It was a tremendous thrill travelling up the river to the three smaller gorges; often you could nearly touch the sides of the riverbank since it was so narrow. Lunch at Shuanglong, and then we climbed along a narrow stairway to the restaurant where we had delicious fresh seafood for lunch.

Following lunch boarded the "willow boats" again and travelled further upstream to the Sky Kissing Precipice; from there the boats turned around and began returning to the M.V. Xiling. It was a marvellous experience taking in so much during such a short period of time.

Along the cliffs of the north of Xiling Gorge is an overhanging narrow mountainous passage ingeniously built as if by celestial immortals, known as Xianren Qiao (Bridge of Immortals).

The precipitous cliff towers a height of over a 100 feet similar to an eagle standing on the bank of the river, known as Eagle Beak Cliff.

It has been claimed that during the Tang Dynasty (618–907 A.D.) the famous scholar Bai Juyi together with his brother Bai Xingjian and their good friend Yuan Zhen visited the cave, hence the name. Many poems and calligraphic masterpieces have been left there by admiring scholars of various Dynasties. (*The Wonderful Charms Of*

The Yangtsze Gorges, an introduction to slides produced by Beijing.)

I arose early the following morning, when our ship entered the second gorge, Wu Gorge, 44 km long (27.34 miles). We saw the Goddess Peak and the Kong Ming Tablet carved upon the wall of the mountain adjacent to the Yangtsze River. We passed the town of Beishi on the border separating Sichuan from Hubei, through the Guandukou Pass, marking the end of the second gorge. We passed Padong the most westerly county of Hubei, and also passed Zigiu County the home of Quan Yuan, famous poet of ancient China.

We entered the Xiling Gorge passed "the stone sword" through the Yi-chang ship lock on the Yangtsze River. Docked at Yichang, transferred to a bus to visit a workers' kindergarten, also went through the power station of Ji-Chong. They provided us with an impression of the proposed new dam now under construction; it will dramatically raise and alter considerably the water of the Yangtsze river.

Following a good night's rest we arrived at a place known as Cheng-Ling-Yi where we boarded a local bus along a rather dusty road to see the Yue-Yang Tower built in 716 A.D. during the Tang Dynasty. The tower is 15 metres high (49 feet), rebuilt in 1867 during the Ching Dynasty; it's extremely colourful and picturesque. We were shown through a factory where they make and decorate hand-made fans. The next point of interest was a fish farm, then returned to the ship, spent the evening aboard the ship. By 10:00 a.m. arrived in Wuhan (Hankow) ending the thrilling and adventurous and exciting journey down the Yangtsze River from Chungking.

The first thing in the morning we commenced a tour of the Hubei Provincial Museum where they have displayed a complete set of court musical instruments including bronze bells. They played a recording of the music so we could have some impression of how the bells once sounded. From the museum we were driven to East Lake, walked through the park, visited a free market, which was extremely crowded. After lunch we went on a tour of a large carpet factory. Visited a shop where one of their artists provided a live demonstration of his painting. The final stop was at the ancient Lute Temple, then from the temple we were driven to the train station by 5:00 p.m.. We boarded a train for Guilin (Guangxi Province). The train was rather hot but otherwise comfortable. The train travelled during the night from Wuhan (Hankow) to Guilin arriving the next morning by 9:30 a.m.. Were driven to the hotel where we were assigned. In the morning we were taken to Fubo Hill climbed up 370 steps to receive a spectacular and panoramic view of the city of Guilin (Guangxi Province), the Li River etc. During the afternoon we were taken to the famous Reed Flute Cave, walked through the caves to see a colourful natural rock formations within the cave, hidden deep in Guangming Mountain. The horseshoe-shaped cave is 240 metres deep. We saw stalactite icicle-like deposits of calcium carbonate, hanging down from the roof of the caves beside stalagmite cone-shaped deposits of calcium carbonate rising from the floor of the caves. They are exceedingly beautiful formations similar to a floral display.

The greatest thrill of visiting Guilin was taking a one-day boat tour travelling up the Lijiang River (Li River) 83 kilometres in length (51.57 miles). It was a marvellous experience with picturesque and beautiful scenery. Personally I always appreciated Chinese paintings, however, considered the mountains painted by artists were mostly a figment of their imagination. I now realize it was not imagination but a natural formation of mountains in that region of the country.

Along the banks of the Li River, you could see many fishermen standing on the banks using their large nets. Some used cormorants for catching fish by placing a line around their neck to prevent them swallowing the fish. You could also see water buffaloes peacefully cooling off and lazily swimming in the river with their bodies immersed in water with only their heads, nose and large horns peering out from the Lijiang (Li) river.

The mountains are similar to classical paintings from bygone days with rounded peaks in a sugar-loaf formation a truly beautiful sight to see, they appear so beautiful peaceful, quiet and calm.

It was an ideal place to escape from the hustle and bustle of Kweilin stopping at Yangshuo, situated 80 miles up the Li river from Kweilin city, a comparatively small country set amidst pinnacles of limestone. The surrounding mountain peaks of the country are rugged, steep and delicate, all reflected in the nearby water.

We left our boat at Yangshuo, to board a bus to return to Kweilin (80 miles) crossing a twisting, winding uneven road. The farmers could be seen busily engaged in their harvest; some farmers were beating the rice stalks into a container. They spread the rice to dry along the roadside in the warmth of the sun, while the traffic ran over the grain as it passed.

The enchanting Yangshuo countryside has so many places of interest such as Green Lotus Peak, Shutong Hill, Grand Banyon Tree, and Moon Hill. The bus ride to Kweilin requires nearly one hour and forty minutes.

We flew from Kweilin to Guangzhou (Canton, Kwangtung Province) requiring only 40 minutes. The bus required 45 minutes to drive into Canton city. We dwelt in a hotel known as The White Swan, then after lunch visited a jade factory, now days they use machines rather than carve the jade by hand. The factory had some 500 employees working for them. I purchased a jade carving of a key symbolizing the key to the city of Canton, in former days it was known as the City of Rams.

From there we visited the Temple of Six Banyan Trees, built some 1400 years ago. I eagerly climbed to the top of the pagoda obtaining a bird's-eye view of Canton. The final point of interest visited was the elaborate Chen Clan Association Hall, one of the largest clans in southern China.

Our tour group had visited China for just a little over three weeks. Finally we departed Canton by train for Hong Kong, after experiencing a most satisfying and inspiring tour of China. Time passed rapidly, we all left with mixed feelings, but had many pleasant memories. We had exceedingly fond memories of the various people we met, especially the guides throughout China, their many kindnesses to us following all of the varied experiences we had in the People's Republic of China. The last leg of our journey was a three-hour relaxing non-stop train ride from Canton to Hong Kong.

Naturally I felt exceedingly at home in Hong Kong, since I had lived there for 18 years. I wanted our group members to see something of Hong Kong's natural beauty, have a good experience and impression of the city and its people, which I had come to love and appreciate.

A representative of the Hong Kong Gray Line Tours arranged to take us on a bus tour around Hong Kong Island. Nevin Lim was our capable guide; we were driven to the Tiger Balm Garden near Causeway Bay to see the sights, and driven up to "The Peak" on

Hong Kong Island to obtain a splendid panoramic view of Hong Kong Island, Kowloon and the surrounding islands. Fortunately it was a beautiful clear day so we could clearly see the sights. We were taken to Deep Water Bay and Repulse Bay, famous swimming areas on to Aberdeen. Unfortunately our guide Nevin was not feeling well so he left the tour. He requested me to take his place and serve as the local Hong Kong tour guide, which I did. During the afternoon, I also guided some of our members back to Hong Kong Island to explore the various shopping areas and other places of general interest.

We spent approximately six days in Hong Kong sightseeing and shopping. I also met many of my former friends from the church, visited the Morrison Memorial Centre where my office used to be located. Later we checked into the Canadian Airline office for returning home to Vancouver on July 24, 1987, following a 11 hour flight, weary but content and satisfied with our tour of China and Hong Kong. It was then "home sweet home."

CHAPTER 10

Adventures in Southeast Asia

SOUTHEAST ASIA is a large exciting area to come to know. In the fall of 1955 I was appointed a missionary of the United Church of Canada to Hong Kong. Upon my arrival in Hong Kong my first duty and responsibility was to study Cantonese, the major Chinese dialect spoken in Hong Kong (studied for two years) at the Institute of Oriental Studies of the University of Hong Kong. The students were divided into two sections studying either Cantonese or Mandarin. I selected Cantonese since it was the principle dialect spoken in Hong Kong and Kwangtung province (Guangdong) of China. Mandarin is China's national language, however, at the time Mandarin was seldom used in Hong Kong whereas Cantonese plus the Fujian, Shanghai and other dialects were spoken to a lesser extent.

Chairman Mao Tse Tung was at the helm of leadership for the People's Republic of China from October 1, 1949. I was unable to obtain permission to visit China from the beginning, since I was a Canadian missionary living in Hong Kong; it happened China's travel restrictions prevented me from visiting China. In view of the situation whenever I felt the need for a change I visited Macau, Taiwan, Japan, Korea, Singapore, Malaysia and Thailand, which I will describe.

(1) JAPAN

Since I had arrived in Hong Kong only two years previous, my first journey outside of Hong Kong to Southeast Asia was to participate in a conference held in Japan in 1958. I attended the Fourteenth

World Convention on Christian Education from August 6–13, 1958, held at Seiwa College for Christian Workers, part of Aoyama Gakuin University in Tokyo. It was a splendid opportunity to see some of Japan.

One afternoon a large rally was held in Tokyo's sports arena. The theme of the conference was "Christ is the Way, the Truth and the Life." Delegates gathered from many nations around the world to attend the conference in Tokyo. The delegates also travelled to Kobe, Japan for a portion of the conference.

One Saturday, a children's rally was held at the Fourteenth World Convention in Tokyo's sports arena, August 9, 1958 at 3:00 p.m. At the convention we were introduced to a most meaningful and beautiful song prepared especially for the occasion entitled "We've a story to tell to the nations."

1. We've a story to tell to the nations
    That shall turn their hearts to the right,
    A story of truth and mercy,
    A story of peace and light,
    A story of peace and light.
Refrain:
    For the darkness shall turn to dawning,
    And the dawning to noon-day bright, and
    Christ's great kingdom come on earth,
    The kingdom of light and love.
2. We've a song to be sung to the nations,
    That shall lift their hearts to the lord;
    A song that shall conquer evil,
    And shatter the spear and sword,
    And shatter the spear and sword. (Refrain)
3. We've a message to give to the nations
    That the lord who reigneth above,
    Hath sent his son to save us, and
    And show us that God is Love,
    And show us that God is Love. (Refrain)

Special messages were presented at the rally by some of the following delegates:

William Haddad, Lebanon
Rev. John Havea, Tonga
Rev. Canon T.O. Olufosoye, Nigeria
Negro spirituals were presented by Mrs. Rosa Page Welch. While attending the convention, I made many new friends.

(2) THE REPUBLIC OF CHINA (TAIWAN)

In July 1962 I flew from Hong Kong to Taiwan on a one-hour flight. Taiwan is an island nation located off the south east coast of China. The Tropic of Cancer also runs directly through the centre of Taiwan. Taiwan frequently experiences earthquakes and typhoons; the weather is subtropical, hot with high humidity. In Canadian terms Taiwan could be compared to the size of Vancouver Island, only a little wider. (Length 395 km (245 miles), width 144 km (89.5 miles).) Taiwan is officially known as the Republic of China, from October 1949. It is a separate entity from the People's Republic of China. When I visited Taiwan in 1962 it was under the leadership of president Chiang Kai Shek (October 1949 until 1976, his death). Chairman Mao Tse Tung (Mao Zedong) officially declared the mainland of China as the People's Republic of China from October 1, 1949.

A brief historical note: in 1517 the first Europeans to land on Taiwan's shores were Portuguese sailors, who were exceedingly impressed by Taiwan's beauty. They referred to it as Isla Formosa, a Portuguese term meaning "beautiful island." It was called Formosa until the end of the war in the Pacific in 1945. Now it is referred to as Taiwan, a Chinese name which means "terraced bay."

The Dutch arrived in Taiwan in the year 1624. Attempting to colonize it, they established a capital in the southwestern portion of the island at Tainan. Two years later the Spanish took control of northern Taiwan, but were expelled by the Dutch in 1641. The Dutch were expelled from Taiwan by Cheng Chengkung, known in the west as Koxinga, a Ming Dynasty loyalist general forced to leave Taiwan when the victorious Ching (Manchu) armies arrived from China.

It is my personal opinion that Taiwan is one of the most beautiful and productive islands within the Pacific. In 1995 the population was 20,727,000, a densely populated island. Taiwan consists of many high mountains running down the central core of the island much like a spine; mountains cover at least two thirds of the island. Some mountains exceed 10,000 feet in height. Abundant and fertile terraced rice paddies may be seen running along the sides of the intricately terraced mountains making it a picturesque and exceedingly beautiful sight to behold. In recent years Taiwan has been completely transformed from being primarily and predominantly an agricultural nation to an industrial land during the 1950s. The major industries of Taiwan are high technology, computers, footwear, cement, electronics, plastics, furniture, consumer goods, iron and steel, petrochemicals, machinery, plywood, sugar, bananas, citrus fruits, tea, vegetables, fish etc.

On July 9, 1962 I flew from Hong Kong to Taipei, the capital of Taiwan, where some friends met me. I stayed at the Y.M.C.A. in Taipei. At the time most of my transportation within Taipei City was a pedicab (a three-wheeled bicycle) I visited the Grand Hotel, which has traditional Chinese architecture and visited the Confucian temple. Built in the traditional Chinese style of architecture, it has a colourful and decoratively curved roof. The temple also has endless Chinese ancestral tablets evidence of ancestral worship.

The temperature was exceedingly hot and humid (90 degrees Fahrenheit). I strolled around the Oriental style garden at the rear of the Palace Museum. At the Taipei railway station I was met by Greta Gauld, a United Church medical missionary (nurse) serving in Taiwan. We travelled by train to Tai Chung located near the centre of Taiwan. When I looked out of the rapidly moving train I observed the farmers diligently harvesting their rice crops by hand, the method used by farmers in China for centuries. The scenery was exceedingly beautiful, interesting and picturesque. Upon arriving in Tai Chung we hired a pedicab to go to the Red Cross Centre where Greta worked, her friend Dr. Si escorted us through the Tai Chung General Hospital where she was employed, a modern up to date hospital. A short while later Rev. Wu escorted us on a visit to Tung-hai University (Eastern Sea University) to see the beautiful campus with an ultramodern and attractive chapel. Tung-hai is a Christian university, related to Chung Chi College in Hong Kong where I was assisting; Tung-hai University is an integral part of the thirteen united Christian colleges established in Southeast Asia after 1949.

Rev. Wu also made arrangements for a visit to the National Palace Museum (established in 1957) in Pei-kou, a suburb of Tai Chung a short distance from Tai Chung City. It had a precious and invaluable collection of Chinese antique treasures on display within the museum, such as antique bronzes from the Shang Dynasty (1766-1122 B.C.), and the Chou Dynasties; jade items ranging from the Chou and Han Dynasties, Ming and Ching porcelains, silk tapestries plus embroidery work, beautifully hand painted scrolls, skillfully carved ivory balls etc. All of the antiques originally were an integral part of the National Palace Museum in Beijing, China. The antiques originated from Mainland China and were transported to Taiwan just before the political takeover by the People's Republic of China on October 1, 1949.

(Note: A few years later the Palace Museum collection was relocated in a newer and more elaborate museum situated in Taipei, the capital of Taiwan.)

While touring Taiwan we visited the Tai Chung provincial parliament buildings, attractive modern buildings. The final point of interest for the day was the Chung Hua Pa Kua Shan Buddha, 72 feet tall.

The next day we boarded an express bus travelling to Sun Moon Lake where a modern teachers' hostel had been erected. The buildings are exceedingly lovely structures. Since it was a clear day, we could see endless rice paddies in the process of being planted by hand. I was informed Taiwan harvests three crops of rice annually due to their mild favourable climate. The scenery was a fresh lush green colour. We crossed to the other side of Sun Moon Lake to visit a Taiwanese aboriginal village, a most fascinating and interesting educational experience. The aboriginal people are believed to have originated somewhere from the South Pacific.

I returned to Taipei, reporting to the Chinese foreign office applying for an extension my visitor's visa for a longer period in Taiwan. At that time, all visitors were required to receive permission to travel from one part of Taiwan to the next for internal security reasons. I registered with the local police detachment, so they would know where I was living.

The following day I boarded a train for Keelung the northern sea port in Taiwan to meet the ship, the *Szechuan*, arriving from Hong Kong. The ship carried 100 refugees migrating to Taiwan from the People's Republic of China. They received an enthusiastic and warm welcome of endless numbers of firecrackers. The ship also carried eighteen university students from Chung Chi College, from the Chinese University of Hong Kong, where I was a substitute teacher in social work for two years. The students arrived in Taiwan upon the invitation of the Education Department of the Taiwan government. Originally the students were to be escorted by a Chinese professor from Chung Chi college, unfortunately he suddenly became ill so unable to accompany the students. In view of the problem, Chung Chi College requested I replace him by accompanying them on their educational tour of Taiwan. I happily accepted their invitation to escort the students on their journey around Taiwan, serving as their chaperone. Representatives from the Overseas Chinese Student Association in Taiwan met the ship along with a large enough bus to accommodate the students and their luggage. After landing at Keelung they drove us to the Overseas Chinese Hostel in Taipei, providing accomodation and itinerary for the visit. The predominant languages used during the tour were Mandarin and Cantonese along with a smattering of English.

We settled down in the hostel for the first evening before officially commencing the tour. The next morning we made a visit to the Overseas Student Office in Taipei where we paid our respect. We drove to the Education Department where the officials informed us concerning their plan for our Taiwan visit. They drove us to a Taiwan brewery escorting us through the plant, explained the various steps required for bottling the spirits. We visited an art gallery plus the National Taiwan Science Museum and Planetarium, including a fine display of the various Chinese Dynasties from the earlest period to the year 1910.

We were escorted through the National Medical College which included showing us preserved human bodies for medical research. It was an impressive exhibit providing us with a brief insight into the medical research (Western and traditional) under way. Following lunch we were escorted to the Taipei Provincial Orphanage for Children. The director explained the working of the orphanage. We were taken by train to visit a Taiwan military hospital. Mr. Wu, the local guide, lead us to a few additional points of interest.

The following day we visited the campus of the Taiwan National University where they had 8,200 students. We had an interview with a professor in biology, who presented a slide show concerning the university, explaining special features including a display of ornamental shrubs. We visited the Taiwan Normal School University, where educational workers were trained, including many from Hong Kong. At the time they had 3,700 students. The university library is most modern and up to date in all aspects.

Our tour group was escorted to Yeung Ming Shan, which has a well-groomed park. We visited some of the expansive new buildings erected recently. The Yeung Ming Shan area is where more affluent residents prefer to live. We received a magnificent view of the terraced rice fields and surrounding scenery near Yeung Ming Shan; it has many thermal hot springs centred around Peitou. Returned to Taipei where the parents of one of the students invited all to the Canton Restaurant for a delicious and tasty Cantonese supper.

The following day we were informed Typhoon Kate was heading towards Taiwan, temporarily restricting some of our activities, therefore, we drove to the nearby Taipei Relief Centre in a rural setting. They showed us around a home for mentally disturbed patients, plus a home for wounded and retired veterans. They escorted us through a Taiwan fertilizer company, and visited a reformatory for "wayward boys," observed an exhibit for land reform in Taiwan. We were taken to the site of a new water resevoir project currently under construction. Near the roadside were many watermelons stacked up for sale, nearly four feet high. We purchased some watermelons to take along with us. The bus continued on its route stopping for a visit to Sun Moon Lake where we spent the night. We lived in the teachers' hostel, an attractive and comfortable place; it has a very modern form of architecture.

The next morning we planned to visit the well-known and famous mountain known as Alishan, however, we were informed by traffic police the road was temporarily blocked due to a serious landslide that had occured. They accommodated us in a Japanese style hotel in Tainan. All rooms were in a Japanese style; we slept on tatamis (a Japanese grass mat used for sleeping on the floor), most comfortable. The next day visited the historic and famous Chihkan Tower. In the year 1624 A.D. the Dutch invaded Taiwan, they established their headquarters in Tainan, thirty seven years later the Dutch were likewise successfully expelled from Tainan by Cheng Chengkung, known in the west as Koxinga, a Chinese loyalist who fled mainland China for Taiwan after having been pursued by the Ching (Manchu) Dynasty. Koxinga died in 1662 at only 38 years of age, after having been expelled by Dutch colonialists from Taiwan.

The Chihkan Tower was also built by the Dutch in 1663. Still another Dutch fort was visited known as Fort Anping, located in a suburb of present day Tainan. The Dutch erected a lighthouse originating from the same period. From Tainan we visited to the city of Kaohsuing, a splendid modern seaport. Kaohsuing is Taiwan's second largest city plus her largest seaport. Nearby a tiny island connected with Lotus Lake is established the Spring and Autumn Pavilions, an attractive pair of twin pagodas.

Following breakfast we left Kaohsuing beginning our return journey back to Tai Chung and Taipei. It was a fine day weatherwise; it was interesting to see farmers busy tilling their fields, some planting their rice fields. Taiwan is an island nation that has a tremendous variety of agricultural products. On the way back we stopped to see a huge statue of Buddha taking photographs of it. We drove around for a final view of the Tai Chung parliament buildings and exhibits in the National Palace Museum. Stopped again at the teachers' hostel where we had accommodation for the night, six beds per room. From the hostel we visited Tung Hai University for photographs. Drove up Lion Mountain where several Buddhist pagodas are located, climbed a mountain to visit a monastery, ate a vegetarian luncheon in the monastery.

The next day we drove to Hsinchu and toured the Institute of Nuclear Science located at National Tsing Wah University. We were escorted on a tour of their nuclear reactors, they explained the workings of the reactors, and it was exceedingly interesting and informative. From Tsing Wah we returned to Taipei to the overseas hostel where we resided. Some of us made our way to the Cathay Pacific office to reconfirm our return air passages to Hong Kong. Our final appointment in Taipei was to attend a farewell party at the Overseas Chinese Association reception centre, concluding the 15-day Chung Chi College student tour of Taiwan. All of us immensely enjoyed the splendid educational tour of Taiwan; it was carefully planned and prepared, leaving a deep impression upon our minds and hearts for years to come.

(3) SINGAPORE, MALAYSIA AND THAILAND

I had planned on taking a freighter from Hong Kong to north Borneo then to Indonesia on a visit to that familiar and famous part of Southeast Asia, I had heard much about the legendary beauty of the island of Bali belonging to Indonesia. However, one week prior to my departure I received a telephone call from my Hong Kong travel agent informing me the shipping company had cancelled all passengers' travel due to trouble with President Sukarno of Indonesia. He indicated it would be exceedingly hazardous to go, since President Sukarno didn't care for Chinese or anyone connected with them. In view of the situation they cancelled all my travel plans to Indonesia. Sukarno had killed over 10,000 Chinese in Indonesia and was still slaughtering them. I agreed to the cancellation of travel plans to Indonesia avoiding any possible trouble. However, the travel agent immediately arranged for me to visit Singapore, Malaysia and Thailand instead of Indonesia, I was naturally disappointed concerning the cancellation, but agreed with his suggestion the travel agency cancel my travel plans to Indonesia.

July 17, 1963 I flew from Hong Kong to Singapore on the first leg of my annual vacation. The plane flew via Bangkok Thailand then to Singapore, approximately a four hour jet flight. My first night was spent in the Seaview Hotel in Singapore, but it was too elaborate and expensive for my pocket book. The following day I found the y.m.c.a. had a room, therefore decided to accept it. Living at the y.m.c.a. was quite convenient and far less expensive $8.00 (Malaysian currency) per day $56.00 per week. It was nearer the downtown core, close to the National Museum formerly called the Raffles Museum, which greatly pleased me, since I enjoy going through museums, a favorite side interests of mine. I soon discovered the museum had splendid exhibits of natural history including birds, animals and reptiles, plus a fine prehistoric collection of tools, and artifacts originating from Malaysia, Singapore, Borneo and Indonesia. I spent nearly two hours browsing through the museum.

The tourist association was exceedingly helpful so I decided to take a Siakson Coach Tour, including the Queen Elizabeth Walk near the waterfront, past the city council and the Supreme Court building and near the Polytechnic and the highest hill in Singapore for a panoramic view of the city. Drove down the hill to a rubber sorting wharehouse, observed the way rubber is made into sheets. I visited the Haw Par Villa (Tiger Balm Garden fame). I drove to the Botanical Garden to see some of Singapore's famous orchids. I visited Jade House to see a splendid jade collection. During the afternoon I went on a tour including the University of Singapore, past the Ford factory and Hume Industries, crossed the causeway separating Singapore from Malaysia, visited the Malayan state of Johore Bahru, a traditional Japanese garden in Johore, then to Abu Bakar mosque, a stylish and attractive mosque built in the Middle Eastern style of architecture with domes. Saw the sultan's palace located high upon a hill and had an opportunity to go and visit a factory where they produce *batik*, an Indonesian type of cloth, the process for producing batik was demonstrated and explained to us, how they use wax to transfer the patterns on to the material. I returned to Singapore to visit the Kranji War Memorial, where 24,000 soldiers are remembered, from the Japanese period of occupation during the Second World War a most impressive sight. The memorial is beautifully arranged. From there we visted a rubber estate observing the way rubber latex is collected from the rubber trees into small cups. Passed by the Singapore Turf Club (race course) back to the Y.M.C.A., went for supper at Swee Kee's to eat Hainan chicken and rice as well as soup, a famous and delicious dish.

I always enjoyed swimming so boarded a Red Line bus travelling outside Singapore city enroute to Changi beach, which is fronted by clean, wide, sandy beaches or *katong* located on the eastern coast. The countryside is picturesque with tropical palm trees and lovely vegetation. Malaysian thatched huts built among the palm trees, including Western style cottages. The road passed by the prisoner of war camp and a former Royal Air Force base, with planes sitting on the airfield. The Changi beach winds its way having miles and miles of beautiful golden sand, a tremendous place to relax and unwind.

I also took time to attend a Protestant church in a pleasant colonial style church building with plenty of fresh air, the Wesley Methodist church located on Fort Canning road not far from the Y.M.C.A. where I was living. The minister was Dr. Gunnar J. Teilmann. It happened to be ecumenical Sunday, so Dr. Teilmann used as his topic "the tragedy of a divided church." During the p.m., I visited Dr. P.K. Kwan who drove me around to see Trinity Theological

College the principle theological seminary in Singapore. Dr.Kwan also escorted me to three of the water reservoirs in Johore, plus the botanical garden and Singapore University. The Kwans were exceedingly hospitable and kind in every respect.

The Cathay Pacific travel agency in Singapore helped me plan and arrange my itinerary: travelling by train from Singapore, up the Malayan Peninsula to Malacca, Kuala Lumpur, Penang, then Bangkok, Thailand. Before leaving Singapore I visited the Van Kleef Aquarium. They have a splendid selection of tropical fish of all sizes, shapes and colours.

On July 25th I left Singapore by train to commence my journey up the Malayan peninsula travelling by second class from Singapore to Bangkok, Thailand. It cost me only $71.00 (Malayan currency or $24.00 u.s.). The train departed Singapore at precisely 8:00 a.m., crossed the causeway from Singapore into Johore state, Malaya. The rail route travelled up the centre of the Malayan peninsula. The terrain consisted mostly of rolling hills with some hills higher than others. I observed endless rubber tree plantations scattered along the route, including bananas and tea trees. Following lunch I got off the train at Tampin, taking a pedicab into Tampin, where I transferred to a public bus travelling to a Malayan village. It was most interesting driving past country homes built on stilts serving as protection from water, animals, snakes and other reptiles. In Malacca I hired a pedicab to a Government Rest Home (hotel) it cost me $7.00 Malayan per day. The room was clean and comfortable. I went for a walk to Porto di Santiago, symbol of the state of Malacca built by the Portuguese. Visited the old museum built in the style of a Dutch home, extremely interesting.

The following day I enquired regarding guided tours available from a Malacca tourist agency. Mr. Lim Leong Kim took me on a walking tour of Malacca including the old town square, the government buildings are decorated in a pinkish salmon colour, the custom originated from the Dutch period, walked through their modern legislative building plus the residence of the governor. I was taken to the ruins of old St. Paul's Church where St. Francis of Assisi had been buried, until his remains were exhumed and transferred to Goa in India. Guided back to Porto di Santiago I had visited the day before, built by the Portuguese. The guide decided we hire a pedicab which drove us to the Cheng Hoon Teng Temple established during the 17th century and dedicated to the Buddhist goddess Kwan Yin claiming to be the oldest Buddhist temple in Malacca, also visited the earliest mosque in Malacca, plus its famous minaret that is quite ancient. We drove to Lord Buddha's temple, back into Malacca past many homes erected high on stilts for their own protection. We returned to Malacca and visited St. John's Fort an ancient Portuguese form of architecture, received a magnificent view over the straits of Malacca. We stopped at Sam Poh's Well extending back in time to Raja Iskandar from the 13th century founder of Malacca.

On July 27th I took a bus returning to Tampin, the bus left the depot and stopped to let a passenger off, when the bus stopped, they couldn't get it going again. The bus was jam-packed full of Chinese and Malaysians a truly multi-cultural group plus myself. We patiently sat waiting for another bus to come along to pick us up. However, I was fearful of missing my train connection. We waited for half an hour before a relief bus appeared. Transferred to the new bus, we saw the way another bus had slipped and turned over into the ditch. It made me wonder if we would be next. The bus passed many rubber estates and rice paddies, it was exceedingly picturesque. Finally we rattled into Tampin approximately 24 miles from Malacca, hired a taxi to take me to the railway station, I was amazed that I arrived at the station in time to board the train, which happened to be 25 minutes late. Soon I was on my way to Kuala Lumpur, 250 miles north of Singapore. I got a room at the Kowloon Hotel in Kuala Lumpur the capital of Malaysia. A modern and up to date hotel it cost me only $12.00 Malayan per day. Besides I went to a movie on the life of J. F. Kennedy.

In Kuala Lumpur I planned to take a guided tour of the city, however, discovered it was far too expensive, so decided to travel by local bus. I took the bus to the university of Malaya, impressed by the friendliness of the local residents who were helpful at all times. At the main entrance to the university of Malaya is a beautiful mosque with it golden domes. I visited a former Chinese professor of mine who taught me at the University of Hong Kong. His office was located in the arts building. His name was Mr. Cheng Yi he gave me a real welcome, I was his first friend from Hong Kong to visit him since he had moved to Malaya. He invited me home to have lunch with him and his family. Following lunch Mr. Cheng guided me around the University of Malaysia, including the library where the librarian also came from Hong Kong. Mr. Cheng drove me to see the brand new Merdeka Stadium, located on a hill, exceedingly modern and up-to-date.

The following day I continued my sightseeing, drove past their modern and attractive railway station built in the Moorish style, returned to see the Merdeka Stadium. When I arrived at the stadium it happened students from all over Malaysia were gathered preparing for the Malaysian celebrations to be held on August 31, 1963. One of the dances spelt out Malaysia with hundreds of students preparing for the event. The boys were practicing their gymnastics for the occasion, quite a sight. In the stadium I met Mr. Thong Poh Chiew who was exceedingly friendly, he offered to take me sightseeing around Kuala Lumpur. The Merdeka stadium incorporated an Olympic standard swimming pool. Mr. Thong drove me to see some of the city's beautiful and attractive gardens. Mr. Thong was a school teacher, we visited his home, drove out of the city to see the famous Batu Caves, one of the scenic wonders of Malaysia, the caves rise 400 feet high, we climbed up 271 steps to enter the caves where there is a Hindu altar, most interesting and educational. From the caves we drove to a natural hot spring where the water is so hot you can hardly place your hand into it without burning yourself. The next point of interest was a reservoir that supplies Kuala Lumpur with fresh drinking water. Returned to Kuala Lumpur and drove to the Selangor Sports Club for a fresh drink of coconut juice. It is really amazing the friendliness and willingness of the Malayan people towards visitors to their country, leaving a deep and lasting impression upon me.

Still another time I took a bus to Templer Park, which is 14 miles outside of Kuala Lumpur; I walked around the park known for its beautiful jungle flora. I joined a group of high school students on a picnic in the park. There are some beautiful waterfalls there. From the park I took a bus back to Kuala Lumpur and visited Lake Garden. The gardens are so green and peaceful with running streams, overhanging shade trees. It was great to leisurely stroll around the gardens, so very peaceful and quiet.

My train left Kuala Lumpur at 8:10 a.m. and I scrambled onto the train along with hundreds of other folks. I shared a seat with Tan Jao Eng, a young man travelling as far as Ipoh. He filled me in on tin mining and the raising of rubber trees. I saw more rubber planta- tions and tin mining most of the way. The train crossed an irrigation lake, passed through seemingly endless tunnels. About 5:00 p.m. the train arrived at Ira where all passengers including myself were re- quired to get off, we went aboard a ferry for around 20 minutes. It docked on Penang Island. I hired a taxi to the White House Hotel where I reserved a room.

Since it was Sunday I attended St. George's Anglican Church but unaware of the time when the service began, I had just arrived in time for the sermon. It was a Tamil service (language from southern India); the sermon was in English. I also participated in the service of Holy Communion. Following the service went for a walk by the sea to cool off, stopped for a cool drink. Had lunch at the Magnolia res- taurant not far from the hotel where I was living on Penang Road. I bought myself a guidebook of Penang. Later walked downtown near the Supreme Court, plus the War Memorial located on the wa- terfront where many young boys were busy fishing from the shore- line. I walked to Old Fort Corwalis where the walls still remain standing with some of the old cannons pointing seaward, then went to their lovely modern post office, past the banking area, towards a large Muslim mosque, many were taking a rest lying on the floor of the mosque. Passed a host of Chinese shops on the way to a large city market, returned to the hotel where I was lodging.

Visited the tourist association by the old clock tower to enquire about guided tours they offered. They were exceedingly helpful; I soon discovered it was possible to use public transportation rather than tour buses. Spent the morning walking around various shop- ping centres, bought a coconut for 20 cents Malayan or 7 cents u.s. both the coconut milk and its meat were fresh and delicious. Later I took a bus to Ayer Itam, walked to the Kek Lok Si Temple built in the style of a Chinese palace. The temple was erected in 1890 by a Buddhist priest with funds coming from Buddhists in Malaya, Burma, Thailand and Indonesia. The temple was located on the side of a mountain. The most elaborate and outstanding looking build- ing is a seven-tiered pagoda red in colour, known as the Ban Po Thor, otherwise called the "Million Buddha Pagoda." I walked to the top of the pagoda to receive a spectacular and panoramic view of the area. It has Buddhas of all sizes and shapes most attractive; it is worth the effort going there.

The following day I took a public bus to see the famous Snake Temple at Sungei Klang about nine miles from Penang City. It's a temple where snakes are offered a sanctuary and dedicated to the god Chor Soo Kong the snakes were considered as his disciples. Snakes may be seen all over like on the altar, among the flowers, even on the sides of the walls of the temple. You can also see where some snakes even shed their skins. The snakes are a greenish colour; they mostly live on eggs left out for them to eat. The snake temple was built in 1850 by a Chinese priest. From the temple I took a bus to return to Penang City, took another bus to Lok Si Temple to take photographs. When I visited the temple the day before the weather was too dull for photos. Nearby was a large pond where people feed the turtles. There are literally dozens upon dozens of turtles of all sizes. I took another bus to the foot of Penang Hill, where I rode a cable car to the top of the hill. The distance is about one mile distance or 435 yards. There is a funicular railway; it takes about 24 minutes to travel. The railway rises to a height of 2,270 feet. Most refreshing temperature up on the hill. From the top you can see across the bay separating the island of Penang from the mainland of Malaya. There were many ships in the harbour, reminding me of Hong Kong. I walked around the top of the hill for the scenery, returned to Penang by bus, visited the botanical garden. The gardens consist of 75 acres, a distinct change in atmosphere. Countless monkeys could be seen running around and swinging through the trees. The tiny baby monkeys are cute the way they cling to their mother's breast. The mothers are very protective of their babies. I also went to the water reservoir to cool off and relax for while.

On Friday August 9th I rode on a local tricycle to the railway ferry crossing from Penang where I boarded the ferry to Iri located on the mainland of Malaysia. By 8:30 a.m. I boarded a train heading northwards to the border of Thailand, my visit to Malaysia was officially over. On the train I shared a seat with an American Peace Corps worker, before long another gentleman from Switzerland accompanied us. The train passed through low-lying rolling hills. I could see endless green rice paddies lying before us. By 12:45 p.m. the train arrived at Pedang Besar, the border village crossing from Malaysia into Thailand. Immigration officials checked our travel documents and luggage, the extent of the examination. There was no dining car on the train from Iri to the Thai border. By 2:00 p.m. the train departed the border region. The terrain was low rolling hills similar to Malaysia. The surrounding vegetation quite tropical in appearance as the train steadily rolled through the low-lying hills of Malaysia.

Around 5:00 p.m. the train accidentally ran into and killed a farmer's water buffalo. The train stopped suddenly, and immediately the farmer began negotiating the killing of his water buffalo, the farmer's livelihood was at stake, the farmer was naturally extremely upset blaming the train for killing his water buffalo. The water buffalo is equivalent in importance to a tractor in Canada. Tempers flared, after prolonged debate and negotiation a settlement between the farmer and the railway was evidently reached, both parties finally came to a satisfactory agreement, permitting the train to continue on its journey to Bangkok.

I had little rest during the night on the train since three of us were crowded into narrow seats. Our luggage scattered down along the aisle. Directly across from us were two elderly Thai men chewing betel nuts, somewhat the way a person in the west chews tobacco. The betel nuts turn their teeth a jet black, while the juice mixed with saliva results in the saliva turning a bright reddish colour. They spit the juice into tin cans, periodically dumping the cans out of the open train windows. The saliva tended to splash back on to the passengers due to the motion of the train, the breeze created by the motion of the train, gradually caused our faces to become a reddish colour from betel nut juice.

In spite of the crowded, congested conditions, everyone appeared to be in a rather jovial mood; all heading for the same destination, Bangkok the capital of Thailand.

I did little reading, the train continued to speed onward. At one point I could see the South China Sea from the moving train. The train was travelling parallel to the border of Thailand and Burma. The mountains gradually changed from low-lying hills to rather rough jagged mountains, something you might see in a Chinese painting. Thailand is exceedingly famous for exporting a top quality of rice. Most farmers were busy tilling their land, preparing the rice paddies for their next crop of rice due in a few months time. Most farmers were fully occupied transplanting the tiny rice plants into their fields.

By 11:15 a.m. (Saturday) our train approached the outskirts of Bangkok City; everyone was preparing to get off the train. By 11:25 a.m. the train arrived at the main terminal of the railway station in Bangkok. It was exceedingly crowded with so many people preparing to get off the train at the same time.

There was a terrific scramble trying to hire a taxi in Bangkok, however, the most irritating and confusing problem facing all visitors was hiring a taxi, the taxi cab meters actually function, however, none of their meters seemed to be functioning, at least that was the impression the drivers present to the visitors. In view of the situation they can charge whatever they wish; the tourist is completely at the mercy of the cab drivers.

I had accommodation at the Viengtai Hotel, equivalent to $3.50 u.s. or 70.00 ticuls per day. I had a good-sized room with plenty of light, including a bath and shower needed for the hot weather.

After settling down, I went out for a short walk to discover the hotel was quite centrally located, by Thommasat University, where I met a Buddhist novice dressed in his saffron coloured robe. He spoke good English and offered to escort me around the campus. He also introduced me to some of his teachers. We removed our shoes before entering the classrooms, a fine introduction to some of Thailand's ways and customs.

I felt fully rested after a good night's sleep, ready for a day of sightseeing. By 10:00 a.m. I went on a tour of a few of the principal temples in Bangkok; there was only the guide, the driver of the pedicab plus myself. The first point of interest was Wat Indra Vihan or the "Temple of the Standing Buddha," a tremendously tall statue exceeding 100 feet (30.5 metres) from there we drove to the Marble Buddha Temple, also known as Wat Benchamabopit. It has a traditional style Thai roof that turns upwards. Within the temple is a large benevolent looking statue of Buddha; along the corridors of the temple were some 52 Buddhas. A canal runs parallel to the temple, plus a number of ornamental bridges, it's well worth visiting. From there we went to Wat Po where the large sleeping Buddha is located peacefully reclining, the reclining Buddha is 160 feet (48.76 metres) in length. The grounds surrounding the temple are exceedingly beautiful. You could see temple rubbings made on very thin paper, by Buddhist monks.

The final visit of the tour was to Wat Phra Keo sometimes referred to as the Temple of the Emerald Buddha, the image is made of dark green jasper jade about 22 inches high sitting on a pedestal. They have various kinds of robes they place on the Buddha according to the seasons, spring, summer, autumn and winter. The clothing on the Buddha is changed according to the season. Outside the temple is found a model of Angkor Wat, the most famous structure in Cambodia a neighbouring country. Words cannot adequately describe the beauty and splendour and colour of the buildings within the temple grounds, along side are many strange creatures. It is a genuine pleasure to visit the various temples.

Following a brief rest, I decided to take a guided tour of the National Museum of Bangkok. The previous tour of Buddhist temples opened my eyes, it whet my appetite for seeing more of the wonders and beauty of Thailand. The National Museum was formerly the palace of the Prince Successor. The palace was constructed in 1782 by the Prince Successor from the first reign of Bangkok. The entire compound was donated by King Rama the Eighth in 1926. It's entirely filled with exhibits from Thai culture. The principle emphasis of the museum is the influence of Buddhism. Thousands of statues are present ranging from a few inches to others much higher; some statues nearly reach the ceiling.

The exhibits display the royal throne, ceremonial vehicles, royal barges, plus a display of objects related to the use of elephants within the Thai tradition. Also displayed are military exhibits of guns, lances and drums etc. The entire museum is systematically organized and needs to be seen to be appreciated. The museum reflects the form of architecture used at the time, reflecting the advanced culture of Thailand. Outside the museum are cooked food stalls displaying various delicacies from Thailand, plus medical remedies and treatments. I returned to my hotel quite satisfied with my first venture into Thai culture; it has so much to commend itself.

The following day I opted for an early morning tour to visit the famous floating market tour of Bangok. The city is sometimes compared to Venice, Italy, since it is a city of endless canals. Three Cantonese speaking tourists from Singapore including and myself went on a private tour. The boat headed down the wide river, which is very yellow reflecting the colour of mud, we sped under many bridges joining into the canal. Countless boats were also on the canal. Along the sides of the canal may be seen houses built on stilts similar to what you see in rural areas of Malaysia. Dozens of early morning boats were on the river, transporting their cargo into the city for the day, transporting vegetables, fruits and flowers to the market. Children were playing along the banks of the river waving to the visitors. At one point we stopped at a factory where they produce Thai silk, we saw numerous looms operated by women. It happened August 12th is the Queen's birthday; there were evidently more boats on the river than usual. The boat we rode got tangled up in a traffic jam of vessels, many people could be seen swimming in the river.

The next stop of interest was the Temple of Dawn or Wat Arun. The exterior of the temple is decorated with seashells and broken pieces of imported pottery from China. We climbed seemingly endless steps leading up to the spire to enjoy a splendid view of Bangkok city. From there we were taken to see the royal barge plus a fleet of beautifully carved and decorated boats in the shape of dragons. The royal barge is used to help celebrate special occasions. The birthday of the present king His Majesty Bhumiphol is October 12. The bows of the boats are carved like dragons and other sea monsters; they are painted black, gold and red. It was another day of genuine adventure tracing the proud history of Thailand and her people.

The streets of Bangkok are quite wide and modern, however, they are exceedingly crowded with people and vehicles of every shape and size. The noise pollution is unbelievable with car horns and others blasting throughout the day, as well as bicycles, tricycles, and three wheeled taxis etc. All pedestrians must take extreme caution when crossing the busy streets of Bangkok.

Bangkok is a city of many sights and sounds. One morning around 6:15 a.m., I happened to peer out from the hotel veranda to see a most interesting and colourful spectacle taking place. Buddhist priests and novices dressed in the saffron coloured robes and shaved heads and bare feet grasping on to their begging bowls were receiving gifts of food from a devout Buddhist family. The family had placed a table more than 6 feet in length in the alley were busy distributing food to all monks that passed by. Each monk received a generous portion of food while in turn the donor received merit in the next world for the good deed (alms) performed. Each monk was given a large ladle of rice, an egg, fresh vegetables and banana. The line of people was about 20 feet or more, some carried a lotus flowers in their hands symbolizing the Buddhist faith. I saw more than 50 monks receive food for the day in that way. They bowed politely to the donor to express their deep appreciation and humble gratitude. I personally witnessed the sight for some 45 minutes. Yes, Buddha is indeed their lord and master. The guide informed me the donor family must have been an affluent family who was celebrating an auspicious occasion such as a birthday, or some such event for which they returned thanks to lord Buddha for his love and concern.

Later on the morning I took a grand palace tour. We were driven to the main entrance of the palace grounds, but were informed we weren't permitted to enter at that specific time, because the king and queen were on their way. We waited by the roadside to catch a fleeting glimpse of their majesties when they arrived.

We were shown around the spacious palace grounds and through the royal funeral hall. The temple itself is exceedingly elaborate with paintings reflecting the life of lord Buddha covering the entire walls and ceiling. Finally we were permitted to enter the royal chapel where the world famous emerald Buddha is located. We sat crossed legged on the floor as the guide explained the decor and its significance, plus the ceremonies held at the time. The guide explained the significance of the various robes placed upon the Buddha throughout the year. Monks were busy chanting prayers when we entered the temple. The fragrance of incense permeated the entire atmosphere. No photography was permitted within the temple.

The following day I had a guided tour of Ayudhya and Bangpa-in located about 55 miles north of Bangkok. The passengers on the tour came from France, Sweden, the u.s.a. and Canada. Ayudhya was formerly the old capital of Thailand, however, Thailand was invaded by the Burmese who destroyed Ayudhya due to the rivalry between the two nations. As we drove to the countryside we saw endless rice paddies and children busy herding their water buffaloes, used for ploughing and cultivating the rice paddies. Trucks were lined up for more than a mile waiting their turn to enter Bangkok avoiding the rush hour traffic. The first main stop was the old Summer Palace at Bangpa-in, built in a beautiful Oriental architectural style. A huge statue of King Rama the Fourth had been erected. Some of the rooms in the palace were designed in a typical Chinese style. The temporary residence of King Rama the Fifth for the cooler season. The residence is truly beautiful with Chinese porcelain throughout decorating the palace. The gardens were constructed following the Western style. The wall paintings are something to be seen plus an interesting throne with its nine-tiered umbrella. Upon our return to Bangkok we stopped briefly at the Three Precious Buddha Temple where a large seated Buddha is seated in the temple. The journey also stopped to see a huge corral used for rounding up elephants, including sturdy posts and a concrete wall to contain the elephants keeping them under control. Thai elephants are still very much used as work animals in Thailand.

Near Ayudhya is a huge memorial built in memory of one of Thailand's queens considered as a heroine. She died in a battle with the Burmese. We drove to the ruins of the city, where a large reclining Buddha appears to be comfortable and peaceful in his rest. Ayudhya was the former capital of Thailand about 400 years ago. It served as the capital from 1350–1767 A.D. In 1767 Bangkok was made the present capital of Thailand. In recent years they constructed a huge Buddha with a temple constructed over the Buddha image. Buddhist influence in Thailand is unbelievable it is evident wherever you turn.

Since I arrived at the end of my vacation in Thailand, I went to settle my bill for the six days. It came to 420 bhats the equivalent to $21.00 U.S. for six days plus 425 bhats for tours of Bangkok and surrounding areas. It was difficult to believe it was so cheap considering it included so much. I had lunch at the Trocadero Hotel, did a little last minute shopping before returning to Hong Kong.

Following supper I went to see a performance of classical Thai dancing; it is sedate and artistic. The girls performing turned their fingers and hands backwards and appear so artistic and talented. They are trained in the art of dancing from infants. The movements of their hands, feet and head all have special significance and meaning. There was also an instrumental solo, the Thai version of the xylophone skillfully performed, besides a sword dance, they also used spears and lances, the performance lasted approximately one hour, it was worth while seeing, I was so pleased I attended the artistic skillful and splendid performance.

My visit to Bangkok was a real highlight of my visit to Southeast Asia including Singapore, Malaysia and Thailand. The various cultures and customs are fascinating adding greatly to my visit to Southeast Asia. I left Bangkok on August 16, 1963 from Don Muang Airport back to Hong Kong by Cathay Pacific airlines. Three and a half hours later arrived back in Hong Kong, following a tremendously enjoyable vacation in Southeast Asia, which lasted from July 17 to August 16, 1963. I returned home prepared to go back to work in Hong Kong with vim and vigour with a desire to return to those countries again.

An outside stone table at the Koon Yum Temple, Macau, where the first Treaty of Commerce was signed between China and America in 1844.

Historic ruins of old St. Paul's Church in Macau.

Gateway between Macau and China.

CHAPTER 11

Macau, End of an Era

MACAU IS THE OLDEST European settlement on the south-eastern coast of China. Founded in 1557, it soon became the leading gateway for trade with China and Japan; however, on December 19, 1999, Macau was returned to China's sovereignty (after 442 years). It is now known as a "special administration region" (SAR) of the People's Republic of China. Macau has been assured by Beijing things will remain unchanged for the next fifty years. Macau occupies a strategic position on the Western edge of the delta formed by the Pearl River and the West River. It borders China's Guangdong Province and lies 60 kilometres (37 miles) from Hong Kong.

During the middle of the 16th century, some enterprising Portuguese sailor-merchants brought along with them many of their customs and traditions. The city prospered and these sailor-merchants gradually developed their new settlement with the construction of numerous buildings in the Portuguese architectural style of the time. Palaces, churches, forts, convents, schools, colleges and missions are to this day proof of their faith and the wealth of Macau in the past.

The scenery, the style of the buildings, the colour of their facades, and the climate all give a charming atmosphere to Macau (Macao).

Peaceful, sunny, and restful, Macau was an ideal spot for me to take a holiday. From 1955 onward I frequently used to travel to Macau, since at the time the People's Republic of China at the time would not permit me to visit China, since I was a missionary, considered as an undesirable element. China's leader chairman Mao Tse

Tung (also known as Mao Zedong) didn't wish to have anything to do with a person such as me being a Canadian missionary. However, visiting Macau was a change since it was conveniently close to Hong Kong (only 40 miles away). Macau especially appealed to me since it had numerous interesting and historical points of interest.

Avenida Almeida Ribero, the main street, cuts directly across the city, dividing Macau in half. The hub of the city lies here, at a square adjoining the street, called the Largo Do Senado (town hall) and the rather imposing post and telegraph office building.

The Leal Senado (town hall) was undoubtedly one of the finest buildings in Macau. In its present form, that of a typical Portuguese manor house. Erected in 1876 to be the seat of government, later it became the town hall. It was extensively repaired in 1939 but both the facade and the main hall were kept in their original form. It is claimed the hall is one of the most harmonious and beautiful seen this side of Suez. In one of the wings of the building is housed the oldest European public library in the Far East. Its magnificent woodwork is inspired in the beautiful Coimbra University Library; it holds over 30,000 volumes, some of which are rare specimens of the 16th and 17th centuries. However, unfortunately, many of the books were damaged in 1966 due to the leftist disturbance (riots) in Macau during the Christmas season, which marked the beginning of the so-called Cultural Revolution in China.

Immediately upon entering the building above an arch under which a flight of stairs leads to the upper floor there is a wooden inscription whose translation reads: "City of the Name of God, there is none more loyal. In the name of the King, our Lord, Dom Joao de Souza Pereira, caused this inscription to be set up in witness of the unsurpassing of its inhabitants 1654."

The loyalty shown by the population to the Portuguese crown during the Spanish occupation of Portugal is thus remembered. That is the reason why the municipal council of Macau is styled the Leal Senado, meaning "loyal senate."

Opposite the Leal Senado is the Largo De Senado in the middle of which a statue is erected in honour of a local hero, Vicente Nicolau de Mesquita. A short way across from it stands the Santa Casa da Misericordia (Holy House Of Mercy) Charitable Institution, founded in Portugal in the 14th century by Queen Leonor and established here in 1569 by D. Belchior Carneiro, the first bishop of Macau. Created to minimize the hardships of the poor, its mission is still the same today.

A little further on one comes to the St. Domingos Church, situated at the Largo De S. Domingos. In fine modern Roman-style architecture, is kept today as when it was built by the Spanish Fathers more than three centuries ago.

Further along is the Hospital De S. Rafael, the first Western hospital to operate in the Far East. Founded in 1569, it was rebuilt in 1640 and completely reformed and modernized in 1939. Run by the Santa Casa da Misericordia, referred to above, it dispenses medical care to one and all, irrespective of race, creed, or colour.

St. Francisco Garden, criss-crossed by roadways, now faces reclaimed ground. Yet not so long ago, it formed one of the prongs to the graceful bay of Praia Grande. Near it stands the convent of St. Clara, founded 300 years ago by the Franciscan Sisters of Mary. It also houses the famous girls' school named after Santa Rosa de Lima. A magnificent flight of stone steps leads up to it from the main entrance. At one end of the garden stand the S. Francisco Barracks, occupying one of the best vantage points of Macau.

Going uphill stands the new, modern premises of the Hospital Conde de Januario, the name by which the government hospital is known. It replaces an old structure; immediately next to it stands the meteorological observatory, founded in 1880. The site was originally occupied by the Fort of St. Jerome.

A most comprehensive and certainly the best view of Macau and its surrounding territories and islands is obtained from the top of Guia Hill, which lies a little to the northeast. Covered with luxuriant tropical vegetation, it carries on its highest point its own crown: the Guia Lighthouse, which has the honour of being the first lighthouse ever built on the whole coast of China. It started operating in 1864.

Built on the site of the old Guia Fort there, at its foot, stands a chapel, erected in 1626, dedicated to our Our Lady of Guia. The chapel was at one time attached to the Guia Fort, some of whose cannons may still be seen. Around the hill there is a short, winding motor road from where such landmarks as the following may be seen: government hospital, D. Bosco School, government primary schools, municipal swimming pool, Mong Ha Fort, St. Michael Cemetery, the Temple of Kun Yam, where the first Sino-American treaty was signed in 1844, the Barrier Gate, and others.

Leaving Guia Hill one comes down to what remains of the old Vasco da Gama Avenue and the old Victory Monument, both of which are separated by a couple of government primary schools and the municipal swimming pool. There still stands a bronze bust of da Gama, discoverer of the Cape route to India, surrmounting a pedestal on which is carved a scene from Camões' *Lusiads*. The Victory Monument is so called to commemorate the end of a succession of battles against the Dutch who coveted Macau and tried unsuccessfully to take it during the Spanish domination of Portugal (1580–1640). The monument marks the last battle, which took place in 1627.

Camões Gardens, with its famed grotto, is traditionally known as the place where Camões, the famous Portuguese poet, composed part of his epic *Lusiads*, while living in exile in Macau. This beautiful park is nowadays a most favoured relaxing place for the inhabitants of Macau. It is always decorated with seasonal flowers, and the shadows of the old banyan trees make this spot most attractive.

Immediately on the east side of this park are the Canossa Institute, known as Casa de Beneficencia, the old St. Anthony Church, the Church of Our Lady of Hope, the East India Company Cemetery and the former head office of the famous company. The latter building is now a museum where visitors may see, apart from Chinese objects of art, European paintings, some of which are by George Chinnery, the famous Irish painter. The Church of Our Lady of Hope, the oldest Catholic church of Macau, is better known as St. Lazarus Church, now serving the Chinese community.

In the East India Co. Cemetery (also called the Old Protestant Cemetery) some famous people are buried, such as Dr. Robert Morrison, pioneer Protestant missionary, who, during his stay in Macau from 1807–1834, compiled the first Chinese-English dictionary and translated the Old and New Testaments. Also buried there are his wife, Mary Morrison Chinnery; and many others connected with that period, like Lord John Spencer Churchill, fourth son of the fifth Duke of Marlborough.

The ruins of St. Paul's Church, the leading landmark of Macau, occupies a place of its own. Originally built in 1602 by Japanese Christian artisans, the church is dedicated to the Mother of God. At one time it was attached to the College of St. Paul, where missionaries were trained for work in the vast hinterland of China. Burnt down in 1835 only its facade remains; this is considered a masterpiece in the interpretation of Christian thought, with an Oriental background, by Oriental artists. The front is covered with bas-reliefs representing the fountain and the tree of life, ships, gorgons and apocalyptic monsters. The facade is divided into three tiers. In the uppermost tier is represented Jesus Christ with the dove, symbol of the Holy Ghost, surrounded by the instruments of the Crucifixion, and topped by a Cross of Jerusalem. The centre tier has a bronze statue of the Virgin Mary, flanked by angels in prayer. The lowest tier contains four bronze statues of Jesuit saints, some of whom at that time only beatified, notably St. Francis Xavier. All bronze statues were formerly polychromed. The foundation stone, on the west side, is dated 1602. The name of its architect, Father Spinola, is not however engraved thereon. One has to use binoculars to examine every ornament and inscription on this splendid facade. The steps leading to these ruins add to its magnificence. The style is of the best baroque.

The Cathedral of Macau is situated in the center of the city, a little way from the post office. It is a comparatively new building, constructed in 1849 and entirely redone in 1938. Nearby stands the Bishop's Palace, in the olden days used as the bishop's town house and now used merely as diocesan office.

The Fort of Sao Paulo, in the middle of the Macau peninsula, was built by the Jesuit Fathers in the 16th century and taken over by the government early in the 17th century. Some culverins and old bronze cannons are preserved in embrasures of the fort. At the entrance of the fort there is a bas-relief of St. Paul.

The graceful curve of the Praia Grande Bay is lined by a seaboard avenue where century-old banyan trees lazily give shade and shelter. Government House is situated here, as well as the law courts and several government departments along with a couple of hotels and not a few private residences. In front of the government departments building there is a statue in honour of Jorges Alvares, the first European to reach China by sea. He first came to these shores in the sixteenth century.

On an avenue along the sea wall and leading away from the

statue, stands the new building of the Macau Lyceum. Founded in 1894, it is the highest seat of learning locally. Countless graduates from this lyceum have gone on to Portuguese universities for further studies.

Further along and directly on a bend of the avenue, there stands the most elaborate of the Macau monuments. This is in honour of Amaral, a past governor, who was murdered in 1840 while trying to set up free trade and open new roads here. A fenced-off boulder, near the barrier gate, marks the exact spot where he was assassinated.

On reaching the Bom Parto Fort, this avenue changed its name to Avenida Republica, at whose southern most point yet another fort makes its appearance, named the Barra or the S. Iago Fort, guarding the entrance into the inner harbour. Above and beyond the fort no fewer than three small hills succeed each other; on the one called the Penha Hill, an extremely graceful chapel and a residence are perched on top, this being used as the bishop's residence; on another of the hills called the Barra Hill, there is a lovely walk around it. The district around this hill is very much sought after nowadays as residential quarters.

Near the Barra Fort one should not miss out the Ma Kwok Temple. This is a mariner's temple and is older than Macau itself. Actually the name "Macau" is derived from this temple.

Behind and a little above Government House stands the church of St. Lawrence in modern baroque style, surrounded by a garden. Further away, there rises St. Joseph's Seminary, the oldest seminary and the oldest scholastic institution in the Far East, with its fine baroque church and imposing flight of steps. This is a district where the old days well-to-do families used to live. The style of some of the houses, their patios, and the atmosphere about them, so much resemble some provincial towns in Portugal that one can hardly believe one is at the China doorstep.

Praca Ponte e Horta is situated on the westside of the southern part of Macau peninsula. This square adjoins the waterfront in the inner harbour; facing Lappa Island. It is one of the picturesque sites in Macau with its shops under vaulted arcades, a fountain in the middle, and trees along the pavements; it used to be a very busy center and it looks like a part of an old Latin trading city on the Mediterranean coast.

The influence of Macau on the history of Far Eastern relations extends beyond the sphere of mere commercial interests covering a period of 400 years.

The Dutch East India Company gives an account of their embassy in China in 1655, in which Macau is mentioned in this way: "We sailed along the island of Lantao, thence passing by the most famous city of "Maccoa," and though we came not near her, yet we shall relate what we understood from others concerning the magnificence of this place."

The following are palpable signs of municipal activity: the municipal swimming pool, where Olympic heats can take place within its 50-metre-long pool; the modern marketplaces of St. Domingos; St. Lawrence; Horta e Costa, and Horta do Companhia to the city's 200,000 old people; the municipal dogs' home, where stray dogs are cared for until claimed. It is here too the general vaccination of dogs takes place while facilities are provided for dogs to be left there for observation.

** Note: most of the above information was directly extracted from a tiny booklet entitled "Macau," by the courtesy of the Macau Tourist Department, published in the 1960s.

One additional note needs to be recorded at this time. Macau became the principal gambling centre throughout the decades in the Orient. Macau has been notorious for its gambling in all forms by permission of the local colonial Portuguese government. It is frequently referred to as the Monte Carlo of the East (Orient). Gambling, along with the profits derived from gambling, have been the centre of Macau's economy for countless years. It still remains to be determined whether or not that was for the good or evil of Macau. I am of the opinion it was to the detriment of Macau's society and social development, but needs to be left to time and history.

It should be stated Macau was the oldest foreign settlement in the Far East (1557). Having rounded the Cape of Storms and found the way to India, the great captains of the Age of Discovery turned their thoughts to that other distant land in the Far East. Cathay was known to be densely populated and to have abundance of goods so that trade would be easy and profitable. The legendary Country of the Flowery Kingdom was also a new mission field and the interests of the Portuguese were as much spiritual as material. As an example of missionary zeal the glorious figure of St. Francis is at once recalled. The Portuguese had not yet settled in Macau but already controlled Malacca, which Albuquerque had captured by his military skill and held by his exceptional ability as a statesman. Francis Xavier, a native of Navarre, spent most of his life in the service of Portugal and attained sanctity in the East. From the straits he hoped to penetrate into China, then closed to foreigners, and reach Canton and other parts where he might preach the faith of Christ. This hope sustained him to the last moment of his life, but he died within sight of the forbidden land in a wretched hovel in Sanchoan. There he was buried without funeral pomp and with his native servant as sole mourner. Only later was his incorrupt body taken to Malacca and subsequently to Goa where it still lies—and will always lie under the flag he loved for the sake of which he suffered so much. There was as yet no Macau, an outpost of Western civilization, which so many, including the Chinese themselves, were later to regard as a haven of refuge. However, the eagerness to reach China increased every year. The great adventures of the time spoke of it as a land of wonders where the palaces of the mandarins were covered with gold, where even the common people wore silk, where temples were built with silver and coffins made of precious metals studded with pearls, rubies, diamonds and topazes. People spoke of graveyard jade, which was of incalculable value and was said to have amazing powers in the treatment of the plague and other diseases.

In 1513, two years after Malacca had become Portuguese, a merchant from Frexio de Espada a Cinta, by the name of Jorges, set out on his perilous quest. He is the first Portuguese known to have entered Cathay and a statue in Macau still records the feat. Others followed him like Fernazo Peres de Andrade.

A few years later—encouraged by the illusory success of the mission to Japan which came to an end with the massacre of the Christians in the kingdom of Bungo and in Nagasaki—commissioner Leonel De Sousa obtained from the Chinese authorities for the Portuguese to establish a settlement in Macau. He promised the Chinese viceroy at Canton that they would help him to put down piracy, which was rife along that coast. In addition, the Portuguese in the course of some fierce engagements did destroy the power of these sea-robbers. The Emperor, the Son of Heaven, from his golden throne in the Forbidden City was so pleased with the news that he not only confirmed the permission but also ruled that the Portuguese could henceforth consider themselves lords of that land.

The Portuguese settlement in Macau—these events took place over 400 years ago—became a town, indeed the most important in southern China (excluding Canton, of course) until the rise of Victoria on the island of Hong Kong which the British occupied during the so-called "Opium War." Thus began what has been termed the Period of the Unjust Treaties, which came to an end only with the Second World War.

Macau soon had shipyards, a harbour and lighthouses besides the produce which it traded with Canton and other towns on the coast its ships loaded with gold, fine stuffs and other rich goods did business with the neighbouring lands of Siam, Cochin China, Tonkin and Japan. Macau's population increased. With the profit of this valuable trade hospitals, colleges, monasteries, convents and churches were built. From all over the world missionaries eager to preach the faith in the furthest east used Macau as the starting point for their labours.

Since its inception Macau has always been Portuguese; even during the sixty years during the Spanish usurpation (1580–1640), its loyalty never wavered. For this the home government rewarded it with the title of "City of the Name of God—None More Loyal." The people of Macau went further. They were not content merely to be faithful to Portugal but put up a stout defence against several attacks by Dutch fleets which began in 1603 and ended only twenty years later. And the city has its heroes such as Vicente Nicolau de Mesquita who led the bold advance on Fort Pac Sa Leang.

The persecuted have always regarded Macau as a port of refuge and as a Christian sanctuary. The most famous figure of modern China, Sun Yat Sen, the father of the republic, found a haven in Macau when pursued by the Manchu police. During the Sino-Japanese War, which began in 1937 and to all intents and purposes ended only in 1945 with the American victory in the Pacific, the gates of Macau admitted many thousands of refugees who were given food and shelter.

The ruins of the ancient Church of St. Paul are the hallmark of the city. The tourist who approaches Macau sees this venerable facade rising above the crowded houses and stamping this place with the Western atmosphere that pervades this old fragment of Portugal overseas.

This church was erected between the years 1594 and 1602, and a stone in the Western corner on which is inscribed "Irgini, magni, matri, civitas macaensis libens. An 1602." The stone facade, which stands as a hoary ruin today, was designed by Father Spinola and completed about 1637, the artisans being Japanese Christians who fled Japan due to persecution in the homeland. It was considered a wonder of the time.

Along the lowest of the three tiers are niched four statues of Jesuit Saints, some of who at that time had only been beatified, the most notable among them being St. Francis Xavier. The middle tier contains a statue of the Virgin Mary in the centre flanked by angels in prayer, the fountain and tree of life, a ship and a gargoyle, an apocalyptic monster, and a skeleton dormant. In the uppermost tier surrounded by the objects used in the crucifixion, stands a representation of Jesus Christ with the dove, symbol of the Holy Ghost, surmounted by a Cross of Jerusalem.

Around Guia Hill runs a narrow motor road from which there is a splendid bird's-eye view of the whole of Macau. The lighthouse and chapel in the old fort of Guia may be visited if permission is first obtained from the authorities. The chapel and fort date back to 1626. In 1864 the lighthouse was built, one of the first on the China coast. Its original machinery, entirely of wood, was made locally by a Macau-born Portuguese.

One place of interest for the tourist is the century old Barrier Gate, or Portas do Ceraco. For the visitor it is always an experience to contemplate the tangible signs which mark the frontier between two states, with the characteristic quiet of the Portuguese province on one side and the vast and legendary China on the other—here the green and red standard of Portugal at the mast above the gate, floating over a few miles of Portuguese territory where four centuries of Christian civilization have left their stamp, there the red flag with its five stars waving over the country known as the Great Middle Kingdom.

Within a park, known as Camões Gardens, in a romantic grotto, is the bust of Luiz de Camões, Portugal's greatest poet. In this grotto, according to tradition, Camões wrote part of his epic poem, *Os Lusiadas*, recounting the glories of Portugal. Born in Lisbon in 1524, Camões was the scion of a noble family. In Santarem, whither as a wild and unruly youth he had been banished, he composed many of his shorter pieces. Later he enlisted against the Moors. During his service in the army he lost his right eye by a musket ball. Returning to Lisbon, he found neither his military nor his poetical merits procured him advancement; and he embarked in the year 1553 for the East Indies. First he went to Goa in Portuguese India, and then took part in the occupation of Macau in 1557. Returning from exile he was shipwrecked off Cochin China, saving himself by swimming while holding aloft and above the waves his manuscript of the *Lusiads*. On his return in 1569 his genius was recognised by the king, Dom Sebastiao, who granted him a pension. He died at the age of 56.

The Loyal Senate, in the very heart of the city, is an edifice of character. One is immediately struck by the sobriety of its lines and the nobility of its appearance. For a long time this was the seat of government; it now houses the municipal council.

Over the stairway leading up to the hall is an inscription attesting to the loyalty of the populace to the Portuguese monarchy upon the restoration of Portuguese sovereignty, after the Spanish domination from 1580 to 1640.

"City of the Name of God, there is none more loyal. In the name of the King, our Lord, Dom Joao IV, the governor and captain-general of the city, Joao de Sousa Pereira, ordered this inscription to be set up in testimony of the exceeding loyalty of its inhabitants. 1654."

The splendid public library is in the same building. Its woodcarving in the style of King John V was carried out by local artisans and is a tribute to their skills.

From its earliest days Macau became a centre of religious and humanitarian service. The Jesuits built their hostel there in 1562, and it grew into the Great College of St. Paul, an important university from which scholars were sent to all the Portuguese mission fields in the Far East—Japan, China, Annam, Siam, Laos, Cambodia, Timor and Korea. In 1569 the Santa Casa da Misericordia (The Holy House of Mercy) was founded, a charitable institution which survives to the present day and which established, in 1569, the Hospital of St. Raphael. Macau can pride itself, therefore, on possessing in which almost four hundred years ago, Western medical science and surgery began to be practised on the coast of China and where Chinese became familiar with the gradual development of medicine through the years.

Kun-yam (Kwun Yam) temple, the Temple of the Goddess of Mercy, is celebrated because it is the most important and characteristic of the Chinese temples in Macau.

This temple antedates the coming of the Portuguese, and round it clustered the homes of the Chinese settlers, probably fishermen, who lived there in those times. Constantly victimized by Chinese pirates, the Portuguese came to their rescue and expelled the Corsairs in 1557. In course of time the old temple was displaced by the present structure, with its picturesque pavilions altars and halls.

This temple is also celebrated for the fact the first treaty between the u.s.a. and China was signed within its precincts, in the territory of a third power, Portugal. The stone table erected the occasion may still be seen; at this table Mr. Caleb Cushing, for the U.S. government, and Viceroy Yi, for China, signed the treaty on the 3rd of July, 1844.

Chinese as well as foreign scholars have commemorated Macau's Kun-yam Temple in prose and verse, and its fame extends far beyond the confines of Macau. (*** Note: the above information entitled "Macau" was produced and published by the Tourist Association of Macau in the 1960s.)

CHAPTER 12

The Cultural Revolution
and Hong Kong

MAY 1966 MARKED the dramatic beginning of the so-called "Cultural Revolution" in China, which was decidedly not cultural, but resulted in the opposite effect, it lasted for a total of ten years. The Cultural Revolution was a sad extension of chairman Mao Tse Tung's revolution throughout the China, gradually developed into fanaticism across the length and breadth of the nation. It had a most undesirable and unsettling effect upon China's peoples, that became evident by the way it spilled into Hong Kong, adversely affecting the daily lives of Hong Kong's citizens. The Cultural Revolution had an unstabilizing and unsettling affect upon all aspects of life in China, it resulted in hundreds of thousands of people wishing to leave China to live in Hong Kong or elsewhere wherever refuge safety and security could be found. Many nations fortunately opened their doors and hearts to the endless flood of political refugees arriving from China in Hong Kong. Countless numbers fled China and left for other nations, where they have since made splendid contributions.

The Cultural Revolution commenced in May 1966 in China, it spread like wild fire across the entire continent of China. Mao Tse Tung's little red book with phrases and sayings from chairman Mao used to help justify the actions of the red guards, promoting their cause throughout the land, escalating Mao's concept for struggle and revolution. Countless numbers of China's youth spent their entire time promoting their cause of communism by utilizing the media such as radio, television, and newspapers. Before long

China's Cultural Revolution spilled into Hong Kong and Macau; it promoted riots and civil disturbances in both territories. Macau experienced her difficulties during Christmas 1966, while in May 1967 trouble erupted on the streets of Hong Kong. Ardent and youthful supporters of Mao's cause planted explosive devices in Macau and Hong Kong. Homemade bombs (Molotov cocktails) created havoc and widespread unrest and fear in both territories.

Due to Hong Kong's geographical proximity to China caused Hong Kong to become vulnerable, which helped to relieve some of the pressure from those living in Kwangtung province southern China they fled their homeland seeking refuge. I happened to be living in Hong Kong during that historical and unforgettable period, thus became involved through the Church of Christ in China Hong Kong council in the field of social welfare, by assisting many of the people adversely affected due to the turmoil and general confusion which resulted.

China came under the direct influence of the communists when the People's Republic of China was officially proclaimed by Chairman Mao Tse Tung from Beijing on October 1, 1949. At the time countless numbers fled China to live in Hong Kong, resulting in an acute shortage of living facilities in Hong Kong due to the recent turn of events. Hong Kong was challenged to face a crisis of immense proportions. At the end of the war in the Pacific in August 1945, Hong Kong's population was reduced to about 600,000. When I arrived in Hong Kong in October 1955, Hong Kong's population had increased to nearly three million, but by the time I returned to Canada in the summer of 1973, Hong Kong's population had dramatically increased to between five and six million people.

One of the most crucial and obvious needs to surface was housing and living accommodation. Every street, apartment (flat), staircase or rooftop available was occupied by people to the utmost capacity. The sides of the hills, were literally covered with make shift huts constructed from large cardboard boxes, tin, fibreboard or whatever material the people could lay their hands upon. Accommodation was hazardous, dangerous, and vulnerable to typhoons (tropical hurricanes in Asia), besides torrential floods in the monsoon season.

During the autumn and winter seasons, fires regularily erupted in squatter areas destroying the flimsily constructed homes, all those in the direct path of the fire was destroyed depending upon the direction of the wind at the time. It became a common sight to see black smoke suddenly belching out over one of the many squatter areas whether located on the side of a mountain, or in a residential area. It seemed to burst into flames consuming all in its raging path. Naturally deaths occurred due to fire, but it was amazing how few deaths actually occurred. The refugees were exceedingly quick both in foot and mind escaping from the raging fires that often consumed their homes. One of the greatest obstacles faced was the inability of the local fire department to reach the scene of the disaster quickly enough. The fire department was frequently obstructed due to the narrow streets or their ability to pump sufficient water upon the rapidly spreading flames.

The disastrous fire which destroyed the squatter area of Shek Kip Mei in Kowloon on Christmas Eve 1953 destroyed some 45 acres, rendering more than 50,000 people homeless, which forced the British government to recognize the need and introduce a new squatter resettlement policy as well as establish orthodox low-cost housing to spring into existence.

The Hong Kong government soon introduced a new policy, since large areas were redeveloped into what were known as resettlement areas. Initially they consisted of one-storey structures that were far from being adequate. Their policy was completely altered and converted into erecting multi-storied buildings as established in the Tai Hang Tung Resettlement Area of Kowloon. All new structures were for some time a uniform seven stories high. Each new building was exactly the same height, shaped in the form of a capital H. The buildings were constructed parallel to each other accommodating 2,500 people per building. Each tiny suite within the building measured approximately 10 feet by 12 feet. Washroom facilities were communally shared in the bar portion of the H. Hundreds of thousands of people were forced to live under such crowded, congested circumstances. The ground floor of the structures consisted of tiny shops operated by individual residents, serving a few of the many needs of the people living in the buildings. Numerous volunteer agencies helped transform the rooftops of the H-style buildings into a.m. and p.m. kindergartens or primary schools. They were established by the churches, y.w.c.a. and countless other volunteer agencies. Gradually they were transformed into educational, social or recreational centres for the masses.

At the time the only water supply provided for the public consisted of standpipes located in the resettlement areas. The people would line up to obtain their drinking water. Long dragon-like lines were formed, often fights and disagreements frequently broke out between the various residents as they stood in line for their daily supply of water.

There were no lifts or elevators whatsoever in any of the early buildings. All residents were required to ascend the stairways to their home. The buildings were constructed of concrete, a vast improvement over the former illegal wooden structures. The structures being solid and firm, a tremendous improvement over the squatter huts where they formerly lived.

Employment was a further major problem facing the residents. Since Hong Kong has no raw materials whatsoever of its own, all raw materials were imported from China, Asia or other countries. Among the first locally produced products to appear in Hong Kong markets were plastic goods like toys and artifical flowers. The individual parts of the flowers like leaves, stems and flowers were produced in local factories, being assembled in the homes by children and elderly citizens. The finished products were exported throughout Asia and the entire world. The products were readily accepted wherever they were sold.

The next major industry developed in Hong Kong was textile products. Many of the developers had previously operated large factories in China where they developed their skills and products. The developers transferred their knowledge and skills to the Tsuen Wan and Kwun Tong industrial areas and other locations. Before long they were producing everything from transitor radios and other electronic products. Skilled labourers were trained in all fields exporting the goods around the world. Before long Hong Kong was accused of exploiting cheap labour, however, they perfected and developed their skills sufficiently well to overcome those accusations. Today Hong Kong's factories are among the most modern up-to-date factories in the world. The shortage of water was a further urgent and major problem in Hong Kong. When I first arrived in Hong Kong in 1955, water rationing was an accepted fact of life and already in effect, however, as the population increased especially during the initial stages of the Cultural Revolution the shortage of water became an even more critical problem. Hong Kong has no natural source of water except the rainfall. They depended entirely upon the rainy season, they stored water in large reservoirs or dams, however, it was far from sufficient. For a short period of time they imported drinking water from China by utilizing huge tankers, before long they built a large pipe line into Hong Kong from China's east river situated in Kwangtung Province.

One year because of the severe drought conditions in southern China, Hong Kong became exceedingly short of water, and on account of political reasons China cut off Hong Kong's water supply resulting in an even graver crisis.

The worst scenario I personally recall was the time when water was rationed to four hours of water once every four days. During that period the family I lived with stored water in their bathtub and large barrels. They conserved every available drop of water; the water was recycled for cleaning purposes around the apartment to wash the floors etc. However in the resettlement areas the residents were required to line up to obtain their precious water supply. They carried water in huge buckets. It's nearly impossible for many Canadians, especially British Columbians, to visualize such a shortage of water. However, it was a reality and fact, we had to live with in Hong Kong. Hong Kong is extremely hot and humid during the summer, which caused a genuine hardship and inconvenience for Hong Kong's residents. Nowadays (1999) since Hong Kong is part of the People's Republic of China, they have a more direct access to China's water supply than previously when Hong Kong was a British colony.

Likewise education became a critical problem for Hong Kong. Education is considered a vital and essential requirement for all people, but due to the tremendous influx of refugees it was realized a solution had to be immediately provided. The Hong Kong government sought assistance from the various religious and voluntary agencies to help provide education. As a result many kindergartens and primary schools were established on the rooftops of the resettlement buildings as a temporary stopgap measure, before long generous government grants encouraged religious organizations to construct primary and middle schools, such as True Light and Pui Ying Middle Schools, Ying Wah Boys' and Girls' Colleges, Wah Yan College, the Y.W.C.A. and Y.M.C.A. etc.

Before long primary school education was declared a requirement by the Hong Kong government. Eventually middle school education was included as an essential service. The Chinese people consider education as a complete necessity; you needn't convince them concerning the necessity of an education. The above situation and conditions were all adversely affected by China's Cultural Revolution.

"Silent Witness," the story of Che Kam Kong, the first Protestant martyr in China.

CHAPTER 13

A Silent Witness

THE INSPIRING AND DRAMATIC story of Che Kam Kong, the first Protestant martyr in China. This exciting dramatic presentation was written and presented by the Hong Kong delegation to the Second Asian Church Women's Conference at Petburi, Thailand, November 1962. It was presented as Hong Kong's contribution at the evening worship series on the theme "Christ's Faithful Fishermen." In this series each national delegation shared the story of the life of a man or woman from its church's history that had been a source of inspiration to its church. (Published by the Women's Department of the Hong Kong Council of the Church of Christ in China.)

THE SETTING

In front of the Great East Gate of Poklo City, Kwangtung, China.

TIME

1856-1861

PARTICIPANTS

Narrator
Che Kam Kong
Village elders
Che Family elders
The speech choir
Voice

THE SILENT WITNESST . . . THE UMBRELLA WHICH SPOKE.
Che Kam Kong, the First Protestant Martyr in China

SCENE 1: THE GLAD GOOD NEWS TO POKLO

Narrator:

Before returning to his father, the risen Christ called his disciples together and commissioned them to go into all the world and preach the gospel to the whole creation. He said to them: "You shall receive power when the Holy Spirit has come upon you, and you shall be my witnesses in Jerusalem and in all Judea and Samaria and to the end of the earth." (Acts 1:8)

Down through the centuries, in every land, Christ has called his chosen servants sending them out with the glad good news of the gospel. Just one hundred years ago he called Che Kam Kong giving him the same commission, saying,

Voice:

Che Kam Kong, you shall receive power when the Holy Spirit has come upon you, and you shall be my witness both in your native town of Poklo and in all the eastern district of Kwangtung and also in Hong Kong and to the generations who will follow you.

Narrator:

Christ did not call Che Kam Kong to any easy witness, to an easy success. His joyful vigorous witness cost him his life.

It was the year 1856 and in a small city in eastern Kwangtung province, Che Kam Kong was preparing for a trip to Hong Kong. Most of his journey would be made by boat. His friends and relatives were gathered around him, warning him to be very careful in the big wicked city of Hong Kong. Many strange things could happen to a person there. They especially warned him against the queer looking people from the West whom he would see. Yes, indeed, a simple country man from Poklo must be very careful when he reached that foreign Chinese city.

Village elders: Kam Kong, big brother, be careful in the strange city. It is full of danger. When you return bring us reports of all the strange people and things you see there.

Che Kam Kong: Honorable big brothers, I shall take your good advice and shall be most careful.

Village elders: Beware of the strange foreigners and their strange ways. Beware of the danger that awaits you in Hong Kong.

Narrator: Che Kam Kong arrived safely in Hong Kong with his fellow townsmen who had come to the big city with him. His eager inquiring mind led him into many new and interesting experiences. He walked about the streets and along the sea wall where he saw the ships tied up along the wharf. He had learned that they had come from far away places called England and America. He learned that some of them had taken ninety days to reach Hong Kong. He looked with interest at the many boats from Canton, which were anchored along the shore.

He visited the shops and looked at the curious things which the ships had brought from across the ocean. He saw the huge men with big eyes and big noses. Hong Kong was full of new things to see and hear.

One day he met a man who told him that one of the foreigners was standing at a nearby street corner speaking to the crowd in the Chinese language. This was most unheard of! This was truly most unusual and Che Kam Kong and his companion went to see if it were really true.

Indeed it was true. Che Kam Kong and his companions lingered on the outskirts of the crowd. They watched the speaker and listened to what he was saying.

Voice: For God so loved the world that he gave his only begotten son, that whosoever believeth in him should not perish but have everlasting life.

Narrator: The others drifted away from the listening crowd, but Che Kam Kong remained. He wanted to hear more about this God who loved men. During his stay in Hong Kong he returned often to the place where the missionary from London was preaching. Before he was ready to leave Hong Kong, Che Kam Kong heard Christ speak to him.

Voice: Che Kam Kong, come follow me.

Che Kam Kong: Master, I will follow thee.

Narrator: The time soon came when the men from Poklo had to return to their homes. They were met by friends and relatives who helped them carry all their packages and boxes. The happy excited crowd hurried back to the city and soon disappeared through the great wide-open gate. Only Che Kam Kong lingered behind.

(*Pantomime:* Che Kam Kong walks back and forth, slowly in front of the gate and wall).

Walking slowly along the path leading to the gate, he took a little package from his pocket. Carefully he pulled out the separate pages and looked at them. They were tracts telling of Jesus. They were printed papers telling that God who made all men, loved all men everywhere.

Che Kam Kong knew what he was going to do. He would give these precious papers to his family, to his friends. These papers with their wonderful, good news were the best gift which he had brought home with him from Hong Kong.

(*Music:* chorus of "O Zion Haste," music only.)

Quiet meditation

SCENE II: A WITNESS WHICH CANNOT BE SILENCED

Narrator: A year passed very quickly and the men from Poklo were going back to Hong Kong for another visit. Che Kam Kong was in the boat and with him was a man with whom he had shared the good news of Jesus. This man asked many questions and after hearing all that his friend could tell him had decided to become one of Christ's followers. He believed and had come with Che Kam Kong to be baptized by the London missionary.

The following year, Mr. Che made the journey to Hong Kong again and this time there were two more believers with him. The next year he made a fourth trip to Hong Kong and two other men came with him to be baptized as followers of Christ. By 1860 he had won nine more persons to faith in Jesus Christ. Since the time of his own conversion he had won a total of fourteen people who had become members of Christ's family.

The Christian pastor in Hong Kong was amazed at the result of Mr. Che's witness. Fourteen persons had taken their stand for Christ in Poklo. He knew that God was working through Mr. Che and for his zeal in telling others what Christ meant to him.

In Poklo Che Kam Kong gathered his friends and neighbours into his house and told them about Jesus Christ and the joy which came to a man when he gave his heart to Christ. Forty persons made the decision to worship God and to follow Christ. They asked their neighbour preacher to arrange for them to be baptized. Mr. Che then wrote to Hong Kong and invited the missionary pastor to visit Poklo. It was with great anticipation that the pastor went to Poklo. When he arrived there, he found forty people ready for baptism. It was truly a day of great rejoicing.

Voice: In January 1861 sixteen more men from Poklo City went to Hong Kong so they could be baptized. They joined the Christian church and then returned to their homes to help Mr. Che spread the good news.

The little Christian community in Poklo wanted to establish a Christian church in their own city. They felt they were ready for it. They needed their own church. After discussing the matter and after earnest prayer they invited the English missionaries to visit their town and help them to organize a Christian church. In May 1861 two Hong Kong ministers arrived, not only was a new church established. Forty more converts who were ready to be baptized.

Narrator: God's spirit was working mightily through his faithful servant Che Kam Kong. Within four years, he had won over one hundred of his fellow-citizens to faith in Christ. This was no small matter and the elders of Poklo city were becoming alarmed. So many people were becoming Christians that they were afraid their own Chinese gods might be neglected. They were afraid that the foreign religion would win so many followers that the local gods would be angered and that disaster would fall upon everyone. They felt the only way to stop the new religion was to silence Che Kam Kong.

The elders of Poklo called Che Kam Kong before them and instructed him that he must not preach this foreign doctrine anymore.

Village elders: Che Kam Kong, you must not preach this foreign doctrine any more. We command you to stop this preaching. You will bring disaster upon our city.

Narrator: This threat did not frighten Mr. Che. He kept on preaching and winning converts. Finally the city fathers called his relatives and commanded them to deal with Mr. Che.

Village elders: Brothers of the Che clan, hear us. Your little brother is preaching a strange doctrine in our city. Our Chinese gods are angry. We shall hold the Che clan responsible for putting an end to Che Kam Kong's disobedience to our commands.

Narrator: The Che clan called a family council and of course Mr. Che Kam Kong was included.

Che family elders: Che Kam Kong, the fathers of Poklo City have made us responsible for you. You must stop preaching. You must also stop giving out the Christian tracts. Do you hear us? We must be obeyed.

Che Kam Kong: Honourable elders of the Che family, your little brother hears you.

Narrator: Che Kam Kong's voice was silenced, but he still sought ways of sharing the gospel with his fellow townspeople. He bought a huge blue cotton cloth umbrella and on it printed a verse from the bible in large white characters. He chose the words of Jesus as given in Mark 1:14 "The kingdom of God is at hand. Repent and believe the Gospel, and be baptized."

Che Kam Kong was a brave man. He loved Jesus Christ with a love that was strong and deep. He believed that all men needed Christ. He believed that the gospel was for all men.

(*Pantomime:* Che Kam Kong walks slowly along the city wall carrying his blue umbrella with its life-giving message.)

Quiet music (but no speaking): one verse, "Must Jesus bear the cross alone?"

SCENE III: FAITHFUL TO THE END

Narrator: The Che clan was not satisfied with Mr. Che's method of obeying their command. They threatened him. They also said he was crazy.

Che family elders: Che Kam Kong, we are displeased with you. You have not really obeyed our commands. You must stop carrying that ugly umbrella. You bring disgrace upon your family. Do you hear us?

Che Kam Kong: My elder brothers, I listen to you. However, I would respectfully tell you also to repent and to believe in Jesus Christ.

Che family elders: Silence! You disrespectful man. You dishonour our family. You bring disgrace on our clan.

Narrator: many times the family warned him but as he would not listen nor obey them, they came to hate him. They again warned him to stop.

Che family elders: Che Kam Kong, you bring disgrace upon our family. We warn you once more. You must stop. If you refuse, we shall drive you from Poklo. If you continue to preach, you shall die! This foreign religion is not good for China. It is not Chinese and might destroy our gods.

Che Kam Kong: O esteemed elders of our most honoured family hear me. Jesus loves you. Give up your false worship. Repent and believe.

Che family elders: Silence, silence, begone, o disobedient one!

Narrator: In the end the family employed some ruffians to kidnap Che Kam Kong. They took him to a house in a tiny village called Bamboo Gardens. This was located just outside the west gate of Poklo City. For two days they tortured him. For two days they insulted him. They hung him by his hands and feet from the roof beams of the house.

Che family elders: "Give up this Jesus Christ. Say that you do not believe in him any more and we will set you free. Stop your crazy preaching and all will be well with you."

Che Kam Kong: I cannot deny my Lord ; I believe in Him. Help me, O God.

Narrator: At length they took him outside the city gate to a high bank above the east river. Here they gave him one last chance to save his life.

Ruffians: Deny this Jesus. Say you do not believe in him.

Che Kam Kong: You may kill my body, but you cannot destroy my soul.

Narrator: In great anger they killed Che Kam Kong. They cut up his body in pieces and threw them down into the river below. Che Kam Kong had fought a good fight. He had finished the course.

(*Pantomime:* No acting. Throw spotlight on the great gate as a solo voice sings.)

A noble army, men and boys,
The matron and the maid,
Around the saviour's throne rejoice,
His robes in light arrayed:
They climbed the steep ascent of heaven
Through peril, toil and pain;

O God, to us may grace be given
To follow in their train.
(*Tune:* The Son of God Goes Forth to War)

The above account is the true story of a great and brave man, Che Kam Kong, who was willing to sacrifice his life for what he believed. He left us with an example that will remain for all time and until eternity. May his life truly inspire us to serve the Lord our God with heart, mind and soul in our day and generation.

The story of Che Kam Kong is one of the most significant illustrations of what it means to be a genuine follower of Christ as our Lord and Saviour. May we follow Che Kam Kong's fine example and serve him with heart, mind and soul.

A copy of the Nestorian Tablet in Kowloon Hop Yat Church.

CHAPTER 14

China's Nestorian Heritage

UPON THE OCCASION of the celebration of the 10th anniversary of Kowloon Hop Yat Church, Hong Kong, in November 1967, a replica of the Nestorian Tablet was unveiled. It was reproduced and located just inside the entrance of the church. It's a copy of the original tablet in the Chinese and Syrian languages discovered in China just before the beginning of the 20th century (1890s). The tablet traces the fascinating history of the first Christian contact with China. The initial contact of Christianity with China originated through the Nestorian Church. The Nestorian Church flourished in China within two distinct periods; the first entry in China came during the T'ang Dynasty (618–906 A.D.), while the second entry of Christianity in China appeared again between (1280–1368 A.D.) near the end of the Yuan Dynasty in 1368 A.D.. Nestorianism seemed to disappear within China, however it left behind certain evidences of its presence. The evidence was a number of bronze crosses somewhat similar in pattern to a Maltese Cross, used for many centuries, which was adopted by the leprosarium of Hay Ling Chau in Hong Kong, as may be found in the 1963 annual report. Years later Nestorian crosses were discovered in northern China (during the 1890s).

One of the ministers of the Hop Yat Church in Kowloon prepared and published a brief account in the form of a pamphlet. Rev. David Lew minister of Kowloon Hop Yat Church indicated in his introduction, "We feel it is meaningful due to its historical and educational value to the indigenous church movement and in evangelism."

The Nestorian tablet was discovered at Hsianfu, Sian province in 1625 A.D. i.e. in the fifth year of Tien Chi during the Ming Dynasty. The original tablet was made of granite, about 9 feet high, 3 feet wide and one foot thick, erected on the 4th of February in the year of 781 A.D. It was chiseled in stone by a Christian called Zazbozed, the inscription was written by Ching Ching, a priest from Persia, the calligraphy was the work of Lui Hsin Yen.

The title of the tablet in Chinese script stated, "Tablet of the spread of Ta Ch'in Ching religion to China" consists of 9 large Chinese characters, located on the top of the tablet, "ta ch'in" meaning "eastern Roman empire" and "Ching" religion "illustrious religion." The entire term actually denotes "a branch of Christianity with Nestorian origin" or "the Nestorian Church in Syria and Persia."

The founder of the Nestorian Church, Nestorius, was a native of Syria Euphratensis, who entered a monastery at Antioch where he later became its abbot, and then in 428 A.D. he became the patriarch of Constantinople. A violent controversy ensued when he opposed calling the Virgin Mary "Mother of God." This idea represented extreme Antiochene Christology, which separated the two natures of Christ. In 431 A.D. he was condemned by the council of Ephesus in 436 A.D. He was banished to Upper Egypt where he died several years later. (The doctrine is no longer considered heretical today!) His followers, known as Chaldean or Assyrian Christians, moved and developed their work in east Syria and Persia. From the later 5th century several of the Persian kings supported them then it spread from Edessa eventually to China.

(*A History of the Expansion of Christianity (volume 2), The Thousand Years of Uncertainty* by Kenneth Scott Latourette. Chapter 5: The Spread of Christianity to the East of the Byzantine Empire, Especially Through the Jacobites and the Nestorians, to the Mongol Conquest. The Persian Empire; Arabia; Central Asia; China; India, page 263.)

Alopen, the first Nestorian missionary to China, arrived in 635 A.D. and was welcomed by the emperor Tai Tsung (627–650) A.D. He was granted a temple to house 21 priests. Several more temples were built afterwards. In 725 A.D. the patriarch of Baghdad sent someone to be the archbishop of China. It is believed there were no fewer than six bishops in China at that time. In 845 A.D. there came a persecution and all Nestorian activities were suppressed but we still may trace their history down to the date of the collapse of the Yuan Dynasty in 1368 A.D.

The inscription upon the tablet, largely in Chinese contains the following:

(1) A statement of Christian doctrine and sacraments: the Trinity; God, the creator of heaven and earth; the fall of Satan; the coming of the Messiah who fulfilled the prophesy of the 24 prophets of the Old Testament and after his ascension left 27 volumes of the Bible; the Holy Spirit which cleanses by water, and Holy Communion which should be taken every seven days.

(2) A description of the first arrival of Christianity in 635 A.D. by a Hsianfu missionary from Ta Ch'in named Alopen and of the imperial privileges which he was granted. After relating how Alopen became a lord guardian of the great law of the empire, there follows an account of the fortune of the church from the reign of Tai Tsung (627–650) down to the reign of Teh Tsung (780–783).

(3) An epitome of (2) in octosyllabic verse; and

(4) A series of short additions in the Estrangelo character.

This tablet is the most significant witness extant to the growth of Christianity in China before the 13th century. In 1907 a replica of the tablet was made by a Danish traveller, Fritz Holm, who deposited a copy in 1908 within the Metropolitan Museum of Art, New York. Later the Japanese obtained another one, which is now displayed in the Exhibition Hall, Kyoto University, Japan.

In his book called *Forward Through the Ages*, Basil Mathews, a former professor of church history at Union College of British Columbia (now known as Vancouver School of Theology) provided the following interesting information about the early Nestorian Church. His is a most informative and reliable article regarding the history of the early Nestorian Church. It happened Professor Mathews was a professor of mine at Union College when I studied theology in Vancouver, B.C.. The University of Hong Kong has a most fascinating collection of Nestorian crosses worth seeing located in the Fung Ping Shan Library in Hong Kong.

Professor Mathews indicated "the story of the outreach of the famous Nestorian Church. In Baghdad the fabulous city of the Arabian Nights, amidst the softly flowing Tigris River, a new Christian church grew up from the fifth century onward. The language of its worship was neither Greek nor Latin, but Syriac, the native tongue of its founder. Nestor, an Antioch monk had been patriarch of Constantinople early in the fifth century. Constantly in his spellbinding sermons in Saint Sophia (Turkey) he insisted upon the quite separate natures of Jesus, the son of man, and Christ, the Son of God. Condemned for heresy in 431 (A.D.) by the council of Ephesus, he was driven into exile in egypt. But his doctrine, carried by missionary disciples and manuscript copies of his sermons, spread widely went down the Euphrates River from Antioch to Edessa to Baghdad, that became the world headquarters of the Nestorian Church and the city where its patriarchs lived."

From Selucia-Ctesiphon, near the present site of Baghdad, merchant caravans wound their way along trade routes that climbed through cities of central Asia, along the "Golden Road to Samarkand" and over the "Roof of the World to China" with these Christian Nestorian merchants travelled missionaries.

Hundreds of burial stones of Christians have been found in what was obviously a flourishing Nestorian community south of Lake Balkash in Chinese Turkestan. In Syria, Mesopotamia and Khurasan: south of the Oxus River they were a majority of the population up to the beginning of the thirteenth century.

The most daring and romantic of all these Nestorian venturers was a bishop whose original name nobody knows. He and a young monk started eastward from their home on the plateau of Persia. Tarrying in Khotan to learn something of the Chinese language from a trader, they started again eastward and at long last, were received in the gorgeous palace of T'ai Tsung, the emperor of China, in the year 635 A.D. when Aidan left for Northumberland. So impressed were the Chinese that they gave the bishop the superb name, Alopen, which means, "the man who was sent by God."

"Build a monastery for these men and for twenty-one monks at my expense," said the emperor, "and let them preach their way, wherever they wish in China."

Alopen never returned to Persia, and we should know nothing about him had not a wonderful black stone tablet been discovered in 1625 A.D. on which the whole story was recorded. Engraved in the year 781 A.D. in Chinese characters, the tablet says that the Christian monasteries were built in different parts of China and that a Christian literature had developed. (Note the photograph at the beginning of this chapter.) Cut off from other Christians by the immense distances and forbidding mountain plateaus and deserts, the Nestorian Church in China went into eclipse when a hostile Chinese emperor in 845 A.D. issued an anti-Christian edict.

Other adventurous Nestorians plunged through the Khyber Pass, into north India and sailed down from the Persian Gulf to south India. "There is a Church of Christians in the land called Malabar where the pepper grows," wrote an Alexandrian Christian traveller, Cosmas, from India in the sixth century A.D.. In Kallian he went on, "There is a bishop . . . and ministers from Persia . . . among the rest of the Indians . . . . There is an infinite number of Christians with bishops." The Thomas Christians (Mar Thoma) the Christian community popularily believed to have been founded by the apostle Thomas: from time to time received bishops from the Nestorian patriarch in Baghdad.

Eclipse is not extinction. The light of the Nestorian Church begins to glimmer again in China. The most mighty emperor, as he proclaimed himself in 1206 A.D., Genghis Khan, although a pagan Mongol, married his son to a Nestorian Christian princess of the Mongol Keraits in Western Asia. Their son more famous in history and poetry than even his grandfather, was Kublai Khan (reigned 1260–94 A.D.) who subdued the whole of China. He encouraged Christians from his palace in Peking (then Cambaluc), and we hear of large groups of Nestorians in China, such as the Ongots, north of the Yellow River, most of whom were Christians."

Forward Through the Ages, a publication prepared by Basil Mathews. New York: Friendship Press, Inc., 1951. (64–66)

師 牧 遜 禮 馬

DR. ROBERT MORRISON, FIRST PROTESTANT MISSIONARY TO CHINA.
150TH ANNIVERSARY (1807-1957) OF HIS ARRIVAL IN CHINA

CHAPTER 15

The Flame of Faith

The 150th anniversary celebration of Dr. Robert Morrison's arrival in China. The following was an important lecture presented by Dr. S. C. Leung, chairman of the Hong Kong council of the Church of Christ held in China in "chi to church" Macao (Macau), September 2nd 1957. He stated the following:

We have assembled here to commemorate the 150th anniversary of the arrival in China of the Rev. Dr. Robert Morrison. As he was the first Protestant missionary to China, the date of his arrival at Canton marked the beginning of Protestant Christianity in the country which we all love, China.

Perhaps it will not be inappropriate on this occasion to give a biographical sketch of this great missionary. He was born in Northumberland, England in 1782. His father was an elder in a Presbyterian church, and young Morrison was very religious. He soon became interested in the missionary cause and started to prepare himself for this divine vocation more or less against his father's wishes. He applied to the London Missionary Society for service abroad in 1804, and was later appointed to China. When he was ready to take the journey, he came into his first difficulty. The East India Company which had the monopoly of trade in India and the east, refused to give him passage. This, however, did not deter him from his objective. He made the journey by way of America. Sailing from England on a sailing ship on January 31, 1807, he set his face towards China. Delayed by a gale and overtaken by another on the Atlantic, his voyage to America had taken 109 days, when air travel between London and New York is only an overnight trip now.

Morrison succeeded in securing passage on an American ship for Canton. He was also armed with a letter from the Secretary of State to the American consul in Canton which proved to be very useful when he got there. The voyage from New York had taken him four months. He first set foot on Chinese soil on September 7, 1807.

Morrison was up against an almost impossible situation when he got to Canton. There were three obstacles which seemed insurmountable. (1) The Chinese were prohibited from teaching the Chinese language to foreigners under the penalty of death. (2) The East India Company forbad any person to stay at Canton except on account of trade. (3) Not only was it impossible for Morrison to live in Canton, but residence in Macao was equally difficult owing to the jealousy of the Catholic Bishop and priests of the time. In spite of all these difficulties, Morrison was determined to stick to the mission for which he had come. Having put his hand to the plough, he would not look back.

However, finding a place to stay, the expense of having to keep three servants, the demand of his teachers for high salaries, the suspicion and unfriendly attitude of the people towards him, and the trying weather conditions had all combined to give Morrison much anxiety and impair his health. During the early days he had practically hidden himself in a secluded spot and had set to work in real earnest on the language which he was soon able to master. At first he tried to live like a Chinese, eating Chinese food, putting on Chinese clothes, and even wearing a queue and letting his fingernails grow. In spite of his good intentions, however, he became more conspicuous and aroused greater suspicion, so was compelled to go back to his European clothes.

After eight months stay in Canton, he found it necessary to move to Macao for health reasons. Having greatly improved in health after three months rest, Morrison returned to Canton only to find it a gloomy situation which led to the withdrawal of all British residents to Macao until a settlement had been reached by governments. It looked as if he had better retire to Penang (Malaya) in view of the seeming impossibility to gain a permanent foothold on Chinese soil, but just at the time two encouraging developments took place. (1) He met and married Mary Morton at Macao. (2) He was appointed translator to the East India Company. The first event gave him much encouragement and strength for he now had a life companion with whom he could share intimately his thoughts, plans, joys and difficulties. The second event gave him a legal status whereby he could live in Canton without question. From this time on, Morrison had a double role to play—translator to a British firm and missionary to China. Two major tasks were before him, namely, the compilation of an Anglo-Chinese dictionary and the translation of the Bible into Chinese. In spite of his heavy work in the English factory, he would not allow it to divert all his attention from Bible translation, although to continue this most important duty he had to work far into the night. Neither would he let any opportunity pass without giving religious instruction to his Chinese helpers.

When Morrison celebrated his 30th birthday his heart was gladdened as his Chinese printer brought the first copy of his translation of the Book of Acts. The appearance of this book in Chinese and the story of Morrison's struggle and triumph created a sensation in Great Britain and Ireland, as a result of which a wave of missionary enthusiasm swept over the churches there. The appointment of a new missionary to strengthen the hands of the lonely pioneer was announced at this time.

In the meantime, a Chinese Imperial Edict was issued against the propagation of the foreigners' religion. Thus declared the edict:

"From this time forward such Europeans as shall privately print books to establish preachers, and the Tartars and Chinese who, deputed by Europeans, shall propagate their religion—the chief or principal ones shall be executed. Whoever shall spread their religion shall be imprisoned, wait the time of execution: and those who shall content themselves with following such religion shall be exiled."

In sending a translation of this edict to the London Missionary Society, Morrison added:

"I must, however, go forward trusting in the Lord. We will scrupulously obey governments a far as their decrees do not oppose what is required by the Almighty."

Thenceforth his missionary activities had to be carried on with greater secrecy than ever. Fortunately his Chinese helpers had already caught something of his spirit and stuck to their task at the risk of their lives.

In 1813 the new missionary, Rev. William Milne and his wife arrived at Macao. By this time the Portuguese authorities were ordered by the Chinese government to enforce a law against foreigners landing at Macao unless they were connected with the European factories. All efforts at securing permission for the Milnes to stay on failed. Although Milne was able to spend two months on language in Canton, it became clear it was not advisable for him to remain in Canton or Macao. At this juncture appeared the First Printed copy of the New Testament in Chinese which was the result of Morrison's work. So it was decided that Milne should go on a missionary journey to Java, Malacca and Penang for the dual purpose of distributing the New Testament in the Chinese archipelago, and exploring the possibilities of establishing a new mission headquarters and a Bible-printing headquarters and a Bible-printing depot.

After Milnes's departure for the South Seas, another blow hit Morrison. It was a message from Peking ordering a search to be made for any Chinese professing the Christian religion. Able Yun, one of Morrison's most valuable assistants had a narrow escape. This strengthened Morrison's conviction that a new mission headquarters should be established in a place where it would be beyond the reach of such relentless opposition.

At this time God gave Morrison his first convert. In 1814 Tsae A-Ko (Choi A-Ko), one of his Chinese helpers, decided to become a Christian and asked to be baptized. This was the first fruit of his seven years labour in China. He took Tsao A-Ko to a quiet spot at the foot of a high cliff where there was a stream of pure clear water emptying itself into the sea. There Morrison baptized Tsao A-Ko in the name of the Father, Son and the Holy Spirit. It should be remembered that in memory of this first Chinese Christian, a secondary school was established by the "chi to church" in Macao some years ago. This institution continues to serve as a useful means of witnessing to Christ.

When Milne returned to Morrison after five months, he brought back a rather encouraging report. The plan for what became known as Ultra-Ganges Mission was set up by the two missionaries, and later approved by the London Missionary Society. The programme of the mission included the following: (1) a Chinese free school; (2) a monthly magazine in Chinese; (3) an undenominational mission for work in China, Malay and farther India; (4) printing work in Chinese,

Malay and English; (5) a Missionary Journal for combined missionary work; (6) religious services for the Chinese colonies. From this point on, these two missionaries began to operate from two bases—Canton and Malacca. New financial support was forthcoming.

In 1815 Morrison was dismissed by the East India Company by order of its London office. This move was prompted by fears on the part of the company that the appearance of the New Testament might cause serious consequences to British trade in China. However, his dismissal did not actually take place for his service to the company was found to be indispensable.

Steady progress was being made during the next few years. The first volume of the Anglo-Chinese dictionary came out in print in 1817 and its third volume was finished in 1821. This dictionary was the result of Morrison's laborious work and proved to be his monumental achievement. In 1816 the Anglo-Chinese College was started in Malacca by Milne. In 1819 the translation of the entire Bible was completed. In the same year a dispensary was opened in the suburbs of Canton.

1821-1822 were years of trial for Morrison. His beloved wife Mary died of cholera in Macao, William Milne, his right hand man, broke down in health and passed away in Malacca. The Canton suburbs and the English factory with which Morrison was connected were in flames and destroyed.

In 1824 he took his first furlough in seventeen years. It was possible for him to leave with ease of mind at this time, for his old teacher Leang Afa, who was Milne's first convert at Malacca, had now returned to Canton. Morrison ordained him as the first Chinese evangelist to whom he entrusted the responsibility for conducting worship for the handful of Chinese Christians and enquirers during his absence. Upon his return to England he received a very warm welcome. He also had married again while at home. In April 1826 he and his wife sailed together for the east, and he resumed work immediately at Canton.

The year 1832 marked the 25th Anniversary of Morrison's residence in China. In retrospect, he made the following statement in writing to the London Missionary Society:

"There is now in Canton a state of society in respect to Chinese totally different from what I found in 1807. Chinese scholars, missionary students, English presses and Chinese scriptures with the public worship of God, have all grown up since that period. I have served my generation and must—the lord knows when I will fall asleep. I feel old age coming upon me."

Two years later Morrison's health gave away. He passed away at Canton on August 1, 1834, and was buried in Macao (the old Protestant cemetery). What St. Paul said of himself was equally true with Morrison. "I have fought a good fight. I have finished the race. I have kept the faith."

This brief resumé of Morrison's life and work reveals three qualities of the great missonary's character. First he proved to be a remarkable pioneer. He pioneered in the missionary enterprise in a strange and far off country where he was not only unknown, but also unwelcome. He pioneered in the compliation of an Anglo-Chinese Dictionary which served as a useful means for interchange of Chinese and Western cultures. He pioneered in the translation of the Bible into Chinese through which the word of God was made available to China's millions. He pioneered in the creation of a small Christian community which became the seed of an indigenous church in China.

Morrison was an unconquerable soul. Think of the difficulties he met, the obstacles he encountered, and the hardships he went through. But he refused to be defeated. When one door closed, he knocked at another, and never gave up. He believed that with God nothing was impossible. He may be likened to the man who made the following declaration:

"my right hand is broken;
my left hand is shattered;
my centre is in retreat;
the situation is excellent;
i shall attack."

Thirdly Morrison had exemplified a dedicated life. He never sought comfort, wealth, position or fame. All these years he had to leave his family at Macao while he worked in Canton except when the trading season was over. He even neglected his own health at times. His one dominating desire was to serve God and to share the gospel of love and salvation with the Chinese people who he loved.

God was therefore able to use him as an effective instrument for the extension of his kingdom among men.

Let us take a look at a later picture of Protestant Christianity which Morrison brought to China. What a glorious history it has had under God. The establishment of the indigenous church, the training of the ministry, the development of the laity, the building of hospitals and clinics, the founding of Christian colleges and schools of all grades, the spreading of the gospel through the printed page, and the organization of the Young Men's and the Young Women's Christian Associations, were among the outstanding of the total Christian programme. Christian influence upon Chinese society became so noticeable that it was altogether out of proportion to the number of Chinese Christians in the land. The foundation for all this was well and truly laid by the pioneering missionary and others who followed him.

That the young Chinese church was able to stand a severe test of faith during the Boxer Uprising in 1900 was clear evidence of the strong spiritual basis which Morrison and the early missionaries had planted the ecclesia or Christian church in China. At that time not only were missionaries persecuted, but there was a large number of Chinese Christians who refused to repudiate their faith and met martyrdom courageously.

Even now when the mainland of China has come under a totalitarian and atheistic regime, God has not left himself without witness, I am sure. The same Lord who did mighty works through his faithful servant some 150 years ago, is still moving among his own people. Jesus Christ is the same yesterday, and today, and forever. Let us dedicate ourselves to the unfinished task of the church in China which Morrison and others had so well begun. Let us move forward in the name of our lord and win China and her people for Christ.

Footnote: Dr. Leung Siu Choh, the author of the foregoing lecture held in Macao September 2, 1952 by the Church of Christ in China, Hong Kong Council, was also one of the most faithful Christian leaders who helped witness unto the Christian gospel during the early days of hardship and trial when the present regime took over China. He never faltered or failed the test of time. He courageously witnessed unto his faith. Dr. S. W. Leung later became the General

Secretary of the Young Men's Christian Association for the whole of China. It was my privilege to have known him and his family who were faithful Christians both in China and Hong Kong. Words are inadequate to explain my personal thanks to Dr. S. C. Leung and his devoted family, staunch and faithful Christians to this day. May the Lord continue to bless them as living witnesses by adopting the faith of their fathers firmly rooted and planted in the hearts of the Chinese people to this day.

CHAPTER 16

Amusing Incidents

(1) COCKROACH ENCOUNTER

My first residence in Hong Kong was at the familiar and well-known Church Guest House, located on Upper Albert Road, originally built to accommodate missionaries and other foreign guests travelling back and forth in and out of China to Hong Kong. I was one of the guests who lived there for about three months until I found another suitable location. Like many older style buildings in Hong Kong, the building had become infested with cockroaches, in fact, the largest cockroaches I have ever seen in my life. They were extremely prolific. The cockroaches would eat the starch from the covers of my books as they stood in the bookcase. In view of that I used to paint the covers of the books with varnish or a clear lacquer for protection. Many of the books had hard covers; they all suffered defacement shortly after my arrival in Hong Kong. The cockroaches grew between one and two inches in length; they could fly and entered my bedroom if I left the window open.

One evening after going to bed I woke up to find a cockroach crawling on my pillow, while another time I felt a cockroach crawling across my head between my nose and upper lip. Fortunately my mouth wasn't open at the time or it may have fallen in.

(2) QUIET MEDITATION

Another time I was leisurely sitting on the toilet in the apartment where I used to live, reading a copy of Reader's Digest. As I sat there, suddenly I noticed a huge hairy spider emerge from the drain of the bathtub; it appeared to be about the size of my hand. Hurriedly I jumped up and took the Reader's Digest and chased the spider around in the bathtub, the Reader's Digest suddenly became a weapon in my hands.

(3) WEDDING CAKE DISASTER

Shortly following my arrival in Hong Kong, I was invited to a large marriage banquet held in a popular Chinese restaurant in Kowloon. Some 500 guests gathered for the joyful and happy occasion. Everything was beautifully decorated and arranged, however, the restaurant must have been short of a small table on which to place the wedding cake, evidentally someone had a bright idea and placed the cake on a card table. The restaurant staff were busily rushing here and there attending to last minute preparations, however, one of their staff accidentally touched the card table with his toe, causing the beautifully decorated cake to fall with a thud on the restaurant floor. The several-tiered wedding cake was lying on the floor only a few minutes before the banquet was about to commence. When the cake fell it caused the guests who witnessed the incident (including myself) to gasp in complete astonishment and horror. The waiters immediately scooped up the cake from the floor, later the cake was served to the wedding guests, it was indeed an embarrassing and unforgettable event one never seems to forget.

(4) INSUFFICIENT FUNDS

The Chinese University of Hong Kong was in the formative stage, I happened to be the church's representative on the first board of directors, therefore, many special meetings were held from time to time at the university. I vividly recall one hot muggy sultry summer day a missionary friend and I were attending a special meeting of the board, which lasted for the entire day at the university of Hong Kong. We had spent a long weary day working out details at the university; both of us were extremely tired. My friend invited me to go to her home for supper, however, I declined her kind invitation replying, "No thanks, we are both very weary and tired, let's go to Jimmy's Kitchen for supper," which was a popular American style restaurant in Hong Kong, but was a little expensive. Off we went to Jimmy's Kitchen; both of us decided to order delicious juicy steaks along with baked alaska (cooked ice-cream) for dessert to help pick up our wilted spirits. We were enjoying the tasty delicious supper, when suddenly I recalled I had changed my shirt in the morning accidentally leaving most of my money in the shirt pocket. How could I pay for such an expensive dinner? It happened before the days of credit cards. I explained the embarassing situation to my friend. She lived near the restaurant so replied, let's share the cost of the supper; if we don't have sufficient funds between the two of us, she suggested that I remain behind in the restaurant reading the newspaper, then she would return home to pick up enough money to help pay the bill.

We hesitatingly requested the bill, fortunately we had just sufficent funds between the two of us to just cover the cost of the meal, but not one cent extra to leave as tips for the waiters. We were extremely embarrassed, we paid our bill then left the restaurant without leaving any tips whatsoever, which the waiters always expected at that specific restaurant. I felt I couldn't return to the restaurant again for several months, due to the embarrassing situation that had occurred.

(5) A HUGE RAT

Since I was a minister, I was frequently invited to assist the church under varying circumstances and situations. One Sunday evening I was invited to preach and conduct the sacrament of Holy Communion in the So Uk Chuen Resettlement Estate, Kowloon. The service was held in the primary school auditorium, which belonged to the Church of Christ in China (H.K. Council), a recently established church. Since they didn't yet have a building of their own, they utilized the primary school auditorium for Sunday services.

After I completed my sermon I was about to commence the sacrament of Holy Communion, therefore, turned and began walking towards the altar, however, just as I was walking to the altar a huge rat around the size of a large cat crossed the auditorium stage in front of me. I was totally suprised and shocked to see such a monstrous rat; I had often sung the World War I song "Rats, Rats, Big as Alley Cats," without thinking of the actual meaning of the words as being a fact and genuinely true, for me it was only a amusing folk song. However, now I actually saw such a huge rat with my own two eyes, a rat big as an "alley cat," now it was a fact not a theory. The following day I reported the incident to the school authorities, who informed the pest control department of the city, which took the appropriate action.

(6) A RED FACE

A few years after living in Hong Kong I spent my vacation travelling to Singapore and Southeast Asia. I took the express train from Singapore to Bangkok Thailand. The train passed through Malacca, Kuala Lumpur, and Penang in Malaysia then on its way to Bangkok Thailand running parallel to the border of Burma. In order to receive an idea of how the ordinary citizen travelled, I decided to go third class on the train, since it was much cheaper, but the coaches were hot inside, therefore, all windows on the train were wide open. Seated in front of me were several local residents, who chewed betel nuts (Cantonese: *bun-long*) from a tropical palm tree as they chatted with each other. The betel nuts always resulted in the saliva turning a bright reddish colour in their mouths. Ordinarily they carried a tin can to spit the juice in; when the can was full, they dumped the contents out the open window of the train. The wind sometimes blew the reddish coloured juice back into the train, striking my face, until my face became a reddish colour. Chewing betel nuts also discolours the teeth, turning them a black colour. Betel nuts evidentally give the chewer a pleasant sensation somewhat similar to tobacco. My advice to all travellers if travelling by train, beware of the betel-nut chewers of Southeast Asia.

On the same journey the train on which I was riding accidentally hit and killed a farmer's water buffalo, causing the train to suddenly stop. The accident resulted in a long protracted argument between the farmer and the engineer of the train concerning the matter. It was an exceedingly serious situation, since the water buffalo of Asia is just as important as a tractor for a Canadian farmer. The situation finally resulted in the railway company promising to compensate the farmer for his water buffalo before the train was allowed to proceed on its journey.

(7) BIRD BUSINESS

One of our churches in Yuen Long in the New Territories of Hong Kong had recently been renovated. In order to help celebrate the happy occasion the church invited many friends to celebrate the joyous event; I was one of the invited guests. At the beginning, we all met in the newly renovated church for a thanksgiving worship service, held in the village style church. The birds flew freely in and out of the church, while others perched themselves high upon the rafters during the worship service.

While quietly sitting in the church, one of the birds bombed me from the rafter; its dropping landed straight on my head. The young people sitting behind me saw what happened and began to laugh. I turned around to investigate what they were laughing over; they informed me what had occurred so I too joined in their laughter, what else could I do? After all it was an amusing and unusual incident happening in the village church; we all enjoyed a hearty laugh together.

(8) BED BUG PRECAUTION

During my first missionary term (5 years) in Hong Kong I was appointed the youth worker for the Church of Christ in China (Hong Kong Council). One weekend I was invited to speak to the youth group in Tai-o a fishing village located on the western side of Hong Kong's Lantau Island. I promised to speak and show some of my coloured slides to the youth group; several weeks earlier I had promised to attend the meeting. Unfortunately the day I arrived to keep my appointment I developed an upset stomach. I should have postponed the event, but didn't want to disappoint the youth, since they were so enthusiastic and looking forward to the occasion. The village of Tai-o could only be reached by taking a several hour vehicular ferry ride west of Hong Kong. I decided to go in spite of my upset stomach where I was enthusiastically welcomed by the youth. I ate supper with them, and then was invited to speak to the youth group. I felt so ill, later I went outside and threw up my entire supper. The young people were very sympathetic and helpful. Originally they had planned for me to spend the evening sleeping on the top of the local school desks, however, due to my discomfort they arranged for me to go the local village hotel to spend the night where one of the schoolteachers resided. The teacher had gone to Hong Kong for the weekend, so I was invited to use his bed.

The Tai-o Hotel was a typical village style hotel. Due to hot weather the walls of the hotel only went partially up to the ceiling, so the ventilation would be better. Some of the guests were enjoying playing mah jong during the evening, which can be a very noisey game, the sound is loud and clear, it wasn't conducive to sleeping. The bed was like a flat board with legs on it, the teacher had a woven grass mat stretched over his bed, to help make it cooler than using a Western style mattress. I was quietly resting on the grass mat, when it seemed to me I felt something underneath the mat. I arose to look beneath the grass mat, I discovered little packages of sulfur scattered all around the edge of the bed to help prevent bed bugs, that I had not anticipated. Later I felt it would have been better sleeping on the school desks rather than a grass mat. I certainly didn't rest much during the evening, so arose early to board the early morning ferry and returned to Hong Kong. It was an experience I will never forget.

(9) FRIED RICE PLUS

In 1967 during the leftist inspired riots that occurred in Hong Kong, everything was somewhat tense and uncertain. I had been invited to speak in one of the local churches located in the Mongkok area of Kowloon. We had a fine worship service; afterwards my friends from the church invited me to go to a nearby restaurant for lunch. It was a typical Cantonese "dim sum" style luncheon with delicious shrimp dumplings, steaming hot buns and so on; the luncheon concluded with fried rice. I was busily eating from my bowl of fried rice, when suddenly I felt something rather hard and strange in my mouth, I unobtrusively removed the food from my mouth into my hand to investigate. To my complete and utter astonishment I discovered a huge cockroach that had accidentally fallen into the kitchen wok when the cook was preparing the fried rice, so it ended in my mouth. Immediately I disposed of the cockroach tossing it under my chair, strangely enough I suddenly lost my appetite, but didn't dare mention anything conerning the matter, since I didn't wish my hosts to be embarrassed over the incident. A few years later after I had left Hong Kong, I returned to live in Canada, but years later revisited Hong Kong. My friends invited me to exactly the same restaurant for lunch. While we were eating lunch, I jokingly informed them what had happened several years ago. They laughed and said, why didn't you tell us, then we could have received a free lunch from the restaurant that day! Better luck next time.

(10) A COOL EVENT

After returning to live in Canada from Hong Kong, I was invited to conduct the funeral of a friend. Following the funeral service cremation took place. I rode in the hearse from the chapel to the crematorium. The staff removed the casket from the hearse to the adjacent waiting room where I had a prayer then held a brief commital service. From there the casket was transferred to the furnace room. We could clearly observe everything through a glass window, red-hot flames shot upwards and burned mightily as the coffin was placed into the fire. One of the grandchildren of the deceased also witnessed the event suddenly one of them exclaimed in a fairly loud voice, "Isn't that cool!" It took me by complete and utter suprise, I could hardly keep from smiling to myself following the exclamation; it was a most unusual reaction following a most solemn occasion.

CHAPTER 17

Stroke Recovery: A Positive View

JANUARY 25, 1991 I EXPERIENCED a stroke when unknowingly a tiny blood clot formed on the right side of my brain thus blocking the narrow passage, resulting in me having a stroke, adversely affecting my left arm and leg. The stroke occurred while I was in the emergency department of St. Paul's Hospital, Vancouver. It's now over nine years since the stroke occurred. The following is a brief updated report concerning the stroke. It's my sincere hope this report may be of some help to encourage other stroke victims to carry on and do their best to recover and not giving up hope.

I was a patient in St. Paul's Hospital in Vancouver for exactly two months, where I had the best treatment and care available at the time. It was a period of unbelievable change and adjustments in my life style. It seemed I had arrived at the crossroad of life where it was impossible to predict what may happen next. My Christian faith and firm conviction helped carry me through the difficulties, and providing the necessary courage, strength and desire to recover. Yes, my faith provided the necessary strength and determination to overcome the myriad of problems, enabling me to endure with confidence the many problems and difficulties which had suddenly and unexpectedly arisen.

The hospital arranged for an immediate CAT scan of my brain. They detected a tiny blood clot had formed causing the problem. The hospital arranged for a physiotherapist and other support staff to work diligently determining to what extent the stroke had affected my limbs, balance, memory, eyesight, hearing, perception, attitudes etc.

Every individual stroke is different from that of another, but also has many similarities. I will admit at first it was a difficult, scary, confusing experience trying to understand the problem that had such a devasting and disastrous effect on my regular daily life.

Initially I was unable to concentrate on any specific problem for long. Shortly after experiencing the stroke I discovered I was temporarily unable to read and comprehend the newspaper or understand what I was reading. However, my ability to read and powers of concentration eventually improved with the passage of time until restored.

The following are a few common traits accompanying stroke victims. Impatience is normally exhibited in all stroke patients, an attitude all strokers exhibit immediately following a stroke. In the mind of the stroker, it appears everything must be done immediately without delay. Naturally such an attitude creates genuine problems especially for the caregiver who is endeavouring to provide help and assistance.

My emotions were exceedingly volatile, muddled and confused; at the beginning the slightest matter upset me. I wept at the drop of a hat. It was exceedingly embarassing, especially if a visitor unintentionally mentioned something that directly affected me. My response was frequently an uncontrollable urge to weep. The visitors were puzzled or confounded by what he (or she) had said causing such a tearful and emotional response. For instance, one evening the hospital arranged for a special musical programme for the entertainment of the stroke patients; it consisted of familiar old time music that naturally helped recall many memories. If a familiar musical selection was played it frequently struck a sentimental note causing my roommate and me to break down into tears and weep. Likewise it triggered a similar reaction and response among the other patients attending the gathering. Many of the visitors looked at each other in complete amazement, trying to comprehend what was actually happening. Most visitors were unaware it was a natural and common reaction for stroke patients to weep so easily.

After experiencing a stroke, the patient must begin living his/her life all over again, including a relearning process to perform familiar tasks like dressing yourself due to the loss of an arm or leg because of the stroke. Both the occupational and physiotherapists enabled me to regain many movements again, one step at a time. I recall one day the therapist placed my clothes on my bed in a systematic and orderly fashion, enabling me to observe the way I should dress myself. She helped me place my underwear and trousers on my paralyzed arm and leg, showed me how to place my paralyzed arm into the shirt sleeve, place a stocking on my paralyzed foot; she helped me to regain my balance, so I could stand up when dressing. Assistance was required every time I had to go to the bathroom; it made me feel helpless, similar to being a child again.

Teaching a patient to feed himself depends upon whether it was the right or left arm affected by the stroke presenting a genuine challenge. For sometime I was entirely dependent upon a member of the hospital staff to help me to adjust. It was essential to learn how to cope with so many aspects of life all over again, which requires genuine love, patience and understanding by the caregiver handling so many changes. It naturally depends upon the severity of the stroke the patient had suffered. However, the situation is not as hopeless nor as futile as it first appears, providing the patient has the will, desire, motivation and outright determination and stamina to recover from the stroke. Fortunately I had a patient understanding and loving sister, who stood by enabling me to make the necessary adjustments. It's extremely difficult for a caregiver to adjust to so many changes and accept the situation that occurred.

Having a positive attitude is an essential ingredient for all stroke patients. Recovery depends upon the patient having a positive and co-operative attitude, making a tremendous difference to all concerned. Likewise, it is essential for the hospital staff to exhibit a similar positive outlook and attitude as they perform their daily tasks and responsibilities.

Due to my knowledge and understanding of the Chinese language after having lived in both Hong Kong and Vancouver for many years, the language proved to be a tremendous asset enabling me to assist many older patients of Chinese origin to communicate with the hospital staff due to the language barrier. I frequently helped translate from Cantonese into English for the nurses and other staff members, serving a two-way benefit. I was able to translate for the patients to convey their needs to the hospital staff and vice versa; it provided me with a feeling of worthwhileness assisting other patients and staff in the hospital.

Due to the overcrowdedness of the B.C. medical system, I was transferred from St. Paul's Hospital to Holy Family Hospital in Vancouver for an additional three month's rehabilitation. Holy Family Hospital to where I was transferred specializes in assisting stroke and other patients. Holy Family Hospital is well prepared and equipped having up to date equipment besides qualified staff. I resided as a patient in Holy Family Hospital for three months, before being allowed to return home on a permanent basis.

The major emphasis of the hospital was rehabilitation, enabling the stroke patients regain their balance and adjust to a more normal hospital setting. The program provided regular periods of daily exercise, assisted patients to begin walking again by introducing a special type of cane if required according to the needs of each individual patient. In my specific situation, I required a four-pointed cane for stability in walking, since my knee would not bend as I walked due to the affect of the stroke. They employed a special staff person to take us on daily walks. They also provided short lectures on various interrelated subjects, encouraged patients to return home for the weekends, so they gradually became used to living at home once again.

Before returning home a hospital social worker visited my home to see for herself the actual conditions that existed. In my setting she recommended installation of grab bars for the bathroom and other such convenient devices, including rearrangement of some of the furniture, so the transition could proceed as smoothly as possible for each individual client.

My return home was a welcome move, however, it involved many adjustments such as temporarily using a wheelchair, before going out on my daily walks accompanied by my sister, she walked around the courtyard with me and followed me with my wheelchair in case I became too weary needing to sit down briefly for a rest. After a few weeks the wheelchair was no longer required, since I was steadier on my legs. I was discharged from the hospital around the end of June, therefore, frequently went on short drives and picnics to the parks and beaches during the summer.

The Chinese United Church where I formerly served for many years both in Vancouver and Hong Kong, presented me with an electric scooter, so I could become even more mobile and independent. My electric scooter is a tremendous asset enabling me to be more mobile. I could go by myself to the mall, bank, library, do the family grocery shopping etc. The church saw I was still limited in the distance I could travel by scooter; they also provided a hydraulic lift for the rear end of my car. Due to the hydraulic lift, the scooter could be transported to Stanley Park and other such places like museums etc. The lift has proven to be a genuine asset, I could then transport the scooter on the rear of my car as we crossed the mountains driving to Saskatchewan to visit relatives and friends then return to Vancouver; still another time we travelled to Smithers, situated in northern B.C. where they were celebrating the 75th anniversary of their city. They likewise invited us to attend the reunion.

Next I decided to write a book by using a computer, the book is called *Crossing Life's Many Bridges*. It enabled me to keep my mind alert and active to prevent me from becoming mentally lazy, or ingrown from sitting around thinking only about myself. The book turned out to be a most beneficial project. The proceeds from the book were sufficient to purchase a new car.

Since I wanted to drive again, I enquired regarding the procedure for recovering my driver's licence. Holy Family Hospital tested my eyes, ears and general mobility; they referred me to the G.F. Strong Rehabilitation Centre in Vancouver for follow up. The G.F. Strong Hospital has a special driver's training course designed for individuals like me to be re-examined, so I could drive once again. They thoroughly tested my driving skills and ability to drive by testing my eyesight and hearing. The instructor responsible for conducting the driver's course informed me I would require a minimum of three lessons (two hours per session). Later he informed me, my driving skills were quite satisfactory, in view of that he recommended me for the formal driving examination, I passed the test on my first attempt. Initially I was issued a driver's licence for a one-year period. When my licence was about to expire the licencing department of the province issued a new licence for five years, the normal period of time. The licencing department is extremely cautious issuing of a driver's licence to former stroke patients, making certain he/she is properly qualified.

I became an active member of the Stroke Recovery Association of

B.C., an organization formed throughout the province to help meet some of the many needs of stroke patients. I became a member of the Coquitlam Stroke Recovery Association (Dogwood Club), which meets every Friday morning in the community centre from 10:30 a.m. until 2:00 p.m. At our stroke club we have fellowship with each other, a regular period of exercise, plus weekly stroke meetings. They invite guest speakers to lecture upon numerous topics, we have special outings and picnics throughout the year weather permitting, and occasionally we meet with other stroke clubs from time to time. Eventually I represented the Coquitlam Stroke Club at the provincial level four times per year, meeting with other strokers scattered throughout the province. It's an organization that attempts to meet some of the various needs of its many members, and helps keep us in touch with others who have a similar problem of being handicapped by stroke.

I still maintain close contacts and links with the Chinese church in Vancouver where I attend regularly. Frequently I am invited to speak at the worship services, conduct marriage ceremonies for those requesting such a service, besides conduct funeral services in Cantonese for those requiring such service. I am completely convinced the more involved stroke victims are encouraged to remain within the local community the better for them and all concerned. It enables other people within the community to realize, recognize and understand that a stroke is not necessarily the end of the road, but may lead to new forms of service, providing the individual stroker is determined to maintain his/her mobility to resume regular activities again as soon as physically possible.

From personal experience and conversation with other stroke patients from various clubs, we feel many family physicians need more experience and knowledge concerning their stroke patients, especially following up on a stroke victim. The ordinary practitioner seems to know little about stroke recovery. Stroke recovery is possible, provided the clients are encouraged to participate in stroke recovery activities and have the opportunity to meet other strokers on an individual and social level, observing how to overcome their problems and difficulties. Many family doctors need to further update their information about strokes provided by the medical schools, by providing such information they would be able to help more stroke patients to be salvaged and encouraged to carry on with their daily life.

Further information and details regarding stroke recovery may be obtained from the Stroke Recovery Association of British Columbia, or individual provincial offices across Canada. They should enquire from their local physicians and hospitals, who will happily provide all the information required. By co-operating and sharing information all will benefit.

Note:
Partners In Recovery
Stroke Recovery Association of British Columbia
Suite 109, 119 West Pender Street
Vancouver, B.C., v6b 1s5
Phone (604) 688-3603)

CHAPTER 18

Epilogue

During the brief span of the past seventy-four years of the 20th century, phenomenal changes occurred. It's often difficult to fully appreciate and understand how so many changes could possibly occur within such a relatively short span of time. It may help to provide a brief background of a few of the dynamic changes one individual as myself has experienced and witnessed. I personally find "change" most challenging and exciting. Time is an element that cannot be rolled back nor controlled. Change and time steadily move forward. We need to be sufficiently flexible to acknowledge time and change as facts of life that include invaluable lessons for each of us to learn. To illustrate my point, oil and gas lamps were used to provide light when I was child. On a daily basis the lamps had to be prepared for use, the wicks trimmed and the glass chimneys cleaned. Prevention of fire was a major hazard that had to be considered; it was part of the routine. Before long the use of electricity was introduced into the life of the ordinary individual, which included the use of the electric light bulb. Today electric lights are commonplace taking many forms and are universally accepted and used around the world. The concept of the electric light was not introduced to the general public until after the first quarter of the 20th century.

When I attended elementary school I lived on a farm in southeastern Saskatchewan. The principle means for travelling to school was by horse and buggy (democrat), however, with the approach of winter we used a team of horses to draw the sleigh as it moved over the snow. Occasionally the temperature would dip to minus 50 degrees

(Fahrenheit) or lower. Wind combined with snow and frost frequently meant school had to be postponed.

At the time all farmers in Canada used horses to help cultivate the land, the implements were all drawn by horses as they sowed the fields in the springtime. The ripe grain was cut by binders, then stooked by hand. At the time steam engines (iron horse) were one of the principle sources of power used to operate the threshing machine, however, steam engines were large, awkward and clumsy, before long the steam engine became obsolete as the farms became increasingly mechanized. Most implements were drawn by horses. Eventually both horses and steam engines were replaced by tractors.

Due to the acute shortage of manpower during the war years (1939–45) a serious situation developed. The farms were becoming increasingly mechanized, out of necessity horses were gradually replaced, combines cut and threshed the grain in one single operation replacing threshing machines. Modern technology was the key to progress, preparing the way for modern farming to emerge as it exists in Canada today.

In my opinion the most momentous occasion of the 20th century was the invention, use and explosion of the atomic bomb for the first time in human history. The atomic bomb was dropped over Hiroshima, Japan, endeavouring to conclude the war in the Pacific. The result was Hiroshima was 75 percent destroyed on August 6, 1945 at 8:10 a.m., killing approximately 150,000 people, besides destroying all buildings and property within the destructive path of the bomb. Due to the effect of radiation, the bomb also killed countless numbers of people and defaced others. The atomic bomb marked the unleashing of nuclear energy for the first time in the history of the world.

I recall in 1955, when I first went to Hong Kong as a missionary, I boarded a Norwegian freighter. The freighter required six weeks to cross the vast expanse of the Pacific. However, due to the extensive development of aircraft during World War II, modern technology forged ahead with leaps and bounds, creating many kinds of aircraft having the ability to carry passengers. Air travel soon became more convenient and speedy; nowadays only eight hours are required to cross the vast expanse of the Pacific ocean by jet airliner. Modern communication is still another factor that needs consideration. For centuries all mail was transported from one destination to another by foot, pony express, trains, trucks, ships and eventually air mail, crossing both land and sea. Likewise with the invention of the radio, it made extensive use of the airwaves for transmitting the latest news. Before long even greater and more dramatic advancements were introduced into the field of communication by the invention of television. Before long communication satellites were developed providing instantaneous communication. All newsworthy events that occurred in one part of the world were immediately known on the opposite side of the globe. The invention of the computer completely and thoroughly revolutionized the entire field of communication, including e-mail. All such communication made the world appear even smaller in size, it seemed the world had shrunk both in size and shape. Space travel rapidly developed during the latter part of the 20th century, transforming science fiction into reality within one generation. I vividly recall the news concerning the first Russian cosmonaut orbiting the earth in 1961. While eight years later American astronauts were hurtling through space towards the moon by a lunar module "Apollo," that resulted in the first moon landing on July 20, 1969. The first man to walk on the surface of the moon was Neil Armstrong, which resulted in complete astonishment and excitement all around the world, firing the minds and imagination of all people and nations. Life consists of a continual series of beginnings from the earliest time to the present, evident as we examine the ancient wisdom communicated through the sacred writings of the Holy Bible, the Koran or other such ancient sources. The opening statement in the Book of Genesis in the Old Testament in the Bible boldly proclaimed, "In the beginning, when God created the universe, the earth was formless and desolate." The above affirmation indicates a basic trust and faith in God as the creator of the universe. While other theories exist regarding the creation of the world, like the Big Bang theory, which claims the world began with a tremendous explosion. It also claims the Big Bang occurred out of the clear blue sky. For me to accept such a theory requires even greater faith than trusting in the divine creation of the universe. The Big Bang theory leaves countless questions still unanswered.

Each day leads us a step further in the process of life. I believe individuals should use their skills and wisdom for the benefit of all people in the world. I likewise believe we are placed here to help further God's will and purpose. On the other hand if we waste our time, we need to be prepared and willing to face the consequences of our choices and actions when standing in the presence of the creator, the Lord God.

We have already entered the year of the millennium, 2000, therefore it's important for us to pause and consider what the new millennium may contain for all nations and people, so we may attempt to chart the course of human history to determine the direction we ought to move. I believe we should use the years that lie ahead of us in a meaningful and constructive manner for the benefit of future generations. It's important to live for a specific and worthwhile cause and purpose, not only drift along in a meaningless manner wherever the current or tide may happen to lead us. God created each individual as unique within the universe having a specific purpose. It is up to us to discover the direction God would have us go, rather than aimlessly drift through the world without any aim or purpose. The analects of Confucius written some 2500 years ago proclaimed, "All within the four seas are brothers." Confucius was one of China's and the world's greatest and wisest philosophers and moralists. He was figuratively speaking on behalf of all mankind and nations as he made the profound statement, "All within the four seas are brothers." Our Christian faith mirrors and reflects a similar concept, the brotherhood of man and the fatherhood of God. We are all children of one God, irrespective of the colour or pigment of our skin, the language we speak, the culture or land from which we originate. Our hopes and aspirations are basically the same, in spite of obvious differences. It's essential and necessary for us to live in peace and harmony with our neighbours from around the world, since God created the world for us to enjoy and appreciate as our earthly dwelling place. It's my earnest hope and prayer that as we cross the many bridges of life, we will be ready and willing to extend a helping hand to all in need. Our wants, desires and aspirations may vary, but the final outcome is the same. I believe we were all created equal in the sight of God; therefore, we need to be willing to extend the hand of friendship, fellowship and brotherhood to our neighbours, ignoring minor differences that may appear to separate or divide us. The Lord our God created us to love each other and to share the world he provided for us to live. We should never forget to remind ourselves of such a basic and essential fact of life. May the good Lord abide, guide and direct us through the adventurous and exciting journey of life. The words of the beautiful inspiring song "One World" express a sincere desire for peace and good will for all living creatures on planet earth. The words express my sentiments far better than I am able to do myself.

> One world, built on a firm foundation,
> Built on a firm foundation of peace
> What a wondrous sight, freedom's flame alight,
> In a world where war shall cease:
> One world, built on love and peace
> When God smiled, bright sunlight,
> Flooded hills and plains:
> Songbirds filled green valleys
> With their glad refrains—
> All things God created,
> It is great love to share,
> Now let men and nations join
> And shout it everywhere:
> One world, built on a firm foundation:
> One world, no longer cursed by war;
> Let no mortal change the Master's plan
> One great world at peace once more:
> One world, one world,
> One world at peace forever more!

(Words by John W. Bratton, music by Geoffrey O'Hara, 1945.)